Public Service Media and Policy in Europe

Public Service Media and Policy in Europe

Karen Donders

First published 2012 by
PALGRAVE MACMILLAN

Palgrave Macmillan in the UK is an imprint of Macmillan Publishers Limited,
registered in England, company number 785998, of Houndmills, Basingstoke,
Hampshire RG21 6XS.

Palgrave Macmillan in the US is a division of St Martin's Press LLC,
175 Fifth Avenue, New York, NY 10010.

Palgrave Macmillan is the global academic imprint of the above companies
and has companies and representatives throughout the world.

Palgrave® and Macmillan® are registered trademarks in the United States,
the United Kingdom, Europe and other countries.

ISBN 978–0–230–29096–9

This book is printed on paper suitable for recycling and made from fully
managed and sustained forest sources. Logging, pulping and manufacturing
processes are expected to conform to the environmental regulations of the
country of origin.

A catalogue record for this book is available from the British Library.

Library of Congress Cataloging-in-Publication Data
Donders, Karen, 1983–
    Public service media and policy in Europe / Karen Donders.
        p.   cm.
    Includes index.
    ISBN 978–0–230–29096–9
    1. Public broadcasting—Europe.   2. Broadcasting policy—
    Europe.   I. Title.
    HE8689.7.P82D665 2011
    384.54094—dc23   2011029571

10   9   8   7   6   5   4   3   2   1
21 20 19 18 17 16 15 14 13 12

Printed and bound in the United States of America

Contents

List of Figures and Tables

Figures

Tables

List of Abbreviations

AVMS	Audiovisual Media Services Directive
BAI	Broadcasting Authority Ireland
EU	European Union
MS	Member States
PSB	Public service broadcasting
PSP	Public service publisher
PVT	Public Value Test
SGEI	Services of general economic interest
TWF	Television without Frontiers Directive
VRM	*Vlaamse Regulator voor de Media* [Flemish Media Regulator]
WTO	World Trade Organization

Preface and Acknowledgements

This book is the culmination of four years of research into Europe's relevance regarding the evolution from public service broadcasting (PSB) to public service media. Confronted with an apparent disagreement about this topic between scholars in the field of media and communications studies, the book provides an in-depth account of the European Commission's involvement in the area of PSB. It somewhat provocatively asserts that the application of European rules has in fact contributed to public service media, asking Member States (MS) to develop more clearly spelled-out and transparent policies for their public broadcasters. In so doing, the European Commission has indeed sometimes gone beyond its competencies. More importantly, MS have failed adequately to modernise public broadcasters and their role in public service media.

In this monograph, *Public Service Media and Policy in Europe*, I disentangle the variety of elements that come into play when MS, public broadcasters, private media players and the European Commission meet in a state aid procedure, which is inherently a battlefield on which the validity of state subsidies is decided. Intrigued by the apparent disagreement about the topic and the dominantly negative appreciation of the European Commission's policies, I wrote a PhD dissertation on this topic. This book is an updated and shortened version thereof.

I owe gratitude to my supervisors, Prof. Dr Caroline Pauwels and Prof. Dr Fabienne Brison, for their advice and the numerous inspiring discussions. In addition, I wish to thank Prof. Dr Jo Bardoel, Prof. Dr Peter Humphreys, Dr Monica Arino and Prof. Dr Sebastian Oberthür for their comments on my work. My appreciation also goes to the Institute for European Studies (IES) (Vrije Universiteit Brussel), which funded my research, and the Center for Studies on Media, Information and Telecommunication (IBBT-SMIT) at the same university. I wish to thank all my colleagues for the exchange of ideas and their support, in particular Hilde, Hans, An V, Sophie, Tim, Birgit, Wim, Alexander, Katja, Hannelore and An M.

As one may notice when reading *Public Service Media and Policy in Europe*, a number of representatives from the European Commission, media ministries, public broadcasters and private media companies have contributed to my work, sharing their insights on Europe's role in the area of PSB. I especially thank Ross, Julia, Renate, Marc, Ben, Lut, Sandra, Helga and Marit, not only for answering my questions but also for reading and commenting on parts of my PhD dissertation.

Finally, this book not only is the result of transpiration and inspiration but also benefited from the support of family and friends. A special word of gratitude is also appropriate for my best friend Ben, my twin Inge, my parents-in-law, my parents and my partner Jan for being so caring and compassionate during the finalising of my PhD dissertation and this manuscript.

Karen Donders

1
Introduction, Aims and Methodology

Context

Public service broadcasting in transition(s)

Public service broadcasting (PSB) is a policy project under revision in Europe. Since its inception in the 1920s, public broadcasters (in most European countries entrusted with the provision of PSB) have been lauded and criticised. Under monopoly, public broadcasters were said to be elitist. Elevated goals of citizen emancipation resulted in programming policies that were developed on the basis of producer, rather than consumer, preferences (McDonnell, 1991, p. 12; Hilmens, 2002, p. 64). After the liberalisation of the broadcasting sector in the 1980s, public broadcasters were forced to adapt their strategies: no legitimacy without an audience. Efficiency, ratings and public management were introduced in public broadcasting and, admittedly, the late 1990s saw a revival in the service. Public broadcasters, and also the project of public intervention in the broadcasting sector, proved to be resilient (Collins et al., 2001). However, the renewed success of public broadcasters provoked opposition from both governments and private broadcasters. The latter alleged that the broadcasting of entertainment, sports and fiction on the one hand and advertising activities of public broadcasters on the other hand distorted the market. Politicians questioned the success rates of public broadcasters, but in fact there was a catch-22: public broadcasters without mass appeal faced legitimacy issues as tax or licence fee payers should benefit from their offers, but too much audience success (and what is too much?) gave rise to concerns about commercialisation. These concerns remain omnipresent and are intensifying as public broadcasters are now launching Internet services.

Towards public service media?

PSB seems to evolve into public service media (Bardoel and Ferrell Lowe, 2007; Iosifidis, 2010; Jakubowicz, 2010). The contours of a public service media project remain unclear at present; public broadcasters are effectively providing services other than 'pure' radio and television broadcasts. Some new activities, like the BBC's iPlayer, are very successful and have been applauded for offering content to a wider audience, while other services have met with fierce criticism. Dating websites, online calculators and forums on the weather forecast seem more difficult (although not impossible) to align with a public service ethos (Moe, 2008b). The concept of public service media is operationalised in Chapter 4 of this book. For the moment, it suffices to say that public service media in this book are regarded as a policy project that represents a future stage in PSB. It is still focused, but not solely concerned with, public broadcasters. Pre-set policy objectives, a level of accompanying regulation and an expansion of the PSB project to new media platforms qualify a project as public service media. The concepts of public service communication (Tambini and Cowling, 2004; Iosifidis, 2010) and public service content (Ofcom, 2007) are not used throughout the book. Admittedly, these concepts are more platform independent and put citizen involvement at their core. However, whereas the evolution toward public service media is already taking place, the concepts of public service communication and public service content embody a longer-term perspective on the future of PSB. In addition, public service content disconnects PSB and public broadcasters and is often associated with a system in which all organisations can apply for public funding of media services. Given the book's focus on public broadcasters, the public service content concept is less suitable.

European involvement

The future of PSB as a policy project and public broadcasters is increasingly determined by a vast number of actors including public broadcasters themselves, national governments, private media companies, the EU institutions and, regrettably, to a lesser extent, citizens. In particular, there seems to be a structural tendency of PSB becoming a more important policy issue for the European Commission ('Commission'). Since the 1990s, the Commission (and more specifically its Directorate General for Competition) has investigated the compliance of public broadcasting funding schemes with the European common market (Bardoel and Vochteloo, 2010; Wheeler, 2010). It has done so on the basis of the competition policy framework. More specifically, the state aid rules (also referred to as 'state aid control') allow the Commission to check whether the subsidies or indirect aid mechanisms of Member States or 'MS') are duly taking into account internal market goals (Bavasso, 2006; Antoniadis, 2008).

The Commission's interventions began in the 1990s and have intensified ever since. In the early 1990s, the first private companies' complaints against the funding of public broadcasters were filed with the competition authorities of the Commission. These complaints, regarding TF1 (France), SIC (Portugal), Telecinco (Spain) and Mediaset (Italy), gave rise to furious reactions of MS and public broadcasters. They argued that the Commission was not competent to intervene in this policy domain and feared for the Commission's economic approach towards the issue. Initially, the Commission stalled decision taking for that reason. From the late 1990s onwards, complaints of the private sector increased, however, and Director General (DG) Competition started its investigations in a variety of aid schemes focusing on the launch of thematic channels, dual funding and the broadcasting of sports programmes by public broadcasters. Some of these investigations were completed rapidly, while other decisions were issued only after the Commission succeeded in drafting some specific guidelines for the funding of public broadcasters in 2001 (EC, 2001). After the publication of these guidelines (commonly referred to as 'Broadcasting Communication'), the number of Commission investigations and decisions increased. These affected public broadcasters in Portugal, Italy, Spain, France, the UK, Germany, Flanders, the Netherlands, Denmark, Ireland and Austria (Antoniadis, 2006). Since 2003, the Commission – acting upon private sector complaints – has focused on public broadcasters' expansion into new media markets. It has asked MS to implement a so-called *ex ante* evaluation for new media services. Public broadcasters would require a prior government approval in case they wish to expand their services portfolio beyond what is already covered by the relevant legislative acts. This demand and other elements of decision practice resulted, in 2009, in the update of the Commission's guidelines for the funding of PSB (EC, 2009a).

Hence, it seems that the Commission is taking its task to enforce competition rules in the broadcasting, and by extension media, market seriously. This affects the margins that MS have to develop public broadcasting policies that are oriented towards the complexities of a new media environment. In other words, the transfer from PSB to public service media is no longer a matter of MS only, but is affected by the policies of 'Europe'.

Research aim

This book investigates, firstly, to what type of public service media project Western European countries should evolve and, secondly, how this evolution is affected by the policies of the Commission.

Dominant assertions about European intervention

Opinions on European state aid control and its (potential) meaning for and impact on PSB, especially in Western Europe where public broadcasting is traditionally a well-entrenched institution, differ greatly. Put simply, some claim the Commission's state aid control is going too far, whereas others maintain it is not sufficiently far reaching. The private media sector is supportive of the Commission's policies (ACT et al., 2004; Biggam, 2009). On the other hand, most scholars in the field of media and communications studies, public broadcasters and a number of MS are highly sceptical of the Commission's intervention. Overall, criticism – be it from a political or academic perspective – on the Commission's state aid control is threefold. Firstly, it is said that the Commission does not take into account the specific – cultural – nature of public broadcasting. For this reason, Bardoel and Ferrell Lowe (2007, p. 12) disapprove of Commission intervention in the field of public broadcasting, wondering 'how the Commission can so blithely treat PSB from a deterministically economic perspective when the entire enterprise isn't about that and is in fact explicitly about the countervailing importance of the socio-cultural dimension'. Secondly, critics are of the opinion that the Commission intervenes in a policy area that falls, following the principle of subsidiarity, within MS' competencies (Holtz-Bacha, 2005). A third point of criticism relates to the actual scope of public broadcasters' activities. It is argued that the Commission aims, inspired by market failure theories on broadcasting, to limit public broadcasters' activities to services that are not readily available on the commercial market (Jakubowicz, 2010, p. 12; Michalis, 2010, p. 40). Entertainment, sports and new media services would then fall outside the public service remit. Setting out from public broadcasters' expansion to new media markets, some stakeholders and scholars fear that the Commission 'might be closing the door to PSB's modernisation and adaptation to the realities of the information society' (Jakubowicz, 2007b, p. 12).

In short, the mainstream appreciation of the Commission's policies in the field of PSB has been negative so far. Against the background of the new media environment, it is forecast that the Commission will hamper the evolution from PSB to public service media. The latter is allegedly marginalising public broadcasters from the mainstream to the margin (Moe, 2008a; Bardoel and Vochteloo, 2009).

Research argument

After nearly 20 years of Commission intervention with PSB, and in the light of the Commission's 2009 update of the guidelines that are used to assess the funding of public broadcasters, one needs to assess in an evidence-based manner whether the intervention of the Commission indeed went as far as some aspired and others feared.

This book questions mainstream academic and political discourse and the common hypothesis in communication sciences that the Commission marginalises public broadcasters. It argues that the Commission has, while indeed shaping MS' room to preserve, to develop and adapt public broadcasting policies, not marginalised public broadcasters' activities. On the contrary, European interventions foster the ongoing transfer from PSB to public service media, trigger welcome reflections on what public service mission suits the digital era and, at the same time, render stakeholders more accountable and responsive with regard to the functioning of public broadcasters. The aim of this book is to investigate both this argument and the claim of marginalisation.

The argument is not that the Commission itself pursues the emergence of a sustainable public service media policy; this could hardly be expected to be one of the distinctive goals of European competition policy. The line of reasoning is that the dynamics of the negotiation process (at the European level) between the different stakeholders and the dynamics initiated by the commitments that MS make (at the national or regional level) to alter certain aspects of public broadcasting policy strengthen the transition from PSB to public service media.

Methodology

The book's findings are based on policy analysis and case studies. The first method is grounded in Loisen's media policy framework (Loisen, 2009, inspired by work of Nobel Price winner Douglass C. North) and

Mosco's political economy of communication paradigm (Mosco, 1996). This concretely means that the analysis focuses on:

- Ideas: what are the dominant ideologies on PSB?
- Institutions: who is in charge of PSB policy?
- Interests: what are the power relations between the actors involved?

The elements listed above are, according to Mosco's paradigm, situated within a wider time frame and their social, economic and political context. Moreover, this book sets out from a normative approach evaluating in what way PSB should evolve into public service media, what public service media are and how the Commission can support this transition. The latter corresponds also with Mosco's element of praxis (i.e. scholars should also attempt to influence policy processes).

Flanders, Germany and the Netherlands have been selected as case studies. The selection of cases originates in the research aim, which is to illustrate that the involvement of the Commission with PSB has facilitated – or at least contributed – to the transfer from PSB to public service media. This aim implies, first and foremost, that the selected countries should have been confronted with European involvement in their PSB policies. Secondly, a public service media element should be present in dealings between the selected MS and the Commission. Finally, this book looks only at encounters between MS and the Commission that have been closed on the basis of a formal decision outlining a number of required alterations of policy for public broadcasters. On the basis of these criteria, Germany, Flanders, Ireland, Austria and the Netherlands can be selected. Germany, Flanders and the Netherlands are discussed in this book as they reveal sufficient divergences (e.g. size of market, lobbying intensity of private actors) and similarities (e.g. strong public broadcasters, resistance to EU intervention) in order to draw meaningful conclusions.

The case studies are, conforming to widespread definitions, operationalised as 'single unit studies' that examine a spatially bound phenomenon during a confined time period (George and Bennett, 2004; Gerring, 2007). Indeed, European involvement is examined regarding how it affects the evolution from PSB to public service media in Germany, Flanders and the Netherlands. The time period varies for the three cases, as European involvement in Germany started in 1999 and ended in 2007 (EC, 2007b), whereas for Flanders and the Netherlands European investigations were opened in 2003 and closed in February 2008 and January 2010, respectively (EC, 2008b, 2010). General lessons can be drawn from the case studies. The uniqueness of each MS PSB system makes wide generalisations impossible. This is not problematic as such since, as Flyvbjerg (2006, p. 224) points out, 'Concrete, context-dependent knowledge is... more valuable than the vain search for predictive theories and universals'. In other words, the in-depth knowledge of some examples can teach us a lot about the overall strategies of the Commission in affecting PSB policy at the national level. At the same time, these can also illustrate how different countries cope with and define the transition from PSB to public service media.

Sources

The main sources used to collect and process relevant data were:

- relevant secondary literature;
- official (both public and non-disclosed) documents of the Commission, involved MS authorities, the Council of Europe, the European Parliament and the European Courts;
- documents of interest groups and other involved stakeholders (e.g. public broadcasters, private broadcasters, publishers, etc.);
- over 70 in-depth, semi-structured expert interviews (most face-to-face, between spring 2007 and autumn 2010) with representatives of the Commission, public broadcasters, private broadcasters, regulators, publishers, interest groups and academia;
- press coverage on PSB, new media and European involvement; and
- attendance at seminars and conferences on this topic organised by involved stakeholders, the Commission and academia.

Structure of the book

This book is divided in three parts. Excluding the introductory chapter, Part 1 includes three additional chapters. The second chapter provides a historical overview of PSB in transition, while the third critically evaluates the different theoretical insights in this regard – with a specific focus on the transition to public service media. The concept of public service media is explored further and operationalised in Chapter 4.

Part 2 includes four chapters, each looking at a different aspect of the involvement of the European Community and, in particular, the Commission with PSB policy. Chapter 5 examines the overall aims and outline of internal market policies in the audiovisual sector. The core elements of the Commission's competition rules when applied to PSB are addressed in Chapter 6. Chapters 7 and 8 investigate the actual policies of the Commission in the area of PSB. Chapter 7 does so from a historical angle, while a more thematic approach is followed in Chapter 8.

Finally, Part 3 consists of four chapters. The concrete consequences of European involvement for PSB in Germany, Flanders and the Netherlands are identified and evaluated. These three chapters are followed by conclusions and policy recommendations.

2
From Public Service Broadcasting to Public Service Media

Since the 1920s public service broadcasting (PSB) has gone through a number of transitions. In order to put current topical debates on public service media and policy in Europe in perspective, this chapter documents these transitions. An analytical distinction is made between three phases: monopoly (1920s–70s), liberalisation (mid-1970s to mid-1990s) and a new media environment (late 1990s onwards). Most scholars make a distinction between two or three phases in the history of public broadcasting. Generally speaking some distinguish between the period before and after liberalisation (Syvertsen, 1997; Levy, 1999; Michalis, 2007), others between the monopoly, liberalisation and digital age stages in PSB history (Collins et al., 2001; Steemers, 2001; Murdock, 2004; Leurdijk, 2007; Bardoel and d'Haenens, 2008). This chapter fits the latter categorisation. Three questions are at the core of this chapter. Firstly, what are the main distinguishing features of each phase? Secondly, who is in charge of public broadcasting policy? Thirdly, how do public broadcasters operationalise their task in each phase?

Monopoly (1920s–1970s)

Before the 1980s there were *strictu sensu* no media markets in most Western European countries. Broadcasting and other sectors such as telecommunications were seen as natural monopolies in which government intervention accounted for optimal outcomes. Dominant assumptions about the public good characteristics of broadcasting and spectrum scarcity resulted in the creation of public monopolies. Governments created public broadcasting monopolies in the 1920s and 1930s and preserved this organisation of the broadcasting market until the 1980s. Only Luxembourg did not establish a public broadcasting organisation. However, private broadcaster CLT-RTL occupied a de facto private monopoly position in Luxembourg until 1991.

The political choice gradually to assign radio and later television to monopolist public broadcasters in Western European countries stood in sharp contrast with American policies. The latter set out from a 'free market of ideas' model in which the market ought to secure a free flow of content and ideas (Mazzocco, 1998; Morris and Peterson, 2000). The opposite idea dominated PSB policies in Western Europe, where the achievement of public interest objectives was said to depend on public protection from inequitable market forces (Hitchens, 2006, p. 12ff; Iosifidis, 2008, pp. 349–50).

Besides this ideological opposition between American and European views on broadcasting, there are several more tangible reasons for the Western European broadcasting monopolies. Spectrum scarcity, political power maximisation and the desire to emancipate citizens in democratic societies all explain the creation of public broadcasters. Even the link with the telecommunications sector, which was already organised as a monopoly in most European Union Member States (EUMS), seemed to make the choice for public broadcasting monopolies self-evident (Raboy, 1995, p. 10).

Technological scarcity

First of all, in phase 1, technological constraints seemed to jeopardise the free entry to broadcasting markets and, as a consequence, a classical case of market failure justified government intervention (Blumler, 1991, p. 7). Scholars like Coase (1947) and West (2004, p. 374), however, have questioned the direct link between spectrum scarcity and public broadcasting monopolies. They argue that scarcity is a basic characteristic of sectors like real estate as well. Consequently, spectrum is a good like any other and should be traded in a free market environment. Scholars like Scannel (1995, pp. 23–4) and Garnham (1990, p. 109) have countered this argumentation, disputing that spectrum and broadcasting are comparable with other economic activities. Moreover, Coase and West too easily ignore that spectrum scarcity was, albeit a logical explanatory factor, not the genuine reason for upholding a broadcast monopoly (Hoffmann-Riem, 1995, p. 82).

The reign of national governments

Public broadcasters were constructed most importantly as a means of ensuring a level of government control over mass media (Garnham,

1990, p. 120; Herman, 1993, p. 87). In other words, those seeking to hold political power sought control over broadcasting (Noam, 1991, pp. 149, 253, 267; Croteau and Hoynes, 2002, p. 87). Since national governments were exclusively competent in the field of broadcasting, the aspirations to seek control of public broadcasters were not in vain. For example, Burgelman and Perceval (1995) convincingly illustrate how public broadcasting in Belgium was an instrument of political elites attempting to acquire political control. In Germany, broadcasting was placed under direct control of the government administration during the Weimar Republic (Humphreys, 1994, pp. 124–6). Even in the UK, several early examples of government influence over editorial strategies can be found. Reference can be made to pressure of the UK government to adapt news reporting of general strikes in 1926 and the Suez Crisis in 1956 (Paulu, 1981, pp. 35–40).

Several authors have illustrated how politicisation was not only about government control of content, but also touched upon the entire organisational structure of public broadcasters. All levels in the public broadcasting organisation became 'infected' by party political appointments. This resulted in bureaucracy, a strong hierarchical structure and a weak competitive basis of public broadcasters (Kuhn, 1988, pp. 177–9; Pauwels, 1995, pp. 75–6).

Even though examples of direct government control over public broadcasting have become more difficult to find, the strong internal politicisation of public broadcasters along party lines remains a central characteristic of public broadcasters' internal organisation – especially still in Southern European countries (Papathanassopoulos, 2007b).

Emancipation of the audience

Besides the aspiration to control broadcasting for own political gain, there was also a genuine belief in the emancipative potential of PSB. Certainly after the Second World War the idea that public broadcasting could contribute to the development and preservation of liberal democracy gained importance (Herman, 1993, p. 88; McQuail, 1998, p. 139ff). Public broadcasters were supposed to inform, educate, elevate and emancipate the masses. These objectives were to be upheld even against the wishes of the audience. Reith's mantra indeed was that 'few know what they want and very few what they need' (John Reith in Hilmens, 2002, p. 64). Hence, paternalism seeped into the PSB project rather soon and complemented the set of elements explaining for the creation and maintenance of public broadcasting monopolies between the 1920s and the end of the 1970s. Admittedly, the emancipative project of public broadcasters has been criticised. Hughes (1988, pp. 53–4), for example, asserted that the Reithian ethos resulted in 'worthy, but ultimately dull programmes, which alienated sections of the audience'.

The emergence of competition issues

Leaving aside the reasons for establishing public monopolies in broadcasting, competition problems did not suddenly emerge after the liberalisation of the broadcasting market in the 1980s. Already before that time, media companies questioned the position of public broadcasters. Certainly, daily press publishers regularly attacked the activities of public broadcasters (e.g. advertising, teletext services) and argued, for example in Germany, for the introduction of private broadcasting in which they could take a stake (Humphreys, 1994). As one would expect, advertisers themselves argued in favour of private broadcasting outlets. Public broadcasters were often not allowed to engage in television advertising, or advertising was permissible only in a very restrictive way (Hughes, 1988, p. 55). The objections to public broadcasters' activities did not, however, result in a widespread political questioning of the monopoly status of public broadcasters until the 1970s.

The lack of competition was not only directly relevant for publishers and advertisers, it also resulted in a weak independent European production sector. Most public broadcasters were indeed not significantly outsourcing production to the independent production sector. This integration of production, programmation and distribution within one single public broadcaster, so Pauwels (2000, p. 26) puts forward, stands in sharp contrast with the USA, where private television networks were obliged to buy programmes with the independent production sector when they started their activities in the 1930s. The fact that such obligations were not put in place in the European public monopolies created manifold problems once the broadcasting market was liberalised. An increasing number of channels had to rely on US content, not necessarily (although an important factor) because US content was cheaper, but because it was available.

Demise of the monopoly

The weaknesses of the public broadcasting monopolies in Western Europe originated in the historical, political and social roots of PSB. Public broadcasters' and, even more so, national governments' strategic choices in shaping the public broadcasting ideal in practice created and reinforced these weaknesses. In spite of that, national political elites used these flaws to argue for the abolition of the public broadcasting monopoly. A free market model was portrayed as the most advantageous organisation for the broadcasting sector (Garnham, 1990; Pauwels, 1995).

Admittedly, a combination of public and private broadcasting was to be preferred over the exclusive reliance on public or private television (Scannel, 1995, pp. 23–4). However, at the end of phase 1, politicians in Western European countries seemed overly to rely on free market ideals and no longer fully supported the ideal of PSB and the institutions accountable to it (Pauwels, 1995).

Liberalisation (mid-1970s to mid-1990s)

After 50 years of monopoly, criticism of public broadcasters intensified and European broadcasting markets were opened up to competition by the end of the 1980s. This shift in broadcasting regimes is, in general, explained by referring to two parallel trends: firstly, the proclaimed end of spectrum scarcity and, secondly, the revival of market-led – to the detriment of interventionist government – policies (Dyson and Humphreys, 1988a; McQuail et al., 1992, pp. 10–11).

The end of spectrum scarcity

To start with, cable and satellite ended the era of spectrum scarcity. In some way, spectrum was and still is as scarce as it was in the 1920s. However, due to new technologies its use became more efficient and, as a consequence, it was possible to license more channels. The technological legitimisation of the public broadcasting monopoly was thus difficult to maintain. A diversity of output could equally be guaranteed in a competitive environment (Dyson, 1985, p. 153).

Undeniably, technological progress and even more so the processes initiated by it strengthened the freedom of information, diversity and pluralism. The 1980s were characterised by the genuine belief in the economic, but also the social and cultural, potential of more broadcasting outlets (Castells, 1996, p. 338). It is only fair to say that some scholars have countered this enthusiasm forcefully arguing that 'spectrum abundance is not the same as pluralism of content' (Barber and Thorburn, 2004, p. 34) and 'the public interest does not disappear because we have broadband cable' (Tracey, 1995, p. 126). Moreover, although liberalisation resulted in more channels, it also gave way to a process of integration and ownership concentration rather soon after the broadcasting market was opened to competition (Venturelli, 1998, p. 220ff; Pauwels and Cincera, 2001; Doyle, 2002a, 2007, p. 137ff).

The rise of market ideology

Next to more efficient spectrum management, the ideological shift towards liberalisation and market-led policy solutions was another, and probably even the most important, reason to end the monopoly phase of PSB. It should be stressed that there was no 'natural' link between the more efficient management of spectrum and governments' apparent desire to open up the broadcasting sector to competition. It is somewhat odd that this causal relation as established as spectrum scarcity was not the most important reason to establish broadcast monopolies. How then could it have been the most important reason to abolish them? Notwithstanding, at the rhetorical level it was an important argument to argue for, and later on when it disappeared against, public broadcasting monopolies. Even scholars heavily criticising deregulatory policy strategies in the media sector adhered to a discourse of declining spectrum scarcity (Negrine, 1985, p. 1; Dyson and Humphreys, 1988a, 1988b; Garnham and Locksley, 1991).

A firm belief in market forces dominated the 1970s and 1980s. The crisis of state intervention and public broadcasting in particular was, as Garnham (1990, pp. 127–8) points out, 'part of a wider political crisis, namely a profound shift in people's attitudes to the state and to the State's proper role in social time'. The consensus on the way to organise public broadcasting disappeared as market failures declined and no longer justified the preservation of the public broadcasting monopoly. The latter was said to inhibit the realisation of the broadcasting sector's economic potential. The offer of more channels, the pursuit of international competitiveness, more jobs, the development of a technological network that not only enabled the offer of more broadcasting services, but also more personal interactive communications services, and so on all called for (de-)regulatory action. In light of this, governments were more than tempted to rely on neoliberal market recipes in order to cope with the recession in the 1970s (Dyson, 1985, p. 154), the logic of which stated that barriers had to be removed where markets worked better (Dyson and Humphreys, 1988a, p. 96).

Public broadcasters were considered to be barriers to the free development of the market. As already hinted at, this was not a natural consequence of the decline of spectrum scarcity: it was, as Pauwels (1995, p. 74) argues, a political choice not to support public broadcast monopolies. The choice for economic recipes based on consumer sovereignty underlied the declining support for public broadcasting from a more ideological perspective. A system had to build up in which, quoting Leon Brittan (former minister of media in the UK, quoted in Tracey, 1998, p. 48), 'the customer rather than the philosopher is king'. Similar arguments, against public ownership and for more freedom for consumers, were put forward by private broadcasters – of which some explicitly questioned the public value of public broadcasters' services in comparison with their own offers:

> For [a] start, I have never heard a convincing definition of what public-service television really is, and I am suspicious of elites, including the British broadcasting elite, which argue for special privileges and favours because they are supposed to be in the public interest as a whole. Such special pleadings tend to produce a service which is run for the benefit of the people who provide it, rather than the viewers who watch it, sometimes under duress, especially late at night, because there is nothing else to watch. My own view is that anybody who, within the law of the land, provides a service which the public wants at a price it can afford is providing a public service. (Murdoch, 2005, p. 133)

The belief in consumer sovereignty crystallised in more down-to-earth ideas about the introduction of pay-television and subscription-based television models (Pauwels, 1995, pp. 91–2).

Liberalisation and a fundamental questioning of PSB followed (Regourd, 1999, pp. 29–30; Chakravarty and Sarikakis, 2006, p. 85ff). It was specifically questioned whether some (if not all) functions carried out by public broadcasters could not be performed (in a more efficient way) by the private sector (Garnham, 1994, p. 11). This was a fundamental breach with the dominant discourse of a 'full-service', full-portfolio or holistic broadcasting model. Related to this, broadcasting was no longer exclusively considered in the light of its social function or public good characteristics (Dyson and Humphreys, 1988b, p. 6). Rather its economic finality became of the utmost importance – an evolution that has been criticised fiercely (among others in Garnham, 1990; Tracey, 1998).

There comes Europe

Market-led policy orientations at the national level were reinforced and to some extent also provoked by actions of the European institutions – most importantly the Commission (Humphreys, 1996,

p. 256ff; Michalis, 2007, p. 139ff). Humphreys illustrates how Member States' (MS') decisions to abolish their public broadcasting monopolies were not enforced top-down by the Commission. Nevertheless, the Directorate Generals for Internal Market and Competition did by all means support and inspire the reforms in the broadcasting sector (EC, 1984, 1997; Donders and Pauwels, 2008).

Assertions on the way forward for broadcasting policy were dominated by free market ideas and an aversion to government intervention (Humphreys, 1996, p. 161; see also the Bangemann report of 1994). This is, for example, apparent in the Commission's green paper on the convergence of the telecommunications, media and information technology sectors in which it upheld that 'the development of new services could be hindered by the existence of a range of barriers, including regulatory barriers, at different levels of the market' and 'given the speed, dynamic and power of innovation of the sectors impacted by convergence, public authorities must avoid approaches which lead to over-regulation, or which simply seek to extend existing rules in the telecommunications and media sectors to areas and activities which are largely unregulated today' (EC, 1997, p. VI).

Concrete 'European' initiatives in the broadcasting market were foremost oriented at the creation of an internal market in broadcasting through measures of harmonisation. This internal market (which is a regulated construct and not a free market *strictu sensu* after all) aimed to further the competitiveness of the European audiovisual industry – and this in order to allow competition with the USA (Papathanassopoulos, 1990, p. 107; Sepstrup, 1990, p. 95).

The two most important instruments through which harmonisation was realised were the Television without Frontiers Directive (1989) (subsequently referred to as 'TWF') and the competition rules. The TWF Directive was approved after difficult negotiations between MS, Commission and other stakeholders. It introduced the country of origin principle, some minimum provisions on public interest objectives and quota provisions for European and independently produced content. The country of origin principle, which allows for transnational intra-European broadcasts in so far these meet the regulatory provisions of the country where the broadcasting signals originate, was groundshaking as it took away MS' right to refuse broadcasting signals that were in breach of their national broadcasting regulation. Few exceptions are admissible under this principle (European Council, 1989).

Next to the above sector-specific attempts to open the broadcasting market, European competition policy played an important role in realising an internal market in broadcasting well. From the 1980s onwards, mergers, pay-television contracts and subsidy schemes were increasingly being evaluated by the Commission on the basis of diverse aspects of competition law. More than once, these investigations clashed with MS' industrial strategies and public interest policies (Pauwels, 1995; Nitsche, 2001). Competition policy did not touch upon the specific issue of PSB yet, however. It was only in the second half of the 1990s that the Commission became a relevant actor in this respect. Before that, Commission officials tried to emphasise their 'neutrality' on PSB (e.g. Da Silva, 1995, p. 40) and preferred not to mention public broadcasting policies within the framework of European audiovisual policies altogether (Jakubowicz, 2004, p. 277).

In short, European and national broadcasting policies became intertwined in the 1980s. However, the impact of European intervention – although new, substantial and often unwanted – should not be exaggerated either. European countries continued to control their policy toolkit in the broadcasting area and, even though bound by general competition and more sector-specific provisions, PSB was still largely a national affair.

New public management in public broadcasting

In phase 2, public broadcasters were confronted with a hostile ideological and political environment. Declining political support was especially apparent at the level of financing (Barnett and Docherty, 1991, p. 37). Although some governments still objected to public broadcasters engaging in commercial markets like advertising, an increasing number of public broadcasters were obliged more and more to rely on commercial revenues. This put public broadcasters in a paradoxical situation. On the one hand, governments insisted more on quality and distinctiveness of public broadcasters' programming; on the other, they were forced to rely on commercial revenues.

Public broadcasters proved to be resilient and adapted to the changed circumstances in two ways. Firstly, as a consequence of governments' cry for reform of public broadcasters in the 1980s (Blumler, 1993, p. 21), a management culture was introduced. Cost efficiency, budget cuts, the lay-off of staff and more professional monitoring of public broadcasters' activities characterised the reform of PSB policy in a number of Western European countries (Vedel and Bourdon, 1993, p. 37; Pauwels, 1995; Grade, 2005, p. 159).

Secondly, public broadcasters shifted programming policies in a more audience-oriented way. In order to legitimise its position as public broadcaster, a vast majority of the audience (not necessarily all at the same time) had to be reached. Liberalisation forced public broadcasters into a logic of competition in the sense that no public broadcaster could afford to lose a majority of its audiences to commercial competitors (Paulu, 1981, p. 26; Price and Raboy, 2003, p. 3). For example, Nossiter (1991) explains that both management and producers referred to a new British Broadcasting Corporation (BBC) at the end of the 1980s where one wanted to see 'bottoms on the seats'. Also, in other countries such as the Netherlands and in regions like Flanders, public broadcasters tried to overcome previous difficulties to grasp the public's preferences (Bardoel and D'Haenens, 2004, p. 169) and connect with the citizens they were supposed to serve (McQuail, 1991, p. 152; Coppens and Saeys, 2006).

In spite of the necessity of a reorientation of often overly paternalistic programming strategies, the increased responsiveness to consumers' needs led to concerns about an alleged convergence between public and private broadcasters' offers (Siune and McQuail, 1992, pp. 194–5; Raboy, 1995, pp. 12–14). After market shares of public broadcasters fell sharply in the 1980s, more 'modern' programming strategies resulted in more stable audience reach results in the 1990s. Pauwels (1995, p. 79) questions whether a strong market position of public broadcasters can be defended if public broadcasters' comeback is based on a strategy that has little to do with realising public service objectives, but everything to do with satisfying the individual needs of 'his majesty the viewer'. She concludes that, whereas during monopoly, paternalism and politicisation prevented public service objectives from being realised, market-oriented strategies were perhaps responsible for the same deficit after liberalisation. The challenge that public broadcasting was confronted with in phase 2 lay in making the good popular and the popular good.

The survival of public service broadcasting

The apparent deadlock between the liberalisation of the broadcasting sector on the one hand and the announced demise of public broadcasters on the other (Tracey, 1998) was eventually not as acute as feared. Public broadcasters were under pressure, yet there remained significant political support and a lot of time and effort were devoted both outside, and above all inside, public broadcasters to meet new challenges (Hulten and Brants, 1992, pp. 127–8).

The new media environment (late 1990s onwards)

The dual broadcasting order that emerged in the 1980s gradually dissolved from the end of the 1990s onwards. A third phase of PSB emerged in which not only public broadcasters delivered public media services; other public institutions such as museums and libraries and, in addition, private companies, delivered services that could qualify as public media services. These are not necessarily part of a publicly subsidised, government-led public service media project, however. In the 1980s and 1990s private broadcasters already claimed they were in fact also delivering public services (Murdoch, 2005, p. 133, publication of a speech originally delivered in 1989). However, in spite of convergence between programming strategies, the boundaries between public and private players and the services they delivered became clearer.

Consequently, PSB has become a policy project that needs to be redefined (once again) (see, for example, Steemers, 2003, p. 125; Barnett, 2006; Jakubowicz, 2007a; Bardoel and D'Haenens, 2008). The context in which public service media have to be conceptualised, operationalised and implemented is in flux, which significantly complicates matters for public broadcasters, private competitors, policy makers and media scholars.

Blurring boundaries, changing consumer habits and abundance

First and foremost convergence – the buzzword of the 1970s and 1980s – gradually became reality from the end of the 1990s onwards. Digital compression technologies were optimised further and, as a result, boundaries between previously distinct sectors like broadcasting, telecommunications and (information and communication technology) were genuinely blurring and, correspondingly, the ways of thinking about regulation in these sectors were being revised (Levy, 1999, pp. 4–5; Bavasso, 2003, p. 398; Galperin, 2004, p. 3ff; Marsden and Arino, 2004, p. 4ff). The blurring of boundaries between sectors increasingly manifests itself in the integrating ownership structures of the broadcasting, telecommunications and ICT sectors (Doyle, 2002a). Mergers, take-overs and partnerships are often at the expense of broadcasting companies who seem ill-suited to face competition with more powerful telecommunications and ICT companies. Business models from the latter sectors are now being introduced in broadcasting: for example, pay-per-view and subscription become more and more widespread revenue streams for broadcasting services.

Consumer habits are changing as well. User-generated content, inter-activity, blogs, citizen journalism and web 2.0 are concepts that dominate debates concerning adaptation strategies of traditional broad-casting undertakings (both public and private) to continue captur-ing consumers' attention. For public broadcasters the evolution from a push- to a pull-content environment is particularly challenging. Bardoel and Ferrell Lowe (2007, pp. 9–17) even argue that meeting changing consumer patterns is one of the core challenges for public broadcasters: within a fragmented and postmodern media environ-ment, public broadcasters' main task is to find ways to connect with citizens.

Finally and perhaps most importantly, the 'digital age' is characterised by abundance. There is more capacity for different types of content and platforms become more and more substitutable (Levy, 1999, p. 5). The observation of abundance fuels liberal and technological deterministic solutions to deal with PSB. Sawers (2000, p. 33), for example, calls PSB 'a paradox of our time', and other scholars like Armstrong and Weeds (2007) question the added value of public broadcasters in a market where there is allegedly an unlimited choice for consumers.

Evolution towards a multi-stakeholder environment

These theoretical arguments against PSB (addressed further in Chapter 3 in this book) are picked up by private media companies. Public broadcasters' new media activities are a thorn in the flesh of pri-vate broadcasters, publishers, DVD retail companies and so on. They attack public broadcasters' activities – arguably in a more forceful and coordinated way at both the national and European level (Donders and Pauwels, 2008).

Although national governments are not insensitive to the arguments of private companies, there seems also to be a shared awareness that some sort of PSB or public service media system might be more essential than ever in a media landscape that offers more diversity indeed, but often at a (higher) price (Steemers, 1999, p. 2ff; 2001, p. 4; Tongue and Harvey, 2004).

Hence, national regulators face the difficulty of enabling and, at the same time, constraining public broadcasters' activities in a com-plex media environment. PSB policy has become the result of multi-stakeholder consultations. During monopoly public broadcasting policy was the outcome of bilateral negotiation processes between public broadcasters and governments. After liberalisation, private broadcasters also gained a say about PSB. At present, other media companies, public institutions (occupied with education, culture, sports, social issues, etc.), various national and European interest groups and supranational bodies such as the Commission have a say in the design of public service broadcasting (Donders and Pauwels, 2010a).

This evolution toward a multi-stakeholder environment is most visible when looking at the increased relevance of Commission initiatives in the area of PSB. By means of the state aid rules it seems that the Commission is affecting national debates on the future of PSB (Humphreys, 2008a; Donders and Pauwels, 2010b; Brevini, 2010). In 2001 and, consequently, in 2009 the Commission communicated what it deemed 'good' subsidies to PSB and the guidelines of good governance it put forward are intrinsically tied to the specific organisation of public broadcasting policy and the definition of public broadcasters' public service task. In addition to the subsidy rules, the TWF Directive (1989) was also updated and a new Directive expanding the scope from television to audiovisual media services adopted in 2007. Oddly enough, however, it seems that the relevance of Community action in PSB is specifically higher when it concerns the horizontal state aid rules more than the sector-specific rules of the Audiovisual Media Services (AVMS) Directive (European Council, 2007) (see following chapters).

Public service media in practice

The crucial question is how to transpose diverging ideas on PSB in policy practice while taking into account the peculiar technological, economic and political circumstances of the 21st century. A conclusive answer to this question is lacking and, for the moment, policy makers seem to focus their attention and efforts on the width of the remit in new media environments (Steemers, 2003, p. 125). This does not mean that policy is not adapted. In many countries, new regulation and experimental control mechanisms have been introduced (Iosifidis, 2008, pp. 353–4). All these experiments set out from the premise that a cross-media role for public broadcasters is necessary and legitimate, but that an expansion into new media should be cautiously (and even suspiciously) watched.

The BBC's Public Value Test (subsequently referred to as 'PVT') is the best-known and often-cited example of how to deal with public service media. For services that can be considered as significant alterations of the BBC's public service delivery, an *ex ante* evaluation of both their public value and market impact has been carried out. The BBC Trust, which is the monitoring body of the BBC, and OFCOM (Office of Communication) are responsible for the analysis (Collins, 2007). The PVT is a dynamic addition to the static Royal Charter; it aims to evaluate whether certain services are covered by the Royal Charter, which is changed once every 10 years only. In that sense, the PVT does not aim to limit the BBC's scope of activities; rather, its objective is to provide solid ground for a legitimate expansion of the BBC's services portfolio. To date, four tests have been carried out concerning the BBC's I-Player service, the offer of a high-definition channel, the launch of a Gaelic channel and the expansion of broadband news videos covering regional news. The first three of these resulted in approvals, with conditions, while the fourth was often linked to concerns of private media companies, technology neutrality requirements and adaptations to foster public interest goals. The news videos were disapproved as they, in the BBC Trust's opinion, embraced little public value and, in addition, would gravely affect regional news providers in the market (BBC Trust, 2009).

In the UK, the design of a public service media system has also been suggested, in which alongside the BBC other companies can take advantage of public funding for public media services. A public service publisher (PSP) would commission content from independent producers, broadcasters and other media companies on the basis of a tender procedure. This requires a universal disclosure of the commissioned content. The idea of a PSP was launched by OFCOM in 2005. In fact, the Peacock Committee had already suggested the creation of a Public Broadcasting Authority in 1986 (Peacock, 1986). OFCOM (2005, p. 6) relaunched the idea as a new means to organise PSB in the digital age. The idea has been lauded for being far more efficient, and also for constraining the BBC's expansion into the Internet (Elstein, 2008; Lilley, 2008, p. 97). It has also been heavily criticised, however, for ending public broadcasters' privileged position and for introducing a market logic into public broadcasting (Iosifidis, 2010, p. 28). The criticism of the PSP model is not so far-fetched as proponents suggest, in top-slicing part of the BBC's licence fee to fund it. This would, as BBC Trust chairman Lyons (2008) pointed out, drive a wedge between the licence fee payer and the BBC and ultimately risks undermining the public's support of the public broadcaster (Iosifidis, 2010, p. 28). Although the idea of a PSP is an interesting one to explore, the financial implications of such an exploration should not be passed on to public broadcasters.

Another more comprehensive strategy for dealing with the evolution towards public service media can be found in the Netherlands, where public broadcasting policy is increasingly focused on functions rather than markets. In other words, the market where an activity takes place is irrelevant in so far as the activity carries out a pre-set public interest function of PSB. Provision of information, entertainment, culture and so on is the function of the various Dutch public broadcasters (WRR, 2005; Broeders et al., 2006). The rethinking of PSB policy can also be more restrictive in nature. For example, in Germany public broadcasters are prevented from advertising and sponsoring revenues in online environments and the Swiss government has limited public broadcasters' Internet activities to services that are directly linked to existing radio and television services (Latzer et al., 2009). To sum up, public service media is at an experimental stage. Policy answers are largely about new ways to control PSB, and fail adequately to consider fundamental questions on its future. Public broadcasters themselves add to the debates, but inspired by doom scenarios they at times also avoid them in an attempt to protect their institution from far-reaching changes. These changes are taking place, however. Public broadcasters are delivering programmes online, deliver generalist and niche services, experiment with new sorts of services, explore the possibilities of interactivity, and continue to cut costs and diversify revenue streams. Public service media exist, albeit without a consensual theoretical and political foundation.

Some concluding remarks

The succinct and fragmentary history of PSB presented above illustrates the fact that PSB is a policy project influenced not only by technological evolutions, but more so by political interests and to a lesser extent social imperatives. Although technological progress has been used to argue for (phase 1) and, later, against the monopoly of public broadcasters (phase 2), the underlying motivation of (not) having a public broadcasting monopoly was linked to political interests. In the 1930s, political power maximisation and an enlightenment ideal about broadcasting led to the political choice to establish a monopoly. In the 1980s, the economic potential of the broadcasting sector and the desire not to miss the train of liberalisation provoked the political decision to end the monopoly status of public broadcasters. Although the liberalisation of European broadcasting markets has often been presented as a straightforward attack on public broadcasters, liberalisation was a messy process and in the 1980s and 1990s governments continued heavily to regulate the broadcasting sector. Of course, this is not to say that the abolishment of monopoly was not a hallmark in the history of public broadcasters. It turned public broadcasters into entrepreneurs that increasingly aimed to reach their audiences while adhering to a public service standard. This evolution from public broadcasting institution to a public broadcasting undertaking was, even in spite of commercialisation, a necessary shift. It resulted in more self-consciousness and reflection. The latter has proved to be particularly necessary as public broadcasters are in the middle of another shift from public broadcasting to public media *entrepreneur*. Public service media strategies are being developed within an uncertain regulatory, technological, economic and financial environment. Again, the future direction of PSB – even if tied to abundance and convergence – is linked with political evolutions and economic interests. In the middle of all this, policy makers should make choices either in favour of or against public broadcasters, between different ways of organising PSB, and about the desirability of evolving into a sustainable public servic media project and the specifics thereof.

3
Perspectives on Public Service Media

The aim of this chapter is not to provide for an exhaustive overview of existing literature on public service broadcasting (PSB) in the digital age. Rather, it aims to sketch the different perspectives on public service media as a viable policy project. A distinction is made between two groups of perspectives that set out from different assumptions and pursue seemingly opposite objectives. The first group of market failure perspectives assumes that government intervention is acceptable in so far it is justified by the existence of a real market failure. In a digital age, it is assumed that market failures and, hence, the need for public broadcasters decline. Social democratic perspectives fundamentally disagree with this view, arguing that PSB and, by extension, public service media are an ideological and political choice in favour of democracy. Government intervention should in that sense not depend on market observations, but on values such as social cohesion, inclusion, diversity and pluralism. Both perspectives propose different future scenarios for PSB. The first rejects public service media, the second strongly propagates them. This chapter further explores the different future scenarios for public broadcasting as they underlie, to a large extent, European policy debates on public service media.

Market failure perspectives

Market failure perspectives set out from the idea that public broadcasting policy is based on the existence of an objective market failure. Hoskins et al. (2004, p. 292) define a market failure as a situation in which the market fails to bring about desirable outcomes. For broadcasting this means that the market is not performing in an optimal or efficient way and under-provides services that are deemed to serve broader social objectives (Doyle, 2002b, p. 64; Whiters, 2003, p. 106). Market failure is often linked to the so-called public good characteristics of broadcasting. Public goods are both non-rivalrous and non-excludable. This means that the consumption of a good does not prevent others from consuming the same good and that it is difficult to charge consumers for the consumption of broadcasting services respectively (Doyle, 2002b, pp. 64–5; Hoskins et al., 2004, pp. 196–7). These public goods characteristics can result in the under-provision of services with positive externalities (e.g. the contribution of news or documentaries to informed citizenship) and the over-provision of services with negative externalities (e.g. the impact of pornography and extreme violence on youngsters' perception of social relations). Government intervention is usually based on reducing negative externalities, while bringing about positive ones. This is not evident as people tend to under-consume services with positive externalities (so-called 'merit goods'). Public broadcasters have to remedy this (Doyle, 2002b, p. 66).

Economic and technological evolutions have put pressure on the traditional market failure rationales for keeping in place big public broadcasters. The UK media and telecommunications regulator OFCOM (2004, p. 11), for example, argues that the market is increasingly providing for a number of public services itself. Under these circumstances, government intervention by means of a public broadcaster has to be re-evaluated. A 'natural' evolution to public service media is by no means acceptable for proponents of a market failure perspective. On the contrary, a gradual dismantling of public broadcasters is argued for. Two possibilities unfold.

Toward a public service publisher

First of all, Elstein et al. (2004) and Peacock (1986, 2004) argue for the abolition of public broadcasters and the creation of a public service publisher (PSP) system in which public services that are under-provided by the market are commissioned through a competitive bidding procedure. Elstein is admittedly more extreme in this regard, as he interprets the PSP system in a very restricted fashion and sees no role at all for public broadcasters. Commercial provision of services is adequate and the public broadcasting system at odds with the current economic reality. Dissolving technological constraints have resulted in more providers and power shifting away from broadcasters to channels and content producers (Elstein et al., 2004, p. 29). Undeniably, there is a more varied offer than 50 or even 10 years ago. However, the idea is ignored (intentionally or not) that an open and competitive market in media remains largely utopian for the moment. Technology in itself does not change the structure of the media market. In their discussion of the UK media market, Elstein et al. (2004) focus mainly on the position of the British Broadcasting Corporation (BBC). However, they fail to recognise the dominant position of BSkyB, which illustrates how media markets have a tendency to concentrate. In fact, technological convergence has only enabled the further integration of the media sector. This is not only apparent in the pay-television sector, but also in the production sector (Ballon et al., 2010). According to Elstein et al. (2004), the latter faces lower barriers to entry into the Internet. Even though this is a truism, the production sector is being confronted with severe pressures to cut costs and, as a consequence thereof, merging activities. In that sense, the abolition of public broadcasters that otherwise would increasingly invest in domestically produced content might further current tendencies of integration and, as such, contribute to a less competitive broadcasting market.

In any case, Elstein et al. (2004) favour a system without public broadcasters. Certainly for new media markets like the Internet, a presence of public broadcasters that goes beyond informing consumers about radio and television activities is undesirable. In fact, it is argued that the BBC uses the licence fee to occupy new media markets and to push competitors out of the market. The BBC should be privatised – in order to protect competition preferably after some of its parts are liberalised – and derive its funding from subscriptions.

Nonetheless, Elstein concludes that the market will still fail to provide some distinct services. These services should be subsidised on a competitive basis. Here, the PSP idea comes in the picture. The privatised BBC could compete for subsidies to provide socially desirable services. In fact, according to Elstein et al. (2004), it is very likely that it would obtain a considerable part of the available subsidies given its experience in the area of public service delivery. A new authority (the Public Broadcasting Authority) should be created to award subsidies (Elstein et al., 2004, p. 20).

Assuming policy makers are not willing to abolish public broadcasters, regulation for public service media needs to be strengthened. A more evidence-based assessment of public service needs in the market must be identified, and the fulfilment of public purposes should be assessed on the basis of verifiable qualitative criteria (Elstein et al., 2004, p. 8). In other words: the abolition of the BBC is the most desirable outcome of any revision of British broadcasting regulation. But if this is not an attainable scenario for political reasons, a small public broadcaster 'light' (*cf. infra*) is acceptable – under strict conditions – as well. Although a more evidence-based approach of public broadcasting policy is argued for in this book, it can be doubted whether any system of control could satisfy Elstein et al. The UK has probably put in place the most extensive set of instruments to continuously evaluate the BBC's activities. According to Collins (2010), this set of control and evaluation instruments is even exaggerated and exemplifies a move towards the 'audit society' in which too much red tape takes attention and resources away from media production and creativity. Taking the extensive control system in the UK into account and Collins' criticism thereof, the suggestion that the BBC is hardly controlled and can free-wheel in new media markets is especially exaggerated.

Peacock is considerably less negative about the BBC. He does not agree with the preservation of PSB as it is today and no longer links PSB with one public broadcaster. However, he does not have a grudge against particular institutions and most ardently defends a PSP system on the basis of consumer sovereignty arguments, rather than statements about the (dys-)functioning of public institutions (Peacock, 1986, 2004).

As early as 1986 Peacock states that 'the consumer is the best judge of his/her own interests' (Peacock, 1986, p. 28; for discussions on consumer sovereignty, see also Peacock, 2000; Sawers, 2000; Knox, 2005, p. 383). Due to technological evolutions, direct pay relations between consumers and providers can be established. Hence, previous market failures in this respect gradually dissolve as 'there is at least a chance of creating a genuine consumer market in broadcasting combined with a continuation of public service, in the positive sense of secure funding of programmes of a demanding or innovative kind' (Peacock, 1986, p. 126). It is important to notice that Peacock acknowledges the need for public service delivery – not least because consumers highly value it (Peacock, 1986, pp. 125–8).

Given Peacock's emphasis on consumer sovereignty and the benefits of competition in the broadcasting sector, his preference for a PSP model to realise public service objectives in the broadcasting sector comes as no surprise. However, he does not plead for a straightforward privatisation of the BBC. Rather, the BBC should become a private non-profit organisation of which the financing is based on subscription and subsidies it can derive from a competitive PSP system (Peacock, 1986, p. 133) organised by a Public Service Broadcasting Council.

The Public Broadcasting Authority of Elstein et al. (2004) is in fact a reinvention of Peacock's Public Service Broadcasting Council idea – launched in 1986. This Council should decide in a highly transparent way and on the basis of clear criteria which programmes to support. Peacock is considerably more flexible on this point than Elstein et al., arguing that all genres (including entertainment) deserve funding. Moreover, against the background of the new media environment, parties other than broadcasters should be allowed to apply for subsidies (Peacock, 2004, pp. 49–50).

The 1986 Peacock report introduced rather controversial ideas about PSB and the BBC into UK political debates. Although it was regularly stressed in the report itself that the Peacock Committee did not advocate for a *laissez faire* broadcasting policy, Peacock and 'his' report have often been considered as the symbol of rising market-oriented policies in the 1980s (Barnett, 2002; Collins, 2002; Fairbairn, 2004). However, the PSP system as outlined by Peacock is far more extensive and inclusive than the one proposed by Elstein et al.; it sets out from the possible value of public service delivery. The idea of extending public service media to companies and institutions other than public broadcasters is also highly valuable and should not be thrown overboard too soon. In a similar vein, it is far too easy to assert that Peacock argues for a gap-filling PSB system, as he has stressed that the delivery of public services should not be confined to certain niche genres.

Admittedly, the ideas of Elstein et al. and Peacock can also be criticised. To begin with, both insist on broadcasting policy being determined on the basis of individual consumer preferences while the ambitions of a society are an equally – if not more – legitimate basis for this. Furthermore, both Elstein et al. and Peacock assume policy change is necessary because of technological change only. This sort of technological determinism that is, moreover, fuelled by a radiant belief in market forces, does not fit easily with reality. For example, some technologies like digital rights management (DRM) protection are used by companies to constrain, rather than enable, consumer choice. Finally, PSB is disconnected from public broadcasters. Although it is not advisable to tie the institution exclusively to the policy project in every discussion, throwing that same link overboard seems too far-reaching and overlooks the corporate heritage of numerous public broadcasters.

A public broadcaster light

A second future scenario for PSB that fits within the broader framework of market failure perspectives concerns the gradual downsizing of public broadcasters to niche public broadcasters. Concretely, a light model of PSB limits public broadcasters' activities to these services not readily available on the market. A broad public service remit would harm private competitors. For that reason, a tighter definition of the public service remit is deemed necessary (Appelman et al., 2005, p. 50; Armstrong and Weeds, 2007, p. 119). In particular, entertainment is excluded from public broadcasters' activities. Overall, light perspectives focus on areas where public broadcasters should not be active. New media, for example, are a 'no-go zone', as are sports, fiction and entertainment (Appelman et al., 2005, p. 52).

Light models of PSB are very much occupied with constraining public broadcasters' activities. To ensure competition in the broadcasting market, public broadcasters should be controlled more vigourously. No engaging project of public service media is outlined. In that respect, light versions of PSB, as proposed in Broeders et al. (2006), Appelman et al. (2005) or Armstrong and Weeds (2007), exemplify rather well private media companies' aspirations.

Some sort of public broadcaster can be maintained. However, the proposal to limit public broadcasters' activities to these services not available on the market and to exclude them *a priori* from sports, entertainment and new media markets is intrinsically an assassination of PSB. Rather confusingly, the argument is made that because public broadcasters' offers are not sufficiently distinctive, they should no longer be allowed to fish in the same ponds as their commercial competitors. A 'pure' profile of public broadcasters is required (Appelman et al., 2005; Armstrong and Weeds, 2007). However, distinctiveness is a concept that applies to public broadcasters' public services in all different markets and genres. It is difficult to understand why, as Appelman et al. (2005, p. 53) put forward, public broadcasters set the standard in news provision and not in entertainment programmes. The misinterpretation of the market failure and distinctiveness concepts in the light model is more threatening than the arguments for a PSP model. Public broadcasters – even if privatised and involved in a bidding process – are still sizeable and competitive. Moreover, a PSP system still accepts the necessity of public service delivery in the new media environment. Proponents of a light model do not share this view; they think government intervention is uncalled for and counter the emergence of public service media through marginalising public broadcasters to US standards.

It must be acknowledged that several economic scholars oppose these predominantly negative market failure appraisals of PSB. Graham (2005) and Robinson et al. (2005) have illustrated that market failures continue to exist in the media sector and that, consequently, a strong case for PSB, and by extension public service media, remains. There is still a gap between the provision of 'Reithian' services by the market and the socially optimal delivery of such services. However, in arguing against the market failure approaches discussed above, it is often not sufficiently addressed what 'Reithian' services are and in what ways they are under-provided.

Social democratic perspectives

Whereas market failure perspectives on public service media are rather disruptive in nature, social democratic perspectives have their attachment to public broadcasters as the core of public service media in common. Public broadcasters are a valuable asset to society (McChesney, 2002; Jakubowicz, 2003; Steemers, 2003; Bardoel and Ferrell Lowe, 2007; Barnett, 2007; Van den Bulck, 2008). Their existence is not based on the existence of market failures, but on the belief in a broadcasting system outside the realm of the market. The latter is ruled by iron-clad laws of price and demand and serves one overall aim: profit making. Public broadcasters, on the contrary, have always been compelled to make programmes and deliver public interest objectives (Tracey, 1998).

In a generalising fashion, social democratic perspectives consider public service media a highly valuable project – encompassing a broad array of genres, platforms and services – that contributes to the democratic needs of society. Public service media should add to the realisation of a public sphere in which all citizens can participate regardless of their market appeal to producers (Barnett, 2002; Jakubowicz, 2007b). The market is often seen as an inferior means of delivering public interest objectives (Brown, 1996; Tracey, 1998; Leys, 2001; Price and Raboy, 2003; Bardoel and Ferrell Lowe, 2007). Garnham (1990, p. 120), for example, argues that the justification of public broadcasting 'lies in its superiority to the market as a means of providing all citizens, whatever wealth or geographical location, equal access to a wide range of high-quality entertainment, information and education, and as a means of ensuring that the aim of the programme producer is the satisfaction of a range of audience tastes rather than only those tastes that show the largest profit'. Moreover, the history of public broadcasters, their trustworthiness and reliability, the embeddednes of a public service ethos (even if partly abandoned at times) and the mix of public service programmes justify the maintenance of a public broadcaster (Barnett, 2006, p. 9). Utopian ideas on the optimal functioning of markets are thus firmly rejected as a basis for media policy (Barwise, 2002, pp. 26–31). Consequently, economic and technological evolutions can not in themselves alter the necessity of public service media. On the contrary, some economic and technological evolutions necessitate the revitalisation of PSB.

In some way, social democratic perspectives on public service media are a combination of ideals and pragmatism. On the one hand, it is upheld that public broadcasters are necessary because they can act relatively independently from market forces. On the other hand, they are necessary because it is observed that the market does not serve significant parts of the audience and under-provides certain services. It is this twofold ideological and pragmatic vision that is transposed in concrete future scenarios for PSB. These scenarios are often ideological and deal with the future of public service media. They also share a manifest and unequivocal rejection of market recipes in the media sector. Many scholars that can be situated within the social democratic perspective on public service media are indeed of the opinion that collective needs are increasingly abandoned to the benefit of individual consumer needs and, above all, private sector interests (Leys, 2001, p. 4; Barwise, 2002, p. 25; De Bens and Paulussen, 2005; Coppens and Saeys, 2006; Bardoel and D'Haenens, 2008, p. 342). Some also counter this pessimism. Emphasising public broadcasters' strategies to survive in a digital environment, these scholars observe that there is still much support for PSB and even public service media. Collins et al. (2001, p. 2) have been particularly active in arguing against dominant assertions about the decline of public broadcasting: 'perhaps the force of these trends is overestimated. European public service broadcasters are deeply embedded within their sustaining societal contexts. It is sometimes too easy to underestimate their durability and legitimacy'. Leaving aside the core assumptions underlying social democratic perspectives on public service media, different future scenarios for public service media can be discerned within the generic group of social democratic perspectives.

Bigger and better public media services providers

Scholars like Bardoel and Ferrell Lowe (2007), Jakubowicz (2007a, 2007b), Leurdijk (2007), Moe (2009a) and Steemers (2001, 2003) can be clustered into one perspective. They all formulate a number of action points that are at the core of policies, aiming to realise public service media. For example, Jakubowicz (2007a) puts forward a six-step strategy on the basis of which public broadcasters can evolve into public media services providers. Most of these action points are also addressed in contributions of the other scholars mentioned above.

Firstly, Jakubowicz (2007a, pp. 31–3; see also Barnett, 2006, pp. 1–2; Bardoel and D'Haenens, 2008, p. 340) stresses that ideology and not technology will undermine the preservation of public broadcasting. Arguments against PSB and public service media should be countered. In this respect, it is primordial to refute all views of public broadcasters as being an exception to normal market conditions.

Secondly, it is crucial to prove that public service media are necessary. As digitisation fuels the further integration of the media sector, diversity and pluralism are under pressure, and local services will be under-provided. These trends should be substantiated in order to illustrate that the market is not functioning optimally (Jakubowicz, 2007a, pp. 33–5). As governments have fewer tools to regulate the media sector, public broadcasters are both a unique and effective means of ensuring quality, diversity and pluralism in various media markets (Humphreys, 2008b, p. 3).

Consequently and thirdly, PSB is automatically and necessarily evolving into public service media. Services that deliver public value are not limited to one platform. The 'B' in public service Broadcasting should for that reason be replaced with the 'C' of Communication or Content, or the 'M' of Media (Jakubowicz, 2007a, pp. 35–8). Public service media can thus only be succesful when carried out by sizeable public broadcasters delivering a vast array of services across platforms (Barnett, 2006, p. 20). As Humphreys (2008b, p. 6) points out: 'Marginalised public broadcasters would not be influential enough to influence the marketplace positively and continue to set the standard for diverse and high quality content production'. In other words, size matters.

Fourthly, the core objectives of PSB must be reaffirmed in every public service media project. A strong public service ethos that is concerned with social cohesion and national identity, and meets individual citizen needs as well, must underlie what public broadcasters do. Consequently, full-portfolio distinctiveness is at the core of such an ethos and should overcome the supposed convergence between public and private sector offerings (Steemers, 2003, p. 128ff). Services are thus to be subsidised because they are important, not because they fit neatly within a particular genre or because they are linked with existing television or radio programmes. A multi-platform conceptualisation of public service media is necessary. Yet, few specifications thereof are provided (see, for example, Bardoel and Ferrell Lowe, 2007, pp. 18–19). This is regrettable, as there is surely no justification for subsidising public broadcasters in new media markets simply because they are the first to enter a market or because one is inclined to think that public broadcasters automatically and 'naturally' deliver public interest objectives. It makes more sense – at least that is the view put forward in this book – to subsidise services of which the inherent objectives are not realised in the market. This is not to say that public broadcasters cannot be active in entertainment or social networking sites. Nevertheless, there must a be clearly spelled out public objective underlying these activities. Being active in markets for the mere purpose of it cannot be a goal of public service media.

A fifth action point that is put forward by Jakubowicz (2007a, pp. 41–2) concerns the funding of public broadcasters. If governments want to see public service media taking ground, sustainable funding is a must. An increasing reliance on commercial funding might result in putting institutional interests before meeting citizens needs (see also Papathanassopoulos, 2007a, pp. 162–3).

Finally, the relation between audiences and the public broadcaster require rethinking. Public broadcasters should treat the audience as active participants and no longer as passive receivers (Coleman, 2002, pp. 94–5; Jakubowicz, 2007a, pp. 42–4). Bardoel and Ferrell Lowe (2007, p. 17) emphasise this point in arguing that a demand-oriented service strategy must replace the traditional supply-oriented programmation strategies of public broadcasters. Although one can hardly dispute the changing relations between content providers and consumers, it should (in the margin) be noted that scholars like Bardoel and Ferrell Lowe (2007) and Jakubowicz (2007a) adhere to a very technological optimist vision on public service media, while criticising market failure perspectives for their similar enthusiasm about new technological opportunities.

To summarise, the scholars discussed above pursue a public service media project in which public broadcasters deliver more services of a higher quality. This is a very valuable point of view that goes beyond platform-dependent discussions on public service media. One should be careful, however, in assuming that bigger public broadcasters are better in delivering public value. Such an assumption would fail to both recognise the structural disfunctions of some public broadcasters and address real-world questions regarding the balance to be struck between public and private service delivery.

Big if necessary and as good as required

The second perspective that can be discerned within the 'school' of social democratic visions on public service media in part remedies the shortcomings of the previously discussed perspective. A more evidence-based perspective on public service media is argued for. The evidence-based perspective largely contends that public broadcasters have to be as big as necessary and as good as required (Barwise, 2002; Collins, 2002; Donders and Pauwels, 2010a). More concretely, this means that public broadcasters are to be maintained and funded on the basis of a licence fee or government grant. Barwise (2002) argues that research shows citizens' attachment to public broadcasters. Moreover, he illustrates that a licence fee ensures that each citizen pays less – this in comparison with a subscription system that allows citizens to opt out. Moreover, the 'messy' reality of PSB in a mixed economy has been proven to deliver benefits to consumers and citizens. According to Barwise, the policy scenarios supported by Elstein and others are at best unproven and have, in fact, already shown their shortcomings (Barwise, 2002, pp. 30–2).

Moreover, the scope and scale of public broadcasters – thus still at the core of public service media – should be determined in a rational way: 'the policy priority should be to state the practical options as clearly as possible and use evidence and analysis, rather than dogma, to assess the likely outcomes of each one' (Barwise, 2002, p. 32). The pursuit of a rational evidence-based public service media project is shared by Collins (2002), who provides more insights on how such a project should appear. Concretely, Collins (2002, pp. 132–6) puts forward the notion that it is necessary to define what the task of public broadcasters is on the basis of four core public service values. It should then be decided whether the scope of public broadcasters' activities is proportional with regard to the goals pursued. Hence, definition and proportionality are two core concepts of Collins' proposals.

The four values Collins puts forward as the basis of public service media policy are quality, universality, independence and diversity ('QUID'). Quality is the most difficult concept to define and measure, but nonetheless it is of the utmost importance in determining the value of public service delivery. There are several types of quality: producer quality, consumer quality, quality as diversity, and so on. Overall,

Collins (2002) emphasises that there is a need for high-quality programmes. One should measure quality systematically through audience surveys, audience reach assessments and peer reviews. Secondly, Collins distinguishes between two types of universality: the ability of people to receive content at an affordable price and the skills to digest content regardless of socio-economic background. With regard to the latter, specific target group policies should be developed. Independence is the third concept of QUID and is defined by Collins as financial independence from vested market or political interests. Finally, public broadcasters' activity is required in areas where diversity decreases. Questions to be answered in this respect include: How much are separate sources of news provision desirable? What sort of diversity is important in determining public broadcasting policy? How should public broadcasters fill diversity gaps? (Collins, 2002, pp. 136–40).

On the basis of these four values and the proportionality concept, public service media and the role of public broadcasters therein should be defined. According to Collins (2002, pp. 144–5), policy makers should do this carefully, realising that blurry boundaries between public and commercial activities, aggressive expansion strategies in new media markets and anti-competitive behaviour do not serve public interest objectives. Moreover, as a side effect, the crowding out of competitors by public broadcasters might perversely endanger diversity and pluralism as well.

Overall, both Barwise and Collins argue from a social democratic perspective that the delivery of public media services by public broadcasters remains important in a new media environment – albeit that it needs to be rationalised and regulated more carefully than before. This approach, combined with elements from other scholars' contributions (situated within both market failure and social democratic perspectives), is followed throughout this book (for the discussion of the position followed in this book, see the following chapter).

The digital commons

A final perspective that merits discussion is Murdock's digital commons conceptualisation of public service media. Murdock puts forward a radical reinvention of public broadcasters' role in the new media environment. Essentially, public broadcasters should not be stand-alone organisations. On the contrary, they should be conceived as 'the principal node in an emerging network of public and civic initiatives that taken together, provide the basis for a new shared cultural space'

(Murdock, 2004, p. 2). The analysis that leads to this role for public broadcasters is twofold. On the one hand, technological evolutions have resulted in the fragmentation of media consumption; smaller groups of people consume a huge quantitative variety of content. This makes it difficult to sustain some sort of public sphere, which is essential in realising full citizenship (Murdock, 2004, p. 4). On the other hand, the media are increasingly subject to a process of commodification. Commercialisation and profit making are at the core of media production, distribution and also, consequently, consumption (Murdock, 2000, p. 39). The observation of these two trends leads Murdock to the conclusion that the realisation of specific information and communication rights is no longer possible (Murdock, 2004, pp. 4–5). In Murdock's opinion public broadcasters should counter fragmentation and commodification and ensure citizens can still access and process information and even engage in its production.

Murdock's assessment on the continuing importance of public broadcasters does not differ from other social democratic perspectives on public service media. However, his focus on participation and the networked environment in which public broadcasters are engaged is much bigger. For Murdock public broadcasters' expansion to new media markets through the launch of digital channels and Internet services is legitimate, but should be more oriented at innovative ways of enhancing citizen participation. Public broadcasters remain too much trapped in a top-down system in which the audience can choose from a menu – admittedly, a more elaborate menu, but without access to the kitchen (Murdock, 2000, p. 52).

Public broadcasters should increasingly focus attention on developing initiatives like the BBC's Creative Archive project, which allows the audience to use the BBC's content archive to create new content itself. The latter, so Murdock (2004, p. 14ff) argues, is an example of moving away from 'cultural in common' (in which public broadcasters following paternalist programmation strategies determined the cultural space of the audience) towards the 'digital commons' (in which the audience and content producers share and jointly create) (Murdock, 2004, p. 17).

In the digital commons scenario as decribed by Murdock (2004, p. 18), public broadcasters must reorganise themselves in order to absorb this new project of the better realisation of citizens rights. This reorganisation should not only be oriented towards a strengthening of the public service project, but also, and increasingly so, towards the creation of a network in which different actors work together to ensure full citizenship. Public broadcasters must be a central node in a new network of institutions like schools, museums and libraries. A digital commons network, in which public broadcasters are the nodal point (the 'hub'), must be committed to free and universal access, reciprocity and collaborative practice. The digital commons must also be global in scope and, as such, enhance the emergence of a global public sphere based on principles of mutual understanding and connectivity.

Murdock's analysis is interesting because it adds to social democratic perspectives that exclusively focus on public broadcasters and their delivery of public media services. It is also challenging because it questions rather fundamental basics of the current organisation of public broadcasters. In Murdock's scenario, participation of citizens is not accidental to some programmes or services, but is considered an essential aspect of service delivery, or rather service construction. Also, the network idea seems truly to answer the question as to whether public service media are to be monopolised by public broadcasters. In Murdock's opinion, other actors also have a role to play and are all nodes in a networked provision of public services oriented towards the delivery of public value and with respect to the different rights citizens ought to have in the information society. The digital commons scenario could be explored further in two ways. Firstly, Murdock might have elaborated on the possible added value that could result from cooperation between private undertakings on the one hand and public broadcasters and institutions such as museums and libraries on the other. Such a cooperation is not necessarily excluded from his digital commons scenario, but it is not touched upon. Cooperation between public and private actors could potentially reach and involve more citizens (than 'pure' public–public partnerships) and, consequently, also contribute to full citizenship. Secondly, Murdock does not reflect upon public broadcasters' economic motives in a liberalised media market, nor does he take into account possible power issues that could emerge in concrete cooperation projects between public broadcasters on the one hand and other public or civic organisations on the other. Public broadcasters like the BBC, NOS (Nederlandse Omroep Stichting) and VRT (Vlaamse Radio- en Televisieomroep) are already cooperating for some initiatives with, for example, the cultural sector (Raats and Pauwels, 2010). The latter is rather fragmented, however, and in comparison with public broadcasters, does often not possess the legal know-how and financial means to be considered equals in a cooperation agreement. For that reason, regulation needs to accompany the scenario suggested by Murdock.

How to align social democratic and market failure perspectives?

At first sight, it might seem that market failure and social democratic perspectives on public service media are mutually exclusive. Indeed, they set out from different knowledge frameworks and are difficult to reconcile. However, it should be possible to find 'the appropriate relationship between public service and the market – within public broadcasters and in terms of societies' overall media ecologies' (Collins et al., 2001, p. 17). The next chapter presents a framework of a sustainable public service media policy project setting out from a social democratic and evidence-based perspective on public service media, but meeting concerns of market failure viewpoints as well.

4
A Framework for Public Service Media

In order to evaluate European policies on public service media it seems both inescapable and desirable to elaborate on the normative position taken in this book. It has already been hinted at before that a social democratic perspective is followed. In particular, the approach in this book can be situated within the strand of more evidence-based models of public service media (see Barwise, 2002; Collins, 2002). This chapter aims to discuss the analytical framework used to evaluate the impact of European policy on public service broadcasting (PSB). The chapter starts with a discussion of the assumptions on which the analytical framework is based. An overview of the main building blocks of the analytical framework follows. Finally, some provisional conclusions on the strengths and weaknesses of the framework are outlined.

Starting points

The aim of this chapter is to identify a 'middle-range' and also more future-oriented policy approach for public service media. It sets out from three core assumptions (derived from the findings in the previous chapters). Firstly, public broadcasters are still well suited to deliver public media services. Secondly, other actors also deliver public media services. This observation does not imply the rejection of public broadcasters, but rather warrants the search for complementarity between new and old providers of public services. Finally, a number of regulatory and policy challenges are to be addressed in the case of a consensus on public service media emerging. The consensus on what public service media are should precede regulatory and policy changes, however.

Public broadcasters at the core of public service media

Public broadcasters should retain a central place in the delivery of public media services, for various reasons. Firstly, both historically and theoretically there is a case in favour of public broadcasters expanding activities to new media markets. Public broadcasters have built a considerable know-how, can disclose publicly funded content and prevent it from staying buried in archives, are considered houses of trust (Debrett, 2007, p. 4) and have already developed digital strategies that illustrate the possibility and also opportunity of fulfilling certain public interest objectives on multiple platforms and in different ways.

Secondly, public broadcasters are a well-known part of the media policy toolkit. In spite of public broadcasters' problems, they have contributed to public interest objectives for over 50 years. For that reason, it seems reasonable to rethink PSB and turn it into public service media. The suggestion to abolish public broadcasters is obviously less realistic and ignores the succesful history of public broadcasting. It assumes that more services and more competition will ultimately serve consumers. However, there is no guarantee that a genuine competitive and efficient market will emerge once public broadcasters disappear. Nor is it certain that public value will be delivered by private media companies on a secure basis to all individuals – including those that are less valuable for advertisers. Consequently, public broadcasters' scope is to expand, albeit not limitlessly. One should carefully reflect on areas where public broadcasters are necessary. No *carte blanche* approach should be adopted.

Thirdly, given the explosion of services in a new media ecology, abundancy of content could be seen as a new market failure that could be remedied in part by public broadcasters. In debates on media literacy, also at the European level, it is emphasised that the majority of the population does not master the skills to find, access, understand and evaluate the flow of online information. An even bigger part does not interact and is not making use of the possibilities to (co-)create content. Public broadcasters can definitely play a role here (see also Aslama, 2010).

Finally, and related to the former point, consumption patterns are changing the new media ecology. Both social responsibility and economic market failure perspectives acknowledge that traditional forms of media consumption are increasingly being complemented by other more experimental forms. Consequently, the evolving playing field changes not only the relations between actors that offer content, but also the relations between those actors and the audience. The latter has different, increasingly cross-media or multi-platform, needs and expectations. This evolution, as Murdock (2004) and Ferrell Lowe (2010) point out, will have important consequences for the way in which the public sphere functions. On the one hand, public broadcasters should offer individual consumers services that experiment with new media and types of interaction. On the other hand, fragmentation should also be countered by public broadcasters in order to continue furthering social cohesion.

Public service media is a shared project

The persisting and convincing arguments for a continuing role for public broadcasters should not lead to a denial of the huge variety of services offered by the market and other public institutions. In the new media ecology, many actors deliver public media services and are, hence, part of the public service media mix. The traditional conflict between public and private broadcasters no longer survives in the new media ecology. Roles of actors are changing, traditional boundaries are blurring and entirely new players are entering the market. For that reason, there is still a role for public broadcasters, but other players also have a valuable role.

In this respect, cooperation between actors to deliver public media services should be encouraged. Ad hoc public service networks are already emerging. The cooperation between public broadcasters and smaller cultural players is far from straightforward, however. Public broadcasters are clearly in a more powerful position than the highly fragmentary cultural sector. Very small cultural players are in turn far less professionalised than public broadcasters (Raats and Pauwels, 2010). In that sense, it is advisable that regulators not only encourage cooperation, but also assess its specific shortcomings in reality and provide for remedies if necessary.

Regulatory and policy challenges are ahead

Finally, pragmatic regulatory and policy mechanisms must be developed. Taking into account the historical embeddedness of public broadcasting and the liberalised new media ecology, regulation should be concerned with consultation, consensus and pragmatism for the purpose of finding a balance between the social democratic objectives of public broadcasters on the one hand and the economic interests of undertakings in the media sector on the other hand. Any consensus in this regard should take into account that public broadcasters also have their own institutional and economic interests. Moreover, a consensus should be oriented at enabling all stakeholders to fulfil their duties (be they public service oriented or economic) and certainly not at excluding public broadcasters from specific platforms.

Overall, the regulation of public broadcasters in a new media ecology should focus on two challenges. Firstly, the public service media project to be delivered by public broadcasters and, possibly, other actors should be defined as clearly as possible. There is a definite tendency towards integration in the media sector (McChesney, 2008, p. 234). In addition, media products continue to reveal specific public and merit good characteristics. Taking both integration trends and the specificity of media into account, the public service remit of public broadcasters should remain holistic in scope and thus, consequently, include a wide variety of services on different platforms and in all genres. This argument easily fits seemingly old-fashioned, but still highly valuable, arguments about the importance of television (Hollick, 1995; Tracey, 1998) and widens the scope of these arguments to other media services (Dahlgren, 2001). Secondly, once the remit of public broadcasters is defined, it has to be operationalised. Accountability on the side of public broadcasters is a must, and government should refrain from too far-reaching political control by introducing independent control and sanctioning mechanisms. Concretely, this means that both internal and external accountability have to be compatible and should reinforce each other.

Building blocks of the analytical framework

In short, the analytical framework describing the main building blocks of a sustainable public service media policy sets out from the three core ideas elaborated above:

1. Public broadcasters should be obliged (not merely allowed) to deliver new media services related to a clearly defined remit.
2. Public broadcasters should cooperate with other public actors and even private media companies for the delivery of some media services (e.g. cooperation with schools on documentaries and other educational services).
3. Public broadcasters' evolution into public media services providers should be accompanied by pragmatic regulation based on consultation rather than conflict.

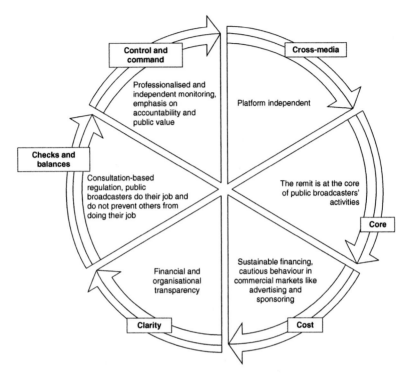

Figure 4.1 Analytical framework: Conditions for a sustainable public service media policy

These three core ideas have been operationalised further and transposed into six concrete conditions for a sustainable public service media policy (see Figure 4.1 above): cross-media, core, clarity, cost, control and command, and checks and balances.

Cross-media condition

The first condition of sustainable public service media policy relates to technology neutrality. Public broadcasters should be active on all relevant platforms in so far as the services they offer on these platforms meet pre-set public interest objectives. In other words: public broadcasters' activities should not be limited to traditional broadcasting platforms. This attachment to the principle of technology neutrality is shared (however, not necessarily put into practice) by European Union Member State (EUMS) and the Commission, which has repeatedly stated that regulation should not be determined on the basis of technological carriers (Reding, 2005). This also conforms with the idea that media companies have to follow consumers, and not *vice versa*.

Core condition

Secondly, the plethora of services offered by public broadcasters should reveal the core values underlying their existence. Public broadcasters' new media services (*in casu* Internet and mobile services) should not be accepted provided they are linked or 'closely related' to existing radio and television services. Some new services linked to existing programmes can exhibit less public value than services that are completely detached from existing radio and television services. Moreover, the requirement of a link between television and radio programmes on the one hand and new media services on the other is a legal swamp. A study by Latzer et al. (2009) on Swiss public broadcasting regulation, which allows public broadcasters to deliver online services in so far as these services are linked to radio or television services, illustrates that the operationalisation of this criterion is far from easy. The Swiss government, for example, allows online services that provide background knowledge for existing television and radio services. It is self-evident that the notion of background knowledge can be interpreted in varying ways.

New services should aim to seize the public value related opportunities that accompany technological revolutions (Debrett, 2007, p. 4ff) and, for that reason, relate to core objectives set by government. These objectives are to be clearly spelled out. Moreover, the services to be delivered should be identified. Basically, the 'amount' of public broadcasting that is needed should be pinned down (Collins, 2002, p. 142). Taking into account the huge diversity of services that can be offered by public broadcasters in the new media ecology, it is advisable to identify sets of objectives for different groups of services and genres. For example, for fiction requirements related to domestic production, innovation and quality can be guiding principles. Social relevance and cohesion can be considered important criteria for documentaries, and one could require that blogs and forums focus on political issues and are, moreover, adequately controlled by webmasters and linked to informative websites. This approach does not *a priori* exclude public broadcasters from certain genres or services, nor does it result in the emergence of core or peripherical services. Rather, it defines core values and objectives (hence, core condition) and links services with these. For the sake of clarity, it needs to be emphasised that the concept 'core' should by no means be equated with a niche public broadcaster!

Cost condition

Of course, the realisation of public service objectives clearly spelled out through the offer of public media services is possible only where public broadcasters are adequately financed. A decline in public funding in some Member State (MS), accompanied by the pressure to raise more commercial revenues, would inevitably marginalise public broadcasters as money is a relevant factor when one aims to make outstanding (and domestically produced) programmes. A more commercial course of public broadcasters (aimed at the generation of more commercial revenues) would inevitably undermine its legitimacy (Jakubowicz, 2007b).

Hence, levels of public funding should be sufficient (in the light of the public service remit) and based on a rational determination of the cost of public services. Moreover, commercial activities on the Internet or in other new media markets should be restricted where possible in order to ensure that the possibilities of these new environments are explored with an eye to better realisation of the public service remit, rather than with an eye to generating more commercial revenues.

Funding is highly dependent on the specific country of a MS. In bigger MS like the UK and Germany, private broadcasters oppose commercial activities of public broadcasters. In smaller MS like Flanders, private broadcasters also oppose commercial communication activities (like advertising) but favour public broadcasters engaging in the offer of pay-television services as well. They take this position as it is impossible to create, for example, a video-on-demand market without public broadcasters' inducement.

Clarity condition

The increasing variety in funding mechanisms and the overall complexity of the new media environment requires public broadcasters to be as transparent as possible. Accountability and control mechanisms make no sense without transparency (Bardoel, 2003; Buckley et al., 2008, p. 193ff). In a similar vein, a lack of transparency also inhibits the emergence of a flexible environment in which creativity can flourish and that allows for cooperation between public broadcasters and other parties (Donders and Pauwels, 2009). However, an advanced level of organisational and financial transparency should never result in the obliged disclosure of confidential and strategic information by public broadcasters; after all, the latter are participating in a market economy. Transparency requirements that are too burdensome might risk undermining public broadcasters' competitive position, and eventually their ability to deliver public value.

Control and command condition

The condition of transparency relates to both the internal and external accountability of a public broadcaster. Control is another vital aspect of accountability, and becomes a crucial aspect of the sustainable public service media project supported throughout this book. Historically, control of public broadcasters raises questions concerning political influence and the fragmented nature of many MS' controlling mechanisms (Curran, 2008, p. 103). However, a public service media project can be succesful only in so far that it succeeds in reaching a balance between the control and editorial independence of public broadcasters (CoE, 2009). Action points in this regard are:

- the introduction of flexible control mechanisms capable of taking into account the fast changes in the media market;
- a rationalisation of controlling mechanisms;
- a professionalisation of controlling bodies; and
- strict codes on public broadcasters' independence regarding programmation strategies.

In short, control should be optimised and aimed at enabling, not constraining, the fulfilment of public interest objectives (Aslama and Syvertsen, 2006).

Checks and balances condition

Finally, an adequate controlling system is not only a prerequisite for the fulfilment of public interest objectives; it also ensures that media markets are not unneccessarily distorted by public broadcasters. After the liberalisation of the broadcasting market in the 1980s, government authorities have the duty to enhance an optimal functioning of the market through both sector-specific and horizontal policies. This is not to say that public broadcasters should not compete in different markets. Yet, there is no public value justification in public broadcasters foreclosing markets or behaving in other anti-competitive and overly commercial ways. Market distortion is to some extent intrinsic to public broadcasting regimes. Policy makers accept this (Coppieters, 2010; Ingves, 2010). Nevertheless, market distortion without more pluralism, diversity, social cohesion or quality is difficult to defend. For that reason, government authorities should carefully balance the interests of consumers, public broadcasters and private media undertakings. This does not mean favouring public broadcasters over private media companies or *vice versa* in different dossiers and at different times. A structural multi-stakeholder and consultation-based regime is necessary in order to ensure that public broadcasters do their job while not preventing others from doing theirs.

In conclusion

In terms of the research question, this book argues that European policy, and state aid policy in particular, has fostered the ongoing evolution towards sustainable public service media policy in Western European MS.

Admittedly, the analytical framework presented has some shortcomings; the conditions decribed above could have been operationalised further. However, the specificity of countries' public broadcasting regimes makes this difficult. In addition, overly tight conditions might risk undercutting the flexibility of the case study approach used to study the influence of European policy on public service media in Germany, Flanders and the Netherlands. A second point of criticism of the analytical framework presented could be a perceived ambiguity. Some might argue that no definite choice is made between different perspectives on PSB. It might even be alleged that market considerations have no place at all in a framework on public service media policy. Nonetheless, public broadcasters are active in a market environment. Perhaps some do not like this situation but it is a reality, however, and one we can not easily escape. For that reason, this framework is not only ideological in adhering to a social responsibility perspective on public service media. It is also highly pragmatic as it situates itself within an evidence-based approach that allows for the introduction of issues like competition concerns that undeniably play a role in policy-making processes.

The combination of ideals and pragmatism in the analytical framework should result in a nuanced analysis of European state aid policy and its impact on public service media. Such an analysis can only add to further policy making.

5
EU Market Integration in the Broadcasting Sector

A study of public service media and policy in Europe would be incomplete without a consideration of the project of EU market integration in the broadcasting sector. The policy of market integration preceded the application of the state aid rules to public service broadcasting (PSB). Due to the European-wide liberalisation of the broadcasting sector in 1989, competition was introduced in a formerly monopolistic broadcasting sector and, hence, the competition rules became more relevant.

This chapter (in part based on Pauwels and Donders, 2011; drawing also from Harcourt, 2005; Harrison and Woods, 2007) follows the chronology of events in the development of a European integrated broadcasting sector and tries to contextualise them. It consists of six parts. The first part discusses the tensions that are inherent to the creation of European policies in the field of broadcasting. Secondly, the Television without Frontiers (TWF) directive is assessed. In part three, a concise description and evaluation of the 1997 update of the TWF directive follows. Part four elaborates on the 2007 Audiovisual Media Services (AVMS) Directive and is followed by an evaluation of the alterations in the European Union's (EU') harmonisation initiatives in the broadcasting sector. Finally and by way of provisional conclusion, the outcome and impact of the European Community's harmonisation initiatives on PSB is evaluated.

Tensions underlying EU market integration in the broadcasting sector

Several tensions influence the evolution of the EU's media policy-making and legal harmonisation activities. First of all, there is the twofold economic and cultural character of audiovisual services (Wheeler, 2004, p. 350). Secondly, there is the division of competencies between the Member States (MS), the European institutions and multilateral organisations like the World Trade Organization (WTO). Thirdly, all of these governmental actors are divided along the lines of either *dirigiste* (i.e. interventionist or even protectionist) or liberal media policies. More interventionist MS include, for example, France, Belgium and Germany, while the UK, the Netherlands and Luxembourg are more liberal. All these tensions mean that policy decisions and compromises are not only difficult to bring about but, ultimately, are not always coherent and may even be internally self-contradictory (Pauwels, 1995).

Market integration as the driving force of European broadcasting policy

In its 1984 Green Paper on *the Establishment of the Common Market for Broadcasting, Especially by Satellite and Cable*, the Commission launched the idea of a single European broadcasting market (EC, 1984), an initiative that was immediately engulfed in tension. The drafter of the 1984 Green paper was Director General (DG) Internal Market, and this was reflected in the more liberal style of argumentation followed throughout the Green Paper (Collins, 1994). The main idea of the Green Paper, as Michalis (2007) points out, was that the fragmentation of broadcasting policies in the EU inhibited the emergence of a truly competitive European broadcasting market, mainly *vis-à-vis* the USA.

After a consultation round, a proposal for a directive followed the Green Paper in 1986. It was argued that the proposed TWF directive could harmonise MS' broadcasting policies. Subsequently, it would empower the broadcasting sector to increase its revenues and take advantage of technological progress. In addition to this, the harmonisation initiative also had a strong political and cultural motivation. There were, and this remains the case today (Pauwels and Donders, 2011), strong beliefs in the unifying forces of television (Wolton, 1990, p. 92).

In spite of opposition against the Commission taking forward such an important harmonisation initiative in a sector subject to MS' competencies, the TWF Directive was finally agreed upon on 3 October 1989. Starting from the 'country-of-origin' principle, the TWF directive harmonised a number of content-related matters such as:

- advertising;
- protection of minors; and
- broadcasting of European and independent programmes.

From the start, the TWF directive was caught between *dirigiste* MS and those that were more liberal-minded. Only two MS (Belgium and Denmark) voted against the TWF directive. However, several points of disagreement remained keenly debated.

Country of origin: Abandoning countries' sovereignty to regulate broadcasting

The first issue of disagreement concerns the 'country-of-origin' and 'mutual recognition' principles that are at the heart of the TWF directive. In accordance with the basic principles of freedom of movement and freedom of establishment, the essence of both the TWF directive (and also the subsequent AVMS directive) is that MS cannot object to receiving programmes from other MS if these programmes, broadcast from abroad, comply with the (minimum) stipulations of the directive. This also means that each MS must ensure that the programmes broadcast from its territory are in accordance with the stipulations of the directive. From that moment, the principle of mutual recognition applies: whatever is permitted in one MS cannot be subject to additional requirements for permission to be granted in another. The only legislation that applies is that of the broadcasting country. Only in exceptional cases, specifically to protect minors, and which are subject to a number of strict but vaguely specified conditions, can an MS suspend the transmission of programmes from another MS.

The introduction of the country-of-origin principle was revolutionary. It makes it virtually impossible for a receiving MS to object to incoming signals, even if the concerned content is not in line with national regulatory provisions. Put simply, the country-of-origin principle infringes the ideal of national sovereignty in the broadcasting field. The principle gave rise to several other political and judicial problems. Most importantly, it was not always clear which EU MS had authority or, in legal terms, held jurisdiction. The principle also seemed to result in forum shopping, that is broadcasters tried to establish themselves in states with the most lenient set of rules. A number of MS tried to maintain the receiving country's right to control and, to this day, some still insist on a weakening of the country-of-origin principle. This attempt is in vain, however. A strengthening of MS' own right to control (other than their own domestic broadcasters) would infringe the basic principle of free movement, and the creation of an internal media market would become a dead issue in consequence.

Content quota

The second point of contention is the quota regime. The TWF directive provides that broadcasters have to broadcast a majority of European productions 'where practicable and by appropriate means' (Article 4). For independent productions a 10% minimum applies (Article 5). For some, these quota provisions should be framed and controlled much more strictly than was originally stipulated in the TWF directive. For others, quota regimes ought to be abolished because they have no effect other than what the market itself already delivers.

The various opinions on quota make clear how fundamentally opinions can diverge when reconciling cultural and economic aims, the means by which these then have to be realised and on which specific level. In the EU, these diverging opinions ultimately resulted in the quota regime being transformed into essentially a symbolic policy. Essentially, it was not legally enforceable and was, moreover, characterised by very vague terminology. Indeed, it is far from clear exactly what a European or independent production is. This in turn has added to legal confusion and ideological disagreement. In practice, however, the quota regime has resulted in the broadcasting of domestic rather than non-domestic European works (De Vinck and Pauwels, 2008). This was advantageous for both the *dirigistes* and the liberals. It was clear to the latter that broadcasters, and hence the market, delivered national and European content without quotas, simply because their viewers demanded it. For the proponents of a more *dirigiste* approach, the dominance of national European content demonstrated that the demand for European non-domestic content, and hence cultural diversity, was still a long way off.

Harmonisation and relaxation of advertising rules

The third point of contention is the rules on advertising. One faction feels that these cannot be framed strictly enough, while others consider that it must be possible to explore opportunities for commercial revenues to the full extent possible, particularly in times of (uncertain or initial) market development and economic recession. Strict rules on advertising render this impossible. Most observers agree that the advertising regime has become increasingly liberal (Valcke and Lievens, 2009). Other criticisms that are expressed in this context concern the fragmentation of advertising regulations and the use of ambiguous terms. Over the years, MS and other stakeholders have also expressed very different opinions on advertising related to children's programming.

Finally, the trend towards systems of co-regulation and self-regulation, and the accompanying belief that these are better approaches because they are most efficient and became established, initially, in advertising regulation.

To summarise, the adoption of the first TWF directive, and the debates and litigation that followed it, resulted in multiple frustrations for both *dirigiste* and more liberal players. The situation of legal uncertainty and new developments in the broadcasting market called for a revision after five years, as foreseen in the original directive.

Updating the TWF directive

The 1997 update of the TWF directive was preceded by vigorous discussion among MS, the Commission and other stakeholders. The contents of the directive were, as was the case with the former directive, highly disputed (Drijber, 1999). Liberal and *dirigiste* approaches were again in opposition and similar issues to those discussed above emerged in heated debates.

The first point of disagreement concerned the quota regime. Some stakeholders, most notably France – in an attempt to protect its own production companies – and the European Parliament, felt that the quota regime was too loosely formulated. There was a need to clarify the wording of the quota articles, to drop the words 'where practicable' and legally enforce a majority of European content. It was felt that the Commission had to follow up on the quota rules more rigidly as, due to the use of vague concepts, US content (omnipresent on the increasing number of European channels) could qualify as European content. More liberal MS and private broadcasters opposed a strengthening of the quota regime. In the end, the quota regulation remained the same (Curwen, 1999; Drijber, 1999, p. 89).

The second point of discussion dealt with the scope of the directive. Most actors did not favour an extension to non-linear services. Although on-demand services were already a market reality, 'the question whether TWFD should apply to broadcasting over the Internet was left without any explicit answer' (Scheuer, 2006, p. 73). Regulatory and technological uncertainties discouraged an update of the TWF directive in this respect.

Opinions also differed in regard to the rules for the protection of minors. Sweden, a country that does not allow children's advertising, was the only country that voted against the 1997 update of the TWF directive, while Belgium abstained. Both countries felt that the directive was too flexible with regard to children's advertising and tele-shopping.

Although the opposition of some countries did not prevent the Commission from adopting a common position on the 1997 update, it did show the unease of some countries with the TWF directive's minimum standards. Countries like Sweden or regions like Flanders have always been strict in their broadcasting legislation *vis-à-vis* the protection of minors. Because of the country-of-origin principle, their position has become hard to sustain. An influx of other MS' broadcasters of children's television put more protective regimes under serious pressure. As a consequence of declining shares of its main broadcasters in the children's television market Flanders, for example, relaxed its rules on children's advertising. In 1991, Flanders introduced a rule that prohibited advertising aimed at children five minutes before and after children's programmes. In 2007, in response to the situation in which the two most important commercial broadcasters in the Flemish market (VMMa and SBS) were confronted with declining shares in the children's market and, hence, decreasing investments by both channels in children's television, the Flemish government decided to eliminate the five-minute rule and develop an ethical code together with the private sector. As a consequence both VMMa and SBS significantly increased their investments in the children's segment of the broadcasting market, although a news magazine programme specifically aimed at children on VTM (the main channel of VMMa) saw the light of day only thanks to government subsidies.

The final point of discussion was related to the so-called events list, introduced in the revised TWF directive of 1997. This anticipated the possibility of popular sports events disappearing behind the walls of pay-television, allowing MS to draw up a list of events that were to be broadcast free-to-air. Whereas the European Parliament argued for a compulsory system, most MS and the Commission advocated for a more lenient approach. As a result, MS can make a list if they so desire.

In summary, the 1997 update did not bring about huge changes (Drijber, 1999, p. 170). The clarification of the country-of-origin principle was important; it entrenched the revolutionary idea of freedom of reception in broadcasting law and confirmed as such, the intentional evolution to an integrated European market in broadcasting.

The AVMS directive

Whereas the 1997 update of the TWF directive contained only minor changes, the 2007 AVMS directive led to more substantial alterations of the 1989 TWF regulations. Above all, it extended the scope of the TWF directive to so-called 'audiovisual media services'. Its primary objective is to encourage a level playing field for companies active in the media market (Reding, 2006).

Dirigiste and liberal approaches opposed once again

An update of the TWF Directive was due in 2002, and took a lot of negotiation by the Commission, the European Parliament and various EU MS (Valcke and Lievens, 2009). Questions about the scope of the directive and the need for regulation of new media markets were central to discussions about the AVMS directive and reflected, once again, the persistent and pervasive tensions between liberal and *dirigiste* approaches towards regulation in the media and telecommunications markets. The consultations on an update of the TWF directive began in 2002. Rapid changes in technology, the need for and development of new business models, as well as fragmented regulation of new media sectors in different MS, convinced most stakeholders of the need for a revision of the TWF directive. A first consultation document was published in December 2003. On the basis of several issue papers, the Commission proposed a first official proposal for a revised directive in 2005. The update of the TWF directive, pending a a co-decision procedure, was then subject to discussions with the European Council and European Parliament (Scheuer, 2006).

Linear vs. non-linear services

The AVMS directive extends the scope of the TWF directive to all audiovisual media services, which are defined by six elements (Article 1), all of which need some additional clarification.

1. Editorial responsibility: this concept implies a level of effective control being exercised over programmes and programme schedules. This means that mere distributors of content, who supposedly do not have control over the content of programmes nor their aggregation, are not responsible to the obligations of the directive.
2. Media service provider: the AVMS directive defines a media service provider as the entity having the editorial responsibility over programming policies.
3. The principal purpose of providing programmes: this element introduces two sub-categories of programmes. There are linear programmes or 'normal' television broadcasting services that are provided for simultaneous viewing on the basis of a programme schedule. This is characterised as so-called 'push' content, whereas

'pull' content refers to non-linear content, that is content that is on-demand and requested by individuals, for example, on the basis of a catalogue of different on-demand services. The distinction between linear and non-linear content is fundamental to the clear understanding of this directive. Along with it, different regulatory regimes are spelled out; there exists a more severe tier of rules for linear services and a 'lighter' tier for non-linear services. This regulatory regime is dubbed the graduated or two-tiered approach. As pull services require active consumer behaviour, a 'light' version is deemed acceptable and desirable (Herold, 2009). All services that have the 'principal purpose' of providing linear or non-linear 'programmes' fall within the scope of the directive. For example, this implies that online content (that contains audiovisual fragments) of newspaper publishers is not covered by the directive. The idea underlying this differentiation is that newspapers do not have the principal purpose of providing audiovisual media services.

4. To inform, to educate and to entertain: this Reithian adage underlies the remit of most Western European public broadcasters. It is unclear how it adds to the clarity of the definition of audiovisual media services as some observers argue that all services, to some extent, fall within this definition.

5. The general public: this element refers to the idea of a mass audience in the communications industry. It is not defined further in the directive, but it means that private forms of communication (like e-mail or chat services) are not covered.

6. By electronic communication networks: as Valcke and Lievens (2009) point out, this last criterion means that the transmission mode used for the delivery of a service is irrelevant as long as the service is delivered via an electronic communications network. In other words, following the principle of platform or technology neutrality, a service fits the definition irrespective of its technological means of transportation.

It is apparent that the concepts aimed at clarifying what an audiovisual media service is are far from clear themselves. Lack of conceptual clarity was already a problem for the TWF directive, and remains a problem for the AVMS directive. Media services provider is defined by reference to 'programmes' and 'editorial responsibility'. Editorial responsibility means the exercise of 'effective control'. The latter principle remains to be defined, however. Also, the difference between linear and non-linear services is vague. Recital 17 of the AVMS directive states: 'it is characteristic of on-demand audiovisual media services that they are 'television-like', that is that they compete for the same audience as television broadcasts, and the nature and the means of access to the service would lead the user reasonably to expect regulatory protection within the scope of this Directive' (European Council, 2007: Recital 17). In light of the fast technological and economic changes in the media and communications markets, the use of a word such as 'television-like' and the observation of direct competition between linear and on-demand services seems to be rather presumptuous.

Reconciling possible conflicts of interests between Member States

The second part of the AVMS directive deals with the contested country-of-origin principle. Recital 27 stresses that the country-of-origin principle remains the cornerstone of European audiovisual regulation and deems it essential for the creation of an internal market. This is a strong commitment by the MS to the frequently contested concepts of mutual recognition and freedom of reception. The provisions on the country-of-origin principle have been extended and are more detailed. Three additional chapters, containing minimal rules on the country-of-origin principle for all audiovisual media services for on-demand services and the exclusive rights to events, were added to the TWF directive's Article 2. In addition to this, an Article was introduced providing for a conciliation procedure between an MS of reception and one holding jurisdiction whenever the first MS feels a broadcaster is circumventing its national legislation. In this case, the Commission strongly encourages bilateral negotiations between two MS, involving talks between the national regulators of both countries. This should enable an 'amicable settlement' of potential problems before the MS turn to legal procedures or unilateral decisions (against the mutual recognition principle).

Accepting product placement

The third aspect of the revised directive deals with another contested issue: advertising regulation. Based on the assumption that technological developments give rise to more channels, more channels lead to more choice, and choice leads to the empowerment of consumers, a relaxation of existing rules on commercial communications was considered necessary (Woods, 2008, p. 63). Technological developments are also a two-edged sword: they fragment the audience and make it possible for viewers to skip advertisements, which tends to reduce advertising income. As a solution, new advertising options such as split screens and product placement were addressed. A number of private broadcasters explored these new possibilities for advertising, even within regulatory frameworks that did not allow them to do so. The minimum rules on advertising have therefore been relaxed significantly in the AVMS directive. Product placement has been introduced as an acceptable form of commercial communications and the quantitative restrictions on advertising have been limited. The rules surrounding tele-shopping have also been refined.

Self-regulation in the media sector

Another aspect that comes to the fore in the directive is the desire for more co- and self-regulation in the media and communications sectors. The AVMS directive says that MS should recognise the role that effective self-regulation can play and encourage it (European Council, 2007: Recital 36). In particular, with regard to children's advertising and programming, an increasing reliance on ethical codes developed by the sector itself is advocated. The emphasis placed on co- and self-regulation derives from a fear of exaggerated Internet regulation. Nonetheless, Commissioner Reding (2005) explicitly declared that a strengthening of regulation was not the objective of the update.

Changing regulation for better or worse?

Did the AVMS directive change things for better or worse? The directive aimed to enhance legal certainty through the introduction of a harmonised framework for 'old' and 'new' services. To some extent the AVMS directive does harmonise the rules, but it remains to be seen whether harmonisation, rather than actual legal fragmentation, will effectively take place. As was the case with the TWF directive, the AVMS directive contains several vague concepts that are to be interpreted by MS in national law. Once MS start implementing diverging definitions of these concepts and the directive's overarching concept of 'audiovisual media services', the scope of the AVMS directive can differ from one MS to another. This in turn can lead to increasing instead of decreasing problems of jurisdiction. As a result, the directive is a political compromise that may prevent the development of harmonised regulation of non-linear services in the internal market rather than creating it. Valcke and Stevens (2007, p. 290) conclude that there should be a single framework for content services covering all different media services, and not only broadcasting. Such an advice should be considered, as the current directive leaves some actors out of the picture. YouTube-like providers and search engines such as Google fall outside the scope of the directive, and this may be defensible. When a revision of the directive was discussed in 2002, YouTube had barely been heard of; now, however, the platform has come to occupy a crucial place. The role of YouTube-like providers may transform them into the key media providers for future generations (Valcke and Lievens, 2009). It seems that the AVMS directive is not future-proof (and assuming that it reflects present-day realities is already risky).

> Unfortunately, these new rules seem still inspired by an old media environment. They hardly try to address phenomena like YouTube or Tudou, YouTube's larger Shanghai clone, and their consequences on the future provision of TV-like services. (Hettich, 2008, p. 1449)

The AVMS directive also tried to find a balance between economic and cultural objectives. Like its predecessor, the TWF directive, the AVMS directive gives MS some scope to introduce divergent rules for reasons of cultural diversity. Some also welcome the fact that quota rules continue to exist and are mainly aimed at stock programmes as a general cultural policy commitment (Herold, 2009). Indeed, the AVMS directive also asks the MS to invite the providers of on-demand audiovisual services to (solely) promote production and access to European works, adding the words 'where practicable and by appropriate means'. Since the quota regime is still not legally enforceable, the limits of the current degree of cultural policy commitment quickly become evident. By giving MS the opportunity to define strict or divergent rules in the name of cultural or social policy interests, these interests do not enjoy the same level of protection as economic and commercial ones. The latter are covered by a statutory obligation while the former are mentioned only as a legal option or possibility.

Public broadcasters' status in the internal market

By means of concluding this chapter, it must be asked whether public broadcasters, once the bastions of the European media landscape, can withstand the storm of all these media harmonisation initiatives aiming to realise an internal market for broadcasting and, by extension, audiovisual media services.

Leaving aside competition rules, the main observation to be derived from this chapter is that public broadcasters, according to the principle of subsidiarity, are locked into a 'give and take' game between the

MS and European Community institutions such as the Commission and the European Courts. When the TWF directive began the liberalisation of the European broadcasting sector amid fears of the marginalisation of public broadcasters, public broadcasters became, admittedly due to the liberalisation of European broadcasting markets, embroiled in the troubled waters of EU state aid policy control. In that sense, internal market and harmonisation policies should certainly not be seen as a lifetime insurance policy for public broadcasters.

To some extent the TWF and AVMS directives trapped public broadcasters in market developments and underlying ideological perspectives on the way in which specific principles of public law can be expressed in the future. After the liberalisation of the broadcasting market at the end of the 1980s and the technological advancements in the 1990s, the idea has taken root within European Community institutions that the market is capable of fulfilling certain public functions. The TWF and AVMS directives aim to further market functioning. This affects the status of public broadcasters – albeit in ways that are difficult to forecast and that remain heavily depended on the give-and-take processes between MS, European institutions and sector.

6
EU State Aid Rules and the Broadcasting Sector

After the liberalisation of EU broadcasting markets, the competition rules became more relevant for public service broadcasting (PSB). Confronted with competition, public broadcasters faced huge challenges adapting programmation strategies more to user needs and shifting internal operations in order to make them more efficient. Private broadcasters immediately questioned public broadcasters, at both the national and European level, seeking to employ the state aid rules – which constrain Member States' (MS') subsidy behaviour – to their benefit.

The European state aid rules are part of the overall competition framework of which the goal is to ensure and preserve workable competition in the EU internal market. For many years, state aid control or EU state aid policy was considered to be the 'ugly duckling' of competition law (Grespan and Bellodi, 2006, p. 327; Pesaresi and Van Hoof, 2008, p. 1). Other areas of competition law occupied with the behaviour of companies were the core business of DG Competition's activities. This has changed since the 1990s, when the Maastricht Treaty furthered state aid control as an essential part of competition policy (Quigley and Collins, 2003; Hansen et al., 2004, p. 202). State aid control by the Commission is now at the heart of the European integration process, aiming to ensure both effective competition and market integration (Nicolaides et al., 2005, p. 1).

In principle, all economic activities – including public broadcasting services – are covered by the state aid rules. As a general rule, state aid (i.e. subsidies, tax exemptions, government loans) is prohibited. There are exceptions to this general rule as, for example, the support of services aiming to fulfil public objectives is covered by a more lenient application of the state aid rules.

Notwithstanding the simple basic principle that state aid is prohibited, the application of state aid rules has proved to be far from a straightforward matter. The state aid framework is characterised by a multitude of ambiguous concepts, exceptions, tests and so on. This chapter aims to clarify the main aspects of the state aid legal framework. In spite of the book's non-legal focus, some knowledge of the state aid rules is indispensable in order fully to grasp the impact of European policies on public service media. A lack of knowledge might, for example, result in granting too much or too little power to the Commission or MS. Firstly, the main state aid principles are discussed. Secondly, the exceptions to the principles are outlined and those specifically relevant for PSB are elaborated upon. Thirdly, the basics of procedural aspects of state aid law are addressed.

A European ban on state aid

Every state aid intervention of the Commission consists of two steps. Firstly, it is decided whether a measure is state aid within the meaning of the Treaty on the Functioning of the EU (TFEU) and, hence, whether Commission intervention is acceptable at all. In the second instance, measures that qualify as state aid are evaluated with regard to their possible compatibility with the internal market. For new measures (i.e. measures not in place before the first internal market rules were specified in the 1950s), MS require the approval of the Commission before effectively implementing them. For existing measures (i.e. all other aid schemes and approved new measures), such an approval is not necessary. Existing measures can be scrutinised by the Commission at all times.

The general rule

Article 107(1) TFEU (*ex* 87(1) EC) determines which measures qualify as state aid:

> Save as otherwise provided in this Treaty, any aid granted by a Member State or through State resources in any form whatsoever which distorts or threatens to distort competition by favouring certain undertakings or the production of certain goods shall, insofar as it affects trade between MS, be incompatible with the common market.

As a general rule, measures that fit the description above are prohibited. In that sense, state aid rules contain an explicit negative presumption against all forms of government intervention (Friederiszick et al.,

2005, p. 3; Crocioni, 2006, p. 90), be it direct government grants, tax exemptions or loans.

Article 107(1) TFEU identifies three criteria with which measures have to comply in order to be regarded as state aid: there has to be a transfer of state resources, the measure must confer a selective advantage upon certain undertakings or sectors, and the support can potentially harm trade between and competition in MS. The funding of public broadcasters normally meets these three criteria. Firstly, the public subsidies granted to public broadcasters such as Flemish VRT or Dutch NPO can be regarded as a transfer of state resources. Secondly, governments support public and not private broadcasters. Consequently, the funding is selective in nature. Thirdly, since most public broadcasters are active in advertising markets and/or programme rights markets, the funding of public broadcasters can result in a distortion of competition. It is not required to prove an actual distortion of competition taking place – the possibility of it occurring is sufficient to qualify a measure as state aid.

Diverging interpretations on the state aid status of the licence fee

The criteria mentioned above are not undisputed, however. First of all, some public broadcasters and MS have argued that a licence fee is not a transfer of state resources – it has no direct effect on state resources or revenues (Arhold, 2007, p. 152; Santa Maria, 2007, p. 19). Scholars such as Katsirea (2008, p. 333ff) and Koenig and Haratsch (2003) agree with such an analysis, arguing that citizens indeed pay directly for the licence fee that is, moreover, often collected by independent collecting bodies and not by the state. Other scholars like Bartosch (2002, p. 182) have counter-argued that the mere existence of the licence fee and its collection by an independent body does not exclude government control, which is the determining factor (also referred to as 'imputability') referring to a transfer of state resources. Several rulings of the European Courts deal with the question of imputability. In general, the Courts have upheld that evidence of state control on a particular undertaking does not automatically establish a link between the financial actions of the undertaking and the state in question (ECJ, 2001, 2002: §52; Hakenberg and Erlbacher, 2003, pp. 432–3). Nevertheless, the line between government control and no control is a thin one and, for the moment, there is no specific case law on the status of the licence fee as a transfer of state resources. No MS has asked the European Courts for an opinion, probably fearing that a negative outcome might set a precedent in this regard.

Altmark makes transport an example for broadcasting

A second area of dispute concerns the selective advantage conferred upon the recipient of an aid. Measures are qualified as state aid if they improve the financial situation of a company and, hence, impair the position of another company (Grespan and Santamato, 2008, p. 273). Is there an advantage if a subsidy offsets the cost of public service delivery, however? Legal scholars have discussed this question extensively and are essentially divided in two camps. The first camp adheres to a rigid approach, following which the goal of an aid scheme does not prevent it from being qualified as state aid. The second group of scholars disagrees, arguing that offsetting the costs of public service delivery can by no means be regarded as an advantage. So-called services of general economic interest (SGEI) enjoy a special protection that justifies such a stance, according to the relevant article:

> given the place occupied by services of general economic interest in the shared values of the Union as well as their role in promoting social and territorial cohesion, the Community and the MS, each within their respective powers and within the scope of application of this Treaty, shall take care that such services operate on the basis of principles and conditions which enable them to fulfill their missions.

PSB is a so-called SGEI (*cf. infra*) and, hence, covered by this special protection. Following a rigid approach to the issue there is no reason to exempt SGEIs from the application of state aid rules (Nicolaides, 2003, p. 561; Rizza, 2003, pp. 67–8). However, Dony (2005) finds this overly radical and adheres to the approach presented by the Court of Justice of the EU (ex-European Court of Justice) in its *Altmark* judgment. The latter is crucial to an understanding of the application of the state aid rules to SGEIs in general and PSB in particular. In the *Altmark* case, the Court dealt with German compensations for universal service obligations in the transport sector. It ruled that measures to the benefit of SGEIs do not constitute state aid if they comply with four criteria: entrustment with a clearly defined public service mission, objective parameters for control, proportionality of government support, and selection on the basis of a public tender or evidence of efficiency (ECJ, 2003: §89–94). Until now, no support scheme for PSB has complied with the *Altmark* criteria of which, in particular, numbers 2 and 4 seem difficult to adhere to (Antoniadis, 2006; Mortensen,

2008). For that reason, most support schemes for public broadcasting organisations in Europe qualify as state aid within the TFEU's meaning.

It comes as no surprise that several scholars have criticised the *Altmark* approach (Bardoel and Vochteloo, 2009; Wheeler, 2010). It essentially makes PSB subject to conditions derived from a case dealing with transport – a sector that is admittedly very different in economic and social terms from PSB.

Admissibility of state funding

Given the state aid status of funding schemes for PSB and the continued existence of these schemes in spite of the state aid rules, an exception to the general prohibition of state aid exists. In fact, there are plenty of exceptions to the state aid rules. There are two exceptions on the basis of which the funding of public broadcasting organisations can be classified as compatible aid. There is an exception clause for cultural aid (i.e. Article 107(3)d TFEU) and for SGEIs (i.e. Article 106(2) TFEU). In addition, the Amsterdam Protocol grants a special status to PSB.

The cultural exception

First of all, state aids can be compatible with the internal market if they promote: 'culture and heritage conservation where such aid does not affect trading conditions and competition in the Community to an extent that is contrary to the common interest' (Article 107(3)d TFEU). This article has not been applied to PSB to date (Psychogiopoulou, 2008, p. 296ff). There are two explanatory factors for this. Firstly, the Commission has argued that the cultural argument can only be invoked when the aid specifically and exclusively addresses cultural goals. As most public broadcasters' task is broadly defined and comprises cultural, social and democratic goals, this is for the moment not the case (Psychiogopoulou, 2006: p.13). Secondly, the exploration of Article 106(2) TFEU (*ex* 86(2) EC; *cf. infra*) has been far more extensive to date. Psychiogopoulou (2006, p. 16) criticises this reliance on Article 106(2) TFEU for undermining PSB and approaching it from an overly economic angle. It is unclear, however, whether the application of the cultural article to public service broadcasting would be more effective, efficient or more beneficial for public broadcasters. The more widespread use of Article 106(2) TFEU is in part due to the more extensive guidance of the Community Courts in this regard. It provides a more solid legal basis for the analysis of politically sensitive and visible cases related to the funding of public broadcasting organisations. In addition, an application of the cultural exception would require a very difficult balancing act that is, in fact, similar to that necessary for the application of Article 106(2) TFEU. Cultural prerogatives of MS' broadcasting policy would still need to be balanced with the Community interest. While Psychogiopoulou (2006, 2008) argues that Article 87(3)(d) attempts to strike a balance between common market and cultural goals, it is argued in this chapter that the cultural derogation of Article 107(3)d TFEU acknowledges that there is a need for striking such a balance. Nevertheless, it is still the Commission that is responsible for striking that balance (a similar remark is made in relation to Article 106(2) TFEU; *cf. infra*).

Exceptions for services of general economic interest

Article 106(2) TFEU provides for a special treatment of services of general economic interest:

> Undertakings entrusted with the operation of services of general economic interest or having the character of a revenue-producing monopoly shall be subject to the rules contained in this Treaty, in particular to the rules on competition, in so far as the application of such rules does not obstruct the performance, in law or in fact, of the particular tasks assigned to them. The development of trade must not be affected to such an extent as would be contrary to the interests of the Community.

The article thus determines that there is a need for a balancing act between goals like market integration and economic efficiency on the one hand and the pursuit of public interest objectives on the other. It states that, although the rules on competition apply to providers of services of general economic interest, these rules should not obstruct the tasks assigned to providers of these services. Hence, this article gives providers of SGEI such as public broadcasters a special status when pursuing the creation of a European internal market.

It is important to know that Article 106(2) TFEU does not exempt certain support measures from the application of the state aid rules. The idea is to provide for a more flexible application of the state aid rules given the societal importance of some services. Nevertheless, certain conditions must be complied with. Firstly, Article 106(2) TFEU can only be invoked when an actual SGEI – clearly defined by MS governments – is concerned. MS have a wide, nearly autonomous, discretion to define what an SGEI is. The Commission can only object to a definition in the case of a clear and undisputable funding of commercial services. Secondly, the aid must be necessary. This means that, in theory, an MS must pinpoint the necessity of the aid in relation to its targeted goals. Thirdly, the aid measure must be proportional. The latter, rather technical, condition requires MS to calculate the cost incurred for providing SGEIs and, consequently, granting an aid that does not supersede the level of this objective cost (Grespan, 2008a, p. 1128; Ritten and Braun, 2004, p. 956).

The assumption is that if state aids for SGEIs comply with these three conditions, market distortions are minimised to an acceptable extent. In that sense Article 106(2) TFEU tries to overcome the 'uneasy space' (Szyszczak, 2004, p. 185) that public services occupy in the new economy and safeguard 'the provision of effective and high-quality services of general economic interest' as 'a key component of the European welfare state' (Anestis and Drakakis, 2006, p. 60). At the same time, the article ensures that providers of SGEIs are also bound by the state aid rules. This opposition, which is an intrinsic part of the article, results, in the opinion of Buendia Sierra (2006, p. 543), in 'regular seismic movement' as Article 106(2) TFEU 'is thus the main point of contact between two tectonic plates moving in opposite direction[s]'. Such a balancing act is politically indispensable, but is, from a judicial point of view, fiercely criticised for its superfluous nature (Nitsche, 2001, p. 137). Moreover, politically speaking it is not always easy to align the European common interest underlying the application of the state aid rules with national public service objectives that underlie the scrutinised state aids.

> In order to understand this point, one must remember that the concept of services of general economic interest contained in Article 86(2) EC is a Community law rather than a national law concept. The public authorities of each Member State are in principle free to decide which public services they wish to guarantee for their citizens, without their decisions having to coincide with those taken in other MS. However, this discretion is limited rather than absolute. The Community concept of services of general economic interest operates a maximum standard beyond which MS cannot go. If this were not the case, a Member State might artificially lay down an unduly wide definition of public service with the sole objective of giving excessive protection to a certain operator. (Buendia Sierra, 2006, p. 549)

The Broadcasting Communication

The special protection of SGEIs is strengthened further for PSB by the so-called Broadcasting Communication – first agreed upon in 2001 and renewed in 2009. The 'Communication on the Application of State Aid Rules to Public Service Broadcasting', or Broadcasting Communication, is a soft law instrument that provides for guidelines on state aid and PSB. It defines those conditions with which an aid scheme must comply in order to be compatible with the provisions in the TFEU. The 2001 Broadcasting Communication in fact clarifies Article 106(2) TFEU and has been tailored to the specific needs of the state aid and public broadcasting issue. The Communication is binding for the Commission when implementing the state aid rules and fits within Commission competences to decide on the manner of application of Article 106(2) TFEU. MS are not legally bound by the Broadcasting Communication, as the document explains only how the Commission is applying the state aid rules in cases relating to PSB. However, in reality, the Communication does also serve as a point of reference for MS. The Communication is an illustration of the Commission's vision on the funding of PSB (Bavasso, 2002, p. 341). At the same time, it also incorporates MS', public broadcasters' and the private sector's ideas concerning PSB. The soft law approach is not unique for public service broadcasting. The Commission has developed interpretations with regard to support schemes in the field of, for example research and development (R&D). These interpretative schemes make sure that the Commission is not confronted with too much controversy in each and every case, thus leading to the emergence of a 'good' state aid policy standard. MS, including those that initially opposed particular interpretative frameworks, are gradually locked in through such a standard (Blauberger, 2008, p. 12).

The starting point of the Broadcasting Communication is twofold. Firstly, the Communication starts from the observation that liberalisation and technological developments make it necessary to apply the state aid rules to aid schemes in the media sector – thus including public broadcasting. The funding of public broadcasters, so the Communication upholds, must be controlled on the basis of, among others, the state aid rules in order to preserve a level playing field. Secondly, the Communication also acknowledges the importance of PSB for European democracies. In addition, it also stresses that public broadcasting is not comparable to any other SGEI; hence, the specific Communication for PSB.

As stated by the recent Commission communication on services of general economic interest in Europe: The broadcast media play a central role in the functioning of modern democratic societies, in particular in the development and transmission of social values. Therefore, the broadcasting sector has, since its inception, been subject to specific regulation in the general interest. This regulation has been based on common values, such as freedom of expression and the right of reply, pluralism, protection of copyright, promotion of cultural and linguistic diversity, protection of minors and of human dignity, consumer protection. (EC, 2001, §5–6)

Essentially, the Broadcasting Communication introduces three conditions – similar to the more general criteria of Article 106(2) TFEU (*cf. supra*) – with which state aids to PSB have to comply. Firstly, the public service remit must be defined in a clear way – there should be no doubt about the public or commercial nature of services. Secondly, the task of public broadcasters must be officially entrusted to the organisations delivering public broadcasting services. Entrustment is to be accompanied by objective and independent control of the fulfilment of the public service obligations. Thirdly, aid must be proportional; in other words, the net cost of a public broadcaster should be determined, and government support cannot exceed this cost (Antoniadis, 2006, Bavasso, 2006). When the Commission investigates the funding of public broadcasters, these three principles guide the investigations and assessment (Donders, 2009).

When the above conditions are complied with, state aid is acceptable and does not overly undermine the aim of realising a European integrated market. Hence, the evaluation of state aid to public service broadcasting is by no means directly concerned with the effective realisation of public interest objectives. MS have to and want to keep this competency to themselves. It is for the Commission to prevent market distortions going too far.

The application of the three compatibility conditions proved to be somewhat difficult when dealing with new media services. For the Commission, it was not clear to what extent activities beyond radio and television broadcasting were also part of the public service remit (Bavasso, 2006, §17–007). This stance provoked serious debates between the Commission and MS on their respective competencies. After two years of discussion, the Commission decided to update the 2001 Broadcasting Communication, asking MS to evaluate public broadcasters' new media services *vis-à-vis* their public value and possible market impact. The 2009 Broadcasting Communication still adheres to the three conditions with which state aids have to comply and has added specifications on new media activities. Having said that, the Commission has explicitly recognised, in its 2009 Broadcasting Communication, the multimedia remit of public broadcasters to be legitimate (Donders and Pauwels, 2010b).

The Amsterdam Protocol

A final element constituting the special status of PSB in the TFEU is the Amsterdam Protocol, annexed to the Treaty in 1997 when MS agreed to the Amsterdam Treaty. Following an earlier initiative of MEP (Member of the European Parliament) Carole Tongue (EP, 1996), this recognises the importance of public broadcasting for European democracies and, as such, introduces a specific status for PSB in the Treaty of the European Communities itself (Coppieters, 2003, p. 266):

> Considering that the system of public broadcasting in the MS is directly related to the democratic, social and cultural needs of each society and the need to preserve media pluralism.

> The provisions of the Treaty establishing the European Community shall without prejudice to the competence of the MS to provide for the funding of public service broadcasting insofar as such funding is granted to broadcasting organisations for the fulfilment of the public service remit as conferred, defined and organised by each Member State, and insofar as such funding does not affect trading conditions and competition in the Community to an extent which would be contrary to the common interest, while the realisation of that public service shall be taken into account.

The Amsterdam Protocol reflects the concerns of MS about the direction in which media policy, under pressure of European state aid policy, was heading in the 1990s:

> This curious clutch of provisions stem from the lively concern of some mainland MS that an all-pervasive force of liberalism is about to crush certain important vested interests of mostly state-owned public undertakings. There is no more stark exposure in the Treaty of the division ... between those who wish to regulate to protect public utilities and those who wish to make them competitive. (Duff, 1997, p. 84)

Various MS (in particular Belgium and France) and interest groups (in particular the European Broadcasting Union (EBU), representing public broadcasters) lobbied in favour of the 1997 Amsterdam Protocol. The meaning of the Protocol has been disputed ever since it was approved in 1997. The Protocol represents a strong commitment to a 'European-style' concept (Humphreys, 2003, p. 2) of public service broadcasting. It is, moreover, vital since it establishes the competencies of both MS and the Commission when dealing with state aid and PSB. On the one hand, it is up to the MS to provide for services of general economic interest, to fund their provision, to define the public service remit and to organise their system of public broadcasting. It remains, on the other hand, the responsibility of the Commission to make sure that the funding of public broadcasters does not affect trade between MS and competition within MS to an extent contrary to the common interest.

As such, the Protocol seems to be, and is generally considered to be, a more specific transposition of Article 106(2) TFEU for PSB. Although the scope and importance of the Protocol are not always that clear, it is obvious that the Protocol – being an integral part of the TFEU – has an important political and legal function. It assured MS that they were still in charge of PSB, but it also made it very clear that the broadcasting sector is in fact a market of economic activity, and therefore subject to normal competition rules. As a component of the TFEU, the Protocol is legally binding and should be taken into account when handling state aid cases. It also served as an important inspiration for the 2001 Broadcasting Communication.

Notwithstanding the strong political signal, the Protocol's political significance is bigger than its legal effectiveness, so Nihoul (1998, p. 348) claims. The Protocol has indeed not resulted in a complete exception for the funding of PSB from the TFEU and is – to some extent – indeed a muddled legal solution for a political problem (Nitsche, 2001, p. 152). One should, however, not overlook the importance of political signals, nor the fact that the Protocol is part of Community Law and, therefore, a legal obligation rests upon the Commission and the Community Courts to take the special status of PSB into account.

Procedural aspects of state aid control

The subtantial aspects of state aid control do not exclusively determine the outcome of state aid cases. Also, procedural rules are important when investigating the effects of European state aid control on PSB.

The procedural rules concerning state aid are specified in Article 108 TFEU (*ex* Article 88 EC) and complemented by case law and more specific regulations (Grespan and Bellodi, 2006). They deal with the competencies of different parties in state aid procedures, different types of state aids, the notification duty of MS and the different phases in state aid investigations. All of these issues are discussed below, with the aim of providing for a better understanding of the procedures that underlie and guide every state aid investigation. The objective is not to dwell upon all the technicalities (for example, concerning time limits) of state aid procedures, however.

Competencies in state aid procedures

The Commission plays a central role in the enforcement of state aid rules. It has the executive power to enforce the state aid rules and first-ranking judicial power to evaluate possible breaches. The European Courts also have judicial powers in this area, and other actors too are involved in state aid procedures – in the first instance, the MS; the Commission and the MS are both directly involved in state aid procedures. The aid recipient, although also affected by the Commission's state aid control, is not directly involved in the procedure. In practice, and this is certainly the case for public broadcasting organisations, the aid recipient is very often informally involved in procedures. More often than not, MS discuss all aspects of the state aid procedure with their public broadcaster(s). Third or interested parties, like private broadcasters, can also be consulted, although in practice their involvement is rather limited. Additional (informal) meetings with the Commission, in which some aspects of the allegations are discussed, usually follow the complaints made. The Community Courts are involved in case MS or third parties (including also public broadcasters) file an action. Basically, this means that they contest the decision issued by the Commission. Other DGs, apart from DG Competition, are also involved in state aid control investigations. As the College of Commissioners comes to decisions on a unanimous basis, there is also an 'inter-service' consultation about the issue of state aid and public broadcasting. In these consultations, DGs Internal Market, Information Society and Media, Communication, Culture and Education are actively involved. However, DG Competition takes the lead. Notwithstanding, it is possible that certain DGs oppose particular aspects of state aid decisions. Other DGs have the potential to accept decisions of DG Competition without comments, with comments or not to accept decisions at all. Decisions are rarely rejected by other DGs. They, however, frequently ask for adaptations. It speaks for itself that DG Internal Market follows a more liberal policy line, whereas DG Culture and Education follows a policy line more oriented towards the objectives of public broadcasting. In general, DG Information Society and Media is situated somewhere in between these two positions.

Types of aid

State aid already in existence before the date of entry into force of the EC Treaty or before accession of the European Communities is termed existing aid (Grespan, 2008b, p. 555ff). In addition, aid schemes implemented two months after notification without Commission intervention, and previously approved aid schemes, are termed existing aid. For this type of aid there is no notification duty. The status of existing aid provides some legal certainty for government authorities and aid recipients. Also, with an eye to legal certainty, small alterations in aid schemes do not necessarily change the existing aid status of such an aid scheme – each is assessed on a case-by-case basis.

Existing aid does not escape Commission scrutiny, however; it is under the continuous monitoring of the Commission (Ritten and Braun, 2004, p. 980). When state aid is no longer compatible, the Commission can instigate negotiations with MS. These negotiations should result in the abolishment of the aid scheme or, and this happens more frequently, in an adaptation of the scheme (Arhold, 2007, p. 190). An adaptation occurs on the basis of a so-called 'Article 17 letter'. Such a letter identifies certain 'appropriate measures' dealing with the adaptation of certain aspects of the aid scheme scrutinised by the Commission. If MS do not agree with the proposed measures, the Commission can initiate the official procedure designed for new aid and can unilaterally impose measures to adjust the aid scheme, a scenario that does not happen frequently. An examination of existing aid can only result in measures for the future, not the past. Consequently, the Commission cannot order a recovery of the aid.

New aid is defined in relation to the concept of existing aid. Aid that is not existing is considered to be new aid. With regard to new aid, the competences of the Commission are wider. Some aspect of negotiation is involved, but there is a more significant leverage power of the Commission. The latter can, if it finds proof of incompatibility (for example, aid is not proportional), require a reimbursement of the aid. Moreover, MS need approval of the Commission prior to the implementation of the aid scheme. If they do not await such approval, there is so-called unlawful or illegal aid.

In principle, the Commission is responsible for the qualification of aid measures as new or existing aid. The qualification can, however, be contested before the Community Courts by MS and the petitioners of complaints (Soltèsz and Bielesz, 2004, p. 134).

Notification duty

The central role of the Commission is enforced by the obligation of MS to notify the Commission of plans to introduce, alter or modify aid schemes (Ritten and Braun, 2004, p. 198). All new aid measures have to be notified to the Commission on an *ex ante* basis and the Commission needs to approve the measures before they can be implemented by MS. Every notification act is followed by a two-month period, during which if the Commission files no objectives and asks no additional questions with regard to the aid scheme, MS are allowed to implement it. Notification is only complete from the moment that the Commission has obtained all the necessary information to decide on the acceptability of the scheme. Hence, it is possible that the whole process might take more than two months. Given the rapid developments in the broadcasting sector, this might be problematic and deliver delays for public broadcasters.

If an MS pursues its policy without an approval or if it has not notified the aid measure to the Commission, this is described as illegal aid. Such aid can be recovered when the Commission finds the aid scheme to be incompatible with the TFEU.

Phases of a state aid procedure

A notification is the starting point of state aid procedures. Another possible cause of a state aid procedure is a private sector complaint. The Commission can also instigate a procedure on its own initiative but, with regard to PSB, the latter has not happened to date. Approximately 20 per cent of decisions are preceded by notifications; all other procedures have been provoked by private sector complaints (Antoniadis, 2008). It should be stressed that investigations dealing with notified aid seem to be 'easier'; these are less conflictual, as they set out from an intentional cooperation between MS and Commission. Notified cases often also deal with singular services offered by public broadcasters and, hence, do not concern the evaluation of the complete supporting systems of public broadcasters.

A state aid procedure stops if the Commission concludes that the notified aid scheme is not state aid within the meaning of Article 107(1) TFEU or is clearly compatible with the TFEU on the basis of an exemption clause. If this is not the case or there are doubts about the scheme, an investigation is begun. The scheme below, based on the research of Soltèsz and Bielesz (2004, p. 135), clarifies the different stages in a state aid procedure (Figure 6.1). There are essentially two core stages in each state aid procedure. A clear distinction must be drawn between the 'preliminary examination' and the 'formal investigation procedure'. The preliminary investigation concerns a rather informal dialogue between the Commission and the MS. Interested parties do not have a formal role. A preliminary examination allows the Commission to form a *prime facie* idea of the aid scheme scrutinised. A formal investigation procedure follows if the Commission has serious doubts about an aid scheme. It begins by inviting interested parties to submit their comments. A formal procedure is more extensive as it results in data and figures that are delivered by both MS and interested parties. This is essential, so Grespan (2008b, p. 570) says, 'whenever the Commission has serious difficulties in determining whether aid is compatible with the common market'.

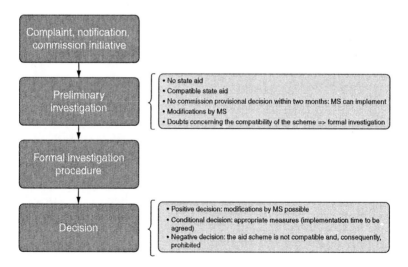

Figure 6.1 Phases in a state aid procedure

In cases where the Commission has doubts about the compatibility of a new aid scheme, it closes its preliminary investigation, after which a formal investigation procedure is opened. The decision to open a formal investigation procedure is published in the OJEU (*Official Journal of the European Union*) in order to ensure transparency of decision taking, and interested parties have the right to comment on it. After this, the Commission takes a final decision.

For existing aid, the procedure is less straightforward as a 'cooperation' procedure is followed. This type of procedure is structured arround three types of 'Letters':

- Article 17 Letter: informal identification by the Commission of measures that would ensure compatibility of the existing aid scheme, dependent on MS' comments and (possible) commitments of MS to alter certain aspects of the aid scheme;
- Article 18 Letter: formal recommendation of the Commission to the MS with 'appropriate measures' that the MS must implement in order to ensure compatibility; and
- Article 19 Letter: opening of a formal investigation procedure in case a MS refuses to adopt recommended measures.

An Article 19 Letter is rare as it exemplifies the impossibility of an MS and the Commission to reach a compromise on a given aid scheme. The Commission usually avoids the use of an Article 19 Letter as it jeopardises a smooth cooperation with MS and lengthens state aid procedures even further. MS, in turn, are bound by a loyalty principle *vis-à-vis* the Commission.

MS, public broadcasters and complainants can bring an action before the General Court or the Court of Justice of the EU against the Commission decision. Often, interested parties or MS ask for an annulment of Commission decisions. The petitioner must illustrate that the Commission's decision contains flaws concerning the competences of the Commission, procedural requirements or the interpretation of the TFEU rules. Interested parties can bring an action before the Community Courts only if they demonstrate that they are directly concerned by a Commission decision. MS and aid recipients are, in general, considered to be directly concerned. Also, competitors of the aid recipient can relatively easy demonstrate their concern as any authorisation to grant aid has a possible consequence for the market position of the competitor.

Provisional conclusions

This chapter has briefly presented the legal framework that applies to the funding of PSB. On the basis of the findings, three concluding remarks are made. Firstly, the assessment of state aid schemes is a complex matter. In all stages of the state aid procedure multifaceted questions and concepts come to the forefront. There is, thus, no simple checklist following which state aid for public broadcasters is deemed to be acceptable or not. Consequently, every state aid assessment, even though grounded in supposedly more objective competition rules and compatibility conditions, is as superfluous in nature as public broadcasting policy itself. Although this ambiguity can be criticised, it also provides considerable and flexible space to search for such a balance on a case-by-case basis. Perhaps, this harms legal certainty. The choice between legal certainty and the need for case-by-case flexibility is a pertinent one indeed.

Secondly, the TFEU itself and the Broadcasting Communication show that state aid control is not a purely legal exercise. The rules require that the Commission makes political choices. This makes it difficult for the Commission to impose unilateral decisions upon the MS. Moreover, the procedural rules would hamper overly aggressive Commission policies. So, on the basis of the assessment of the state aid legal framework it seems that the idea of a Commission 'full frontal attack' on PSB is a myth and can hardly be transposed in reality. The constraints and limitations of the legal framework prevent a 'full frontal attack' strategy from emerging. The latter is a crucial conclusion, as the perception sometimes exists that the Commission, which indeed has considerable leeway in state aid procedures, can 'freewheel' throughout the TFEU against PSB. The analysis of the legal framework indicates that this is not the case – most importantly because the competency to define what a SGEI is lies entirely with MS.

Finally, the chapter also illustrates that the funding of PSB is without question an exception to the general ban on state aid. Even though the research hypothesis is oriented at the 'enabling' rather than 'constraining' effects of state aid policy on PSB, it must be recognised that the overall goal of European state aid policy is the elimination of state aid where possible. Hereby, the idea of market failure, albeit that this concept is not a legal basis for the Commission's analysis, as the only objective justification of state aid is a guiding principle. Hence, it would be incorrect to claim that state aid policy in itself aims to realise PSB goals. The TFEU – which is drawn up by MS! – does not foresee such a scenario and sets out from a scenario in which government intervention is limited or marginalised as much as possible. Hence, it is likely that there is an intrinsic conflict between state aid and public broadcasting policy. However, this does not (yet) exclude the possibility of complementarity either.

7

There and Back Again: A Chronological Perspective on the State Aid Control of Public Service Broadcasting

The assessment of public broadcasting state aid cases by the Commission faces considerable criticism. However, it is unclear whether an analysis of the Commission's evolving state aid policy in the area of public service broadcasting (PSB) supports the arguments made with regard to marginalisation. Can certain priorities and trends be discerned in the Commission's policy and can, in addition, a chronological approach of the research topic validate *ad extremis* the idea of a 'master plan' against the continuation of a holistic PSB model? Put simply, does a succinct historical perspective on the issue of European state aid policy and PSB confirm an increasing role for the Commission as regards PSB and, moreover, indicate an increasingly negative market failure approach towards the financing of public broadcasters? Have the latter, as a consequence, over time more reason to distrust the European Communities' competition authorities?

In this chronological overview an analytical distinction is made between four phases in the Commission's assessment of public broadcasting state aid cases. The first phase is dubbed 'taken by surprise', as it refers to the lengthy period (1992–2000) in which the Commission was essentially clueless about the approach to follow with regard to private sector complaints on the financing of public broadcasting. 'Searching for an approach' is phase two, spans the period 1999–2004 and is characterised by the Commission's and Court's attempts to define some more specific guidelines on the funding of services of a mixed public and economic nature. The third phase is called 'from fragile answers to consolidation'. This is distinctive due to the increasing numbers of closed investigations of public broadcasting aid schemes and the emergence of some standards in the Commission's policy. Finally, in 2009 a fourth phase has emerged as the Commission succeeds in its attempts to consolidate its case practice in a renewed set of guidelines on the funding of public service broadcasting. These new guidelines have already been used in new investigations and, most importantly, revolutionary, encourage Member States (MS) to implement an *ex ante* evaluation of public broadcasters' new media services.

Phase 1: Taken by surprise (1992–2000)

The initial resistance of MS to the Commission's intervention in public broadcasting should be seen in a broader framework than the state aid rules. The 1980s and 1990s were a period in which the Commission, most notably the Directorate General (DG) Internal Market and Competition, and some MS pushed for a process of liberalisation in the media sector. Several European Community initiatives exemplified a strong confidence in market solutions (to the detriment of government intervention). Despite manifold references being made to the importance of cultural exchange and the public interest objectives underlying broadcasting, policy indisputably put forward a market-oriented policy (going against supposed over-regulation) for the broadcasting sector.

Hence, it was no surprise that MS were not amused, to say the least, with the complaints against their funding of public broadcasters. The latter were (and still are) well entrenched and established in Western European societies. For political reasons or because of the firm belief in its significance for democracy, broadcasting seemed too important to be left to the profit-seeking mechanisms of the free market (Burgelman, 1990; Garnham, 1990). As a consequence, public broadcasters have been at the core of most MS media policy for several decades. Notwithstanding MS' criticism on public broadcasters in the 1980s and some MS' support for a more liberal agenda in media policy, a European market-oriented interference with this particular type of policy was considered to be a bridge too far in the EU's integration process. Essentially, concerns were twofold: MS opposed European intervention because it could decrease MS' room for manoeuvre in media policy and, on top of that, EU competencies were mainly inspired by a highly economic project and could not sufficiently take into account cultural and public interest objectives in the field of media policy.

In spite of MS' resistance, competition policy became a real and acute issue in the early 1990s. Private broadcasters started to attack the funding schemes of public broadcasters under both the state aid and antitrust rules. The former govern MS' subsidy behaviour, the latter companies' actions. In any case, the relentless pressures from the private sector necessitated a Commission approach with regard to public service broadcasting.

Private sector concerns

Private broadcasters started to question the funding of public broadcasting in 'Brussels' at the end of the 1980s. In 1987, Screensport (a satellite television company) filed an official complaint with the European competition authorities arguing that the Eurovision system of the European Broadcasting Union (EBU) violated the antitrust rules (Cabrera Blazquez, 2000). The EBU, which has over 100 members – most of them public broadcasters – acquired rights for major events on the basis of the so-called Eurovision system in which most of its members collaborated. Joint acquisition schemes are found to be problematic from a competition point of view, however. It was against the Eurovision system that Screensport, not a Member of the EBU, filed a complaint. The Commission concluded that the system did not violate antitrust principles (Arino, 2004, p. 108; Donders et al., 2007, p. 19). Several companies challenged the Commission's findings before the General Court. The latter indeed rejected the Commission's reasoning.

Leaving aside the specificities of the Eurovision cases, the Screensport complaint, which attacked a specific joint acquisition of rights system, forced the Commission framework for the first time to intervene with the funding and position of public broadcasters under competition law. Several other commercial broadcasters like Métropole Télévision (better known as M6), Gestevision Telecinco, Reti Televissive Italiana and Antena 3 joined Screensport's complaints (Nitsche, 2001, p. 95).

It was after these antitrust complaints that private broadcasters started to explore the state aid rules in order to put pressure on public broadcasters' funding. Telecinco filed the first state aid complaint against the dual funding of Spanish public broadcaster RTVE in March 1992. The company started its activities in 1990. In July 1993, SIC, a Portuguese broadcaster (that began activities in October 1992), raised objections to the funding of Portuguese public broadcaster RTP. Soon after these two complaints, other companies in Italy, France, the UK and Germany followed suit.

Essentially, private broadcasters questioned two aspects of the 1990s' public broadcasting policy. Firstly, they challenged the dual-funding basis of many public broadcasters. The latter indeed derived funding from public pockets and advertising; allegedly, this dual funding gave rise to market distortion and unfair competitive situations. Secondly, private broadcasters questioned the holistic remit of their public competitors who broadcasted a wide variety of radio and television programmes, including entertainment and sports. These genres in particular were considered to be sufficiently catered for by private broadcasters.

Developing a set of guidelines: Mission impossible?

In light of the private sector's complaints and lobbying, and given the General Court's opinion (CFI, 1998, 1999, 2000) that the Commission was obliged to investigate the funding of public broadcasters, the Commission needed to develop a set of guidelines. This would enable an objective analysis of the wave of private broadcasters' complaints.

MS and public broadcasters reacted furiously to the complaints, however, and intentionally slowed down the process of developing the guidelines. What is more, several initiatives were taken to stress the importance of public broadcasting. In 1994, shortly after the first wave of private sector complaints, EU MS signed the so-called Prague Resolution in the Council of Europe. The Resolution stressed the importance of public broadcasting and the need for stability of public broadcasters in European democratic societies (CoE, 1994). In another, and stronger, attempt to limit the Commission's intervention with public broadcasting, MS approved the Amsterdam Protocol. The Protocol, introduced in the Amsterdam Treaty after efforts of former Belgian Prime Minister Dehaene and former German Chancellor Helmut Kohl, acknowledges that public broadcasting 'is directly related to the democratic, social and cultural needs of each society and the need to preserve media pluralism'. The Protocol stresses that, even though the funding of public broadcasters should be in line with the competition rules, the Commission has no discretion to impinge on MS' organisation and financing of public broadcasters. As such, the Protocol attributes a special status to a specific institution. This was, and still is, unique in the EU Treaty as there are no other examples of such a special status. Indeed, public broadcasters and some MS desired a more far-reaching protection of PSB. However, the Protocol represents the best political consensus that could be reached when taking into account all stakeholders' interests. For the MS the Protocol guarantees their regulatory autonomy with regard to PSB; for public broadcasters it is a recognition of their independence; for the Commission it is a clarification of the rules that were already in place; and for private companies it prevented the exclusion of public broadcasters' funding from the state aid rules.

In short, the Commission faced considerable pressure with regard to the private broadcasters' first complaints. Due to MS and public broadcasters' objections, the Commission was at first not very eager to go forward with the complaints filed by the new market players in the broadcasting sector, and stalled decision taking (Smith, 2001, p. 230; Humphreys, 2003, p. 8; Michalis, 2007, p. 169). Next to political pressures, the limited know-how concerning the sector (which had been liberalised only at the end of the 1980s) and the lack of transparency in public broadcasters' organisational and financial structures were no incentive to the triggering of an active Commission. In sharp contrast with MS' and public broadcasters' concerns stands the pressure exerted by the General Court and private broadcasters to take this matter forward.

Hence, at the end of the 1990s, the Commission sought to define a set of guidelines that would enable 'easier' decision-taking on public broadcasting. In 1998, an internal discussion paper was leaked; this proposed a set of guidelines for the analysis of state aid cases concerning the funding of PSB. Frustrated with MS' and public broadcasters' attitude, the Commission seems to have drafted a fierce reaction against the Amsterdam Protocol. The draft document left no doubts with regard to the competencies of the Commission to check for compliance with the state aid rules (Kleist and Scheuer, 2006, p. 171). It pleaded for single public funding and the limitation of entertainment and sports broadcasts on public television. The Commission, for example, proposed 'to exclude from the public service exemption those services (programs) which may be rendered under exactly the same conditions even in the absence of public broadcasters, by private operators and which do not require a stricter public control to guarantee the content of the programs' (EC, 1998, p. 7).

Hence, the draft proposal introduced a market failure approach into public broadcasting policy and attempted to exclude some activities from the public service remit – nonetheless to be defined solely by MS. The latter suspended the negotiations on a set of guidelines with the Commission for some time which led former Commissioner for Competition Karel Van Miert to back down on the issue and to formally declare that a consensus on a uniform set of guidelines for the funding of public broadcasting was not viable. Van Miert explicitly stated that 'Given MS' attitude, the guidelines on aid to public television are dead' (Agence Europe, 1998).

This did not mean that the Commission, hitherto obliged by the General Court, would not investigate the complaints on public broadcasting on a case-by-case basis. Indeed, in the late 1990s it took two decisions in which it – perhaps surprisingly in the light of its 1998 draft proposal of guidelines – accepted a broad public service remit (EC, 1999a, 1999b). Chaos was complete and eventually it gave both MS and the Commission the incentive to search for a compromise behind closed doors (*cf. infra*).

In short, the first initiatives in the field of state aid control and public broadcasting were stretched over a period of 10 years. In this period the Commission avoided taking stance on the issue as much as possible. It simply did not know what to do. The importance of the internal (and leaked) 1998 discussion paper should not be overestimated, nor should it be underestimated. The Commission was reluctant to come to decisions and, in fact, investigations into the French, Spanish, Portuguese and Italian funding of public broadcasters ended only in 2003 and 2005 (these cases were initiated by private sector complaints in the early 1990s!). The prudent decisions involving Germany and the UK were very sensitive towards the specificity of public broadcasting and emphasise how unwilling the Commission was, albeit because of MS' pressure, to prioritise the issue. Overall, the first 10 years of state aid control on public broadcasting had a limited impact on the way in which MS could fund and organise their public broadcasters.

Phase 2: Searching for an approach (1999–2004)

In 2001, all actors involved finally agreed on a set of guidelines (the so-called 'Broadcasting Communication') (EC, 2001). This document put forward a number of good governance principles funding schemes with which public broadcasters should comply: the public service remit should be clearly defined; public broadcasters should be controlled in an objective and independent manner; and aid should not exceed the actual cost of the discharged public service obligations ('proportionality principle'). The Broadcasting Communication leaves it entirely up to the MS to define the public service remit and to decide on the funding model. It thus significantly deviates from the 1998 draft proposal of the Commission. The Commission and the MS – the latter mainly to avoid judicial activism of the European Courts – finally agreed that the application of the state aid rules was a legal fact. Some MS have disputed this in specific cases, but de facto all MS and public broadcasters realised that the struggle for applicability of the state aid rules to PSB was a lost cause. The strategy from that moment onwards focused on curbing the competencies of the Commission in applying the state aid rules.

The 2001 Broadcasting Communication should hence be seen as a necessary means to facilitate the application of state aid law to public broadcasting and maintain the fragile peace established between the Commission and the MS. The consensus was based on an agreement to carefully balance MS' competencies in the field of culture and broadcasting with the Commission's task to assess the possibly adverse aspects of public broadcasting aid schemes. Former Commissioner for Competition Monti (quoted in Nikolinakos, 2006, p. 400) emphasised this, asserting that 'these guidelines will be able to address the need for a level-playing-field while, simultaneously, leaving intact the primary role of public broadcasting in ensuring democracy, pluralism, social cohesion and cultural diversity'.

On the basis of the 2001 Broadcasting Communication, the Commission hesitantly began issuing decisions. In these decisions (six in total), it explored the new guidelines in 'searching for an approach'.

One immediately observes that the six decisions the Commission issued before 2004 were rather diverse. Three closed investigations dealt with specific services, focusing on one particular service being offered by the public broadcaster involved. The other three decisions dealt with ad hoc financing schemes, such as debt rescheduling as opposed to the structural annual and pre-set funding of public broadcasters.

Specific services cases

Two of the three specific services cases have proved milestones in the development of a state aid policy in the area of public service broadcasting policy. The *ZDF Medienpark* case deviates from other 'specific services cases' as it does not concern a thematic channel, but a side activity of one of Germany's two public broadcasters. In 1999, several theme park operators filed a complaint with the Commission against the launch of a specific theme parc by ZDF. They claimed that the theme park would distort competition as the park would benefit from ZDF's brand and public resources. They feared both cross-promotion and cross-subsidisation (EC, 2002b). This decision is the first provoked by companies other than private broadcasters. Even though some commercial broadcasters joined in the criticism of the ZDF Medienpark initiative, it was private theme park operators – undertakings that were not active in the media market at all – that questioned the specific side activity of ZDF (Meza, 1999). Although the Commission is rather critical of side activities, it did not object to the initiative launching a ZDF theme park and contended that ZDF had behaved like a 'normal' undertaking in this project (EC, 2002b, p. 4).

This more relaxed approach altered in the *BBC Licence Fee* (Commission, 2002a; dealing with the launch of digital channels) and *BBC Digital Curriculum* (EC, 2003b) cases. In both decisions, the Commission dealt with new British Broadcasting Corporation (BBC) media activities and appeared to scrutinise the public service remit much more closely. Certainly in the *BBC Digital Curriculum* case, which dealt with BBC online educational software and services, the Commission intervened with the definition of what public broadcasters were allowed to do. The Commission indeed refused to accept that these online educational services were covered by the BBC's public service remit. This refusal, which was based on the perception that the BBC had entered a market in which it had not been active before, added to MS concerns about the Commission's intentions with regard to public broadcasting.

An article written by two Commission officials (Depypere and Tigchelaar, 2004, pp. 20–1) on the legitimacy of public broadcasters' expansion into new media markets added to MS' and public broadcasters' anxiety. These officials argued that the Internet was a many-to-many medium that might require less government intervention than traditional broadcasting services. However, some counter-argued that it was not for the Commission to have any opinion whatsoever on the scope of public broadcasters' activities. The public task definition in regard to radio, television and Internet markets is an exclusive prerogative of the EU MS. Reference was made to the Amsterdam Protocol, which explicitly reinforces MS' competencies in this regard. Once again, the idea that the Commission's state aid control would marginalise public service broadcasting gained ground.

Ad hoc financing cases

In addition to the specific services decisions, the Commission also finalised its investigation into the ad hoc funding of public broadcasters in Spain, Portugal and France. However, these cases – already begun by the mid-1990s – only added to the all-pervading tension surrounding state aid and public broadcasting. Indeed, it should be clarified that these cases dealt with only certain minor parts of the funding schemes of the public broadcasters concerned. The annual funding schemes of the French, Portuguese and Spanish public broadcasters was left for discussion in other, separate, procedures. Two trends come to the fore in these ad hoc financing cases.

Firstly, it is obvious that the Commission increasingly focused on the market behaviour of governments while supporting public broadcasters (EC, 2003c: §86, 2003d: §52). This focus on market behaviour was due to the Commission's use of the *Altmark* ruling of the Court of Justice of the European Communities. *Altmark* concerned the legality of government grants to offset public service obligations in the transport sector. In the ruling, the Court defined a number of criteria with which funding should comply in order to escape the Commission's scrutiny. These criteria were related to the existence of objective criteria to grant public funding and the efficiency of the recipient of the state aid. Put simply, if the funding of public broadcasters complied with the *Altmark* criteria, the Commission would no longer be able to meddle in public broadcasting policy. However, it is far from easy for public broadcasting aid schemes to meet criteria such as based on the characteristics of the transport sector. So, essentially the application of the *Altmark* criteria inserted a market-oriented logic into cases dealing with public broadcasting and suppressed the more generic and value-based logic of the Amsterdam Protocol (Wheeler, 2010).

Secondly, public broadcasters were considered market inhibitors in ad hoc decisions. There was a negative presumption regarding public ownership and too extensive a system of public service delivery in the Commission's and Community Courts' communication (Szyszczak, 2004). This negative presumption, which was highly problematic for public broadcasters having historical roots as public institutions delivering public services, was criticised by several representatives from MS' media ministries and public broadcasters. They maintained that the Treaty's recognition of public service delivery exemplified a strong engagement of the European Communities and its MS towards the maintenance of public service delivery in order to guarantee some of the public values for which Europe stood. As a consequence thereof, so these stakeholders argued, the Commission should not mark public institutions as inhibitors of the common market, but rather as the safeguards of important public values such as pluralism, diversity, democracy and equality.

In this second phase, the Commission thus developed a market distortion approach towards the issue of state aid and public service broadcasting, and gradually analysed complaints on the basis of the good governance principles put forward in its 2001 Broadcasting Communication. A genuine uniform approach was still not present in this phase, however. In spite of the Commission's critical stance on some aspects of public broadcasting funding schemes, it accepted the compliance of all funding schemes with the state aid rules.

Phase 3: From fragile answers to consolidation (2004–09)

It is on the basis of *Altmark* and the 2001 Broadcasting Communication that the Commission from 2004 onwards developed a so-called 'practice'. Whereas from 1992 to 2003 the Commission has issued only nine decisions, 15 were taken in the final five years of European state aid control (2004 to mid-2009). These decisions concerned the funding of public broadcasters in France, Italy, Portugal and Spain (the 'usual suspects'), but also in Germany, the UK, Denmark, the Netherlands, Belgium (the region of Flanders) and Ireland. It is in this more mature phase of state aid control that rather extensive, evidence-based, decisions were taken and the discussion on the matter continued. This does not mean that the state aid debate subsided, however. Complaints from the private sector are on the rise again and an increasing number of non-broadcasters (in particular, publishers) are now filing complaints against – mainly – the expansion of public broadcasters' activities in a new media age (Donders and Pauwels, 2010b).

Two main comments can be made on the multitude of decisions taken in this phase. Firstly, in two decisions public broadcasters were asked to reimburse so-called excess state aid. Secondly, the Commission put forward five action points in a number of decisions and, in doing so, it mainstreamed its investigations.

Reimbursement of aid

Initially, two investigations on public broadcasting in Denmark and the Netherlands led to the reimbursement of 'illegal aid' (aid that is not tolerated within the state aid framework). The Dutch public broadcaster NOS had to reimburse €76.3 million (EC, 2006a) and TV2/Danmark €84.4 million (EC, 2004a) to the Dutch and Danish governments, respectively. These two decisions were highly disputed: they exemplified the first tangible impact of state aid policy and can, as such, be seen as the first formal confirmation of MS' and public broadcasters' fears *vis-à-vis* Commission interference in public broadcasting policy. Both MS brought an action before the General Court challenging the Commission's findings of excess state aid. And, indeed, the General Court (CFI, 2008b) asserted that the Commission had not adequately investigated the Danish funding scheme in order to conclude there was excess state aid. The decision on the Dutch case was upheld by the Court (General Court, 2010). Other single-issue cases led to positive decisions in which the funding schemes were considered to be state aid, but compatible with the principles underlying state aid control of public broadcasting (e.g. EC, 2002b, 2005d, 2008a). The decisions dealing with Spain, Portugal, Italy and France ended 'reform' cases that predominantly focused on the organisational and financial structure of France Télévisions, RTVE, RAI and RTP (EC, 2003a, 2005b, 2005c, 2005e, 2006c, 2006d). The first two principles underlying state aid control did not come to the forefront in the lengthy investigation periods of these cases (over 10 years).

Four action points

The most interesting cases in phase 3 are the whole package cases. Investigations into the funding of the German, Flemish and Irish public broadcasters (respectively, EC, 2007b, 2008b, 2008d) tackled all three principles underlying the Commission's investigations into public broadcasters' funding. In all three cases significant adaptations of public broadcasting regimes or – at least – MS' commitments to changing certain aspects of their funding preceded closure of investigation procedures. Four topics were considered in all three decisions. Firstly, the definition of the remit, in particular in relation to new media services, must be defined more precisely. Secondly, the expansion of public broadcasters' activities to new media environments must be approved *ex ante* by government. Thirdly, there is a need for independent, preferably legally external, monitoring of public broadcasters' activities. Fourthly, and finally, there is a need for increased transparency of the financial and structural organisation of public broadcasters. In this regard, the Commission has asked public broadcasters to limit the accumulation of reserves to 10 per cent of their annual revenues (Donders and Pauwels, 2010b). The demands of the Commission – even if state aid decisions are the outcome of a bilateral negotiation process between DG Competition on the one hand and MS on the other – are somewhat over-reaching and have been criticised by many stakeholders. Most heavily criticised has been the perceived need for an *ex ante* evaluation of new services – including a market impact assessment. The EBU (2008, p. 12), for example, has asserted that 'any decision to introduce an *ex ante* evaluation mechanism for new media activities would, in any case, fall exclusively within the MS' competence, in accordance with the Amsterdam Protocol'. In addition, several public broadcasting representatives firmly disagreed with the Commission's demand for an *ex ante* evaluation; they seriously doubted the discretion of the Commission in this respect. In addition, the Netherlands, which was involved in extremely difficult negotiations with the Commission, took the lead in lobbying with other MS against the requirement for a market impact assessment in any *ex ante* evaluation (Plasterk, 2008).

The Commission's actions thus once again provoked criticism. The emergence of certain practices, moreover, provoked increased academic attention on the issue, most notably in the field of legal studies (e.g. Bavasso, 2006; Buendia Sierra, 2006; Mortensen, 2008; Munoz Saldana, 2008). Whereas media studies' awareness of the matter also increased (e.g. Humphreys, 2007; Moe, 2008a), consideration of the issue in research was mainly limited to negative side-remarks about the presumed impact of Commission policy on public broadcasting (e.g. Jakubowicz, 2007a; Pauwels and De Vinck, 2007). Hence, the very fact that there was a genuine Commission impact (as briefly indicated above) to be observed from 2004 onwards was, in the opinion of many, evidence of the negative influence of Commission policy on public broadcasting policies. The following chapters investigate this assertion in greater depth.

A fourth phase (2009 onwards)

The revival of old issues and the introduction of new topics of discussion is inherent in the Commission's application of the state aid rules in general and to PSB in particular. Case law, whether it concerns Commission decisions or rulings of the Courts, is a dynamic process and, in that sense, it appears that a fourth phase in the state aid and public broadcasting saga emerged in 2009.

Commission proposals to revise the 2001 Broadcasting Communication

On 10 January 2008, the Commission launched a consultation on the revision of the 2001 Broadcasting Communication. It sought to establish its practice of phase 3, use the new guidelines for investigating new complaints and sought an agreement with the EU MS on this revision (EC, 2008c). Former Commissioner for competition Kroes (2008) said, 'We should consolidate our existing case practice and make sure that an updated Communication takes full account of the Amsterdam Protocol and of the new media environment'. For the purpose of revising the 2001 Broadcasting Communication, the Commission invited MS and other stakeholders to offer their opinions.

The revision of the Broadcasting Communication was highly disputed and, given the history of the 2001 Communication, this was no surprise.

And, indeed, one could dispute the necessity of a revision, as the more precision one adds to the established principles of the 2001 Broadcasting Communication, the more one impinges on the discretion of the MS to define the scope of their public broadcasting policy. One of the interviewed experts (involved in the negotiations) said that 'EU MS are autonomous in this field of policy and that is the end of the story'. However, it is not unjustified to strive for a revision given the changed circumstances in the media market.

Overall, the Commission put forward three main action points in this revision process. Firstly, it wanted to include an *ex ante* evaluation principle for the assessment of new services. In one of its draft proposals for a revised Communication, the Commission said that MS should accompany the expansion of publicly funded activities with adequate safeguards in order to fully respect the Amsterdam Protocol. MS should define what new services are and which services shall be subject to a prior evaluation.

Secondly, the Commission asked for additional safeguards in case public broadcasters engage in pay-services. Such services might, in the Commission's opinion, harm the universality of public service delivery of public broadcasters. The Commission did not imply that pay-services can never qualify as services of general economic interest (SGEI), yet such services would need special vigilance in order to ensure that the remit is not defined in a manifestly wrong manner. Herein, special reference was made to the issue of premium contents (in the sports rights market in particular). If premium content were to be offered on a pay-per-view or subscription basis this would qualify as a commercial service; if treated as a public service, this would constitute a manifest error.

A final action point related to the accumulation of capital reserves by public broadcasters. In order to ensure transparency and prevent overcompensation, MS should make sure that reserves are limited to a 10 per cent maximum of annual public compensation. Reserves should be limited by time and earmarked.

Strasbourg resistance

The Commission's action points were immediately criticised by both MS and public broadcasters. The published answers to the consultation that was set up in January and, notably, a conference organised by the French Presidency in Strasbourg from 17 to 18 July, exemplified the tensions surrounding the revision.

In her opening speech to the participants of this conference, former Commissioner Neelie Kroes emphasised that the revision of the

Broadcasting Communication concerned a modernisation, not a revolution. At the same time, however, Kroes made it clear that such a modernisation was necessary. Although recognising the importance of the Amsterdam Protocol – most often associated with MS' competencies with regard to PSB – Kroes also said the Protocol cut two ways. In her opinion, the aim of the revision was to ensure that both sides of the Protocol were complied with. In other words, on the one hand public broadcasting is important and MS define and organise their system nearly autonomously; on the other, the Commission checks whether the funding of public broadcasters violates Community interest.

With regard to the prevention of market distortion, and this is reflected in the enormous importance the Commission attached to MS' implementation of an *ex ante* evaluation for new media services offered by public broadcasters, Kroes (2008) added that there were significant doubts concerning some offers of public broadcasters (i.e. new media offers specifically).

> That means being honest when answering whether all emerging media services serve the social, democratic and cultural needs of a society. When you think of the dating clubs and video games that sometimes proliferate – you have to wonder what purpose they really serve. But the same question can be raised regarding pay per view offers of premium contents which are normally provided by commercial broadcasters. To be able to answer these questions, we need better definitions.

Kroes continued that not only better definitions, but also two-sided Public Value Tests (PVTS) are required to ensure fair competition and good governance.

MS and public broadcasters feared that the Commission was stretching its competencies in its ambition to revise the 2001 Broadcasting Communication. Although these stakeholders understood the underlying rationale for the revision, that is decreasing the number of complaints about the broadcasting sector on the Commission's 'table', they stressed that this argument did not legitimise the inclusion of specific criteria and procedures for the organisation and regulation of public broadcasters at a European level. In this respect, many interviewed representatives of public broadcasters and MS expressed concerns about the competencies of the Commission to ask for certain new rules and instruments, and the so-called 'cost' of an *ex ante* test.

How to wrap things up and reach a consensus

After the first consultations and in spite of the Strasbourg resistance, the Commission managed to publish a first draft of the Broadcasting Communication in early November 2008. Although this draft provoked criticism, it was the starting point of negotiations that ultimately led to the adoption of a revised Broadcasting Communication on 2 July 2009. From the outset, it was clear that this draft would not be accepted by MS and public broadcasters without amendments. These stakeholders opposed the detail of the draft text. Opposition to the revision was led by the Dutch government, involved in a contentious state aid investigation during the update of the 2001 Broadcasting Communication. In these negotiations (eventually closed on 26 January 2010), the introduction of an *ex ante* evaluation was the main stumbling block. During the negotiations of the revised Broadcasting Communication, private competitors filed new complaints with the Commission (during the second part of 2008) concerning, most importantly, the Dutch public broadcasters' expansion of service delivery to new media markets. This resulted in increased tensions between the Dutch government and the Commission. Positions diverged greatly and prompted the Dutch government to resist most aspects of the revision process. For example, in an attempt to stop the Commission from revising the Communication, the former Dutch Minister of Media, Ronald Plasterk wrote a letter opposing the revision, most notably the introduction of principles for an *ex ante* evaluation. This initiative was supported by the vast majority of MS.

The Commission, although determined to take the process of revising the 2001 Broadcasting Communication forward, appeared to be receptive towards the abovementioned concerns and backed down to some extent, claiming:

> If we get indications that the draft text is indeed too detailed: we will have a look at that. We do not challenge the competencies of MS to define the remit. We only want that this process of defining the remit is transparent and that there is accountability. The entire process stays with the MS. It is not the competence of the Commission to do this. But when there is a distortion of competition, it is the Commission's business. I don't think the market impact assessment principles included in the draft are too detailed. They provide for guidance only. If that is not clear, we will, if necessary, put it in capitals in the draft. The draft now is a simple consolidation of procedures so far. The Commission needs to provide more detailed rules concerning competition. It is the MS' role to define. (Lowe, 2008)

This does not mean that the Communication was prepared to revise the Communication at any cost. The Commission insisted that principles like the *ex ante* evaluation of new media services remained at the basis of the revision. A multilaterial meeting in December 2008, in which most MS (except for the UK, Spain, Italy, Greece and Luxembourg) continued to resist a new communication, did not alter the Commission's position in this respect. The Commission clearly stated at several events that it understood some of the concerns regarding, for example, the bureaucratic load of an *ex ante* test and the sensitivities attached to the issue of public broadcasting and state aid, but at the same time it insisted on the maintenance of the *ex ante* test principles in the draft. In this regard, it somewhat provocatively maintained that MS had the choice between a Commission that would stop its investigations of national public broadcasting schemes due to the existence of national instruments to deal with competition problems or an ever more pervasive influence of the Commission in the field of public broadcasting. In other words, if MS did not agree on the inclusion of *ex ante* test principles, Brussels' role as regards PSB was said (threatened) to grow as a consequence of new complaints and a lack of procedures at national level to which complainants might be referred.

In the end, the Commission and MS agreed that, although public broadcasters have the right to expand activities to new media markets, there must be some 'guarantees' to ensure that such an expansion is not overly harming the Community interest. The guarantee envisaged is a test evaluating whether a service is new, is delivering sufficient public value and is not overly distorting the market. This principle was included, provided that the Commission did not overly define the specific aspects of each and every element of such a test.

The new Broadcasting Communication was published on 2 July 2009 (Table 7.1), and still recognises the specific role of PSB in European democratic societies and, more importantly, accepts a multimedia remit that entrusts a wide array of tasks to public broadcasters (EC, 2009a). The new Broadcasting Communication also put forward a new practice for the regulation of public broadcasters; this was inspired by the PVT in the UK and is now spreading to other MS (e.g. Moe, 2010; Van Den Bulck, 2010). Given the fact that the Communication is binding for the Commission only, the latter are *strictu sensu* not obliged to implement an *ex ante* evaluation. Nevertheless, the Commission has stressed that the existence of an *ex ante* evaluation procedure will make it easier and more likely to dismiss private sector

Table 7.1 The revision process

Date	Event
10 January 2008	Commission opens the revision with a questionnaire (consultation of all stakeholders) – the Dutch government invites other MS to join forces against the revision
10 March 2008	Closure of the first consultation
17–18 July 2008	Strasbourg Conference
24 September 2008	The Netherlands sends common position paper (signed by 19 MS) to the Commission
22 October 2008	The General Court (previously the Court of First Instance) annuls the Commission's decision on TV2/Danmark
4 November 2008	First draft Broadcasting Communication published – Commission launches a second consultation
3 December 2008	Debate organised by Rhineland Palatinate (between Dutch government, Commission, ACT and EBU)
5 December 2008	First multilateral meeting between the Commission and the MS
8 January 2009	Hearing EPP-ED in European Parliament
15 January 2009	Closure of second consultation – interventions of MEPs in the European Parliament
10 February 2009	Joint letter from ACT, AER, ENPA, EPC and VPRT to former Commissioner Kroes on the revision of the Broadcasting Communication
8 April 2009	Second draft Broadcasting Communication published – Commission invites MS to comment
5 May 2009	Second multilateral meeting between the Commission and the MS
8 August 2009	Deadline for comments
2 July 2009	2009 Broadcasting Communication published

complaints concerning new media activities and refer private sector representatives to the national or regional competent authorities in this regard. It remains to be seen whether this will actually happen in reality, as it seems that – as can be derived from interviews with the private sector – both the private broadcasting and publishing sectors are becoming more organised in criticising public broadcasters' activities in the new media ecology.

Provisional conclusions

On the basis of this chapter, some provisional remarks and conclusions can be drawn. First of all, an increase in private complaints against the funding of public broadcasters and, as a consequence, a rising number of state aid decisions can be observed. This trend indicates more Commission control. Secondly, the state aid saga remains highly political and it seems that, within the basic legal framework of the state aid rules, judicial aspects of the cases are almost always subordinate to political considerations. Thirdly, there has been a marked increase in attention to the expansion of public broadcasters' activities to new media markets. In particular the revision of the 2001 Broadcasting Communication revealed the tensions between the different stakeholders on the scope of activities of public broadcasters in the digital age. The Commission seems to doubt the genuine public value of some new services offered by public broadcasters. However, it has accepted a public service media role for public broadcasters, provided that the latter's new services are being evaluated *vis-à-vis* their public value and market impact.

In short, this chapter (offering a short-term historical perspective on the issue of state aid and public broadcasting) offers a two-sided answer to the initial research question of this chapter: does a succinct historical perspective on state aid and PSB confirm an increasing role for the Commission in regard to PSB and, moreover, indicate an (increasingly) negative market failure approach towards the financing of public broadcasters? Have the latter, as a consequence, over time more reason to distrust the European Community's competition authorities?

On the one hand, some trends indeed indicate an increasing impact of European state aid control on PSB and, in addition, a more market-oriented approach to the issue. The market-oriented approach of the Commission is rooted in the state aid framework, which is first and foremost aimed at ensuring competition in the internal market. Competition in the media market should be shielded from public broadcasters that are too powerful. In some instances, the Commission has pointed to a market failure approach, doubting public broadcasters' offers of services already delivered by the market. Also, in its draft communication of November 2008, the Commission questions some of the services, like chat-rooms, offered by public broadcasters. In addition, the Commission attempts to force a more market-oriented approach upon the MS (e.g. the introduction of market impact assessment requirements in the 2009 Broadcasting Communication).

On the other hand, although some trends indicate that public broadcasters and MS have justified concerns about Commission state aid control, there is no clearcut evidence of an increasingly negative approach towards state aid and PSB. There is evidence of a more stringent approach towards the issue. A 'master plan' against the funding of public broadcasters does, however, not exist. The fact that the Commission for more then ten years did not know what to do and lacked the legal tools to handle private competitors' complaints illustrates this. It was only after 2001 (with the adoption of the first Broadcasting Communication) that some uniform approach emerged which is, at first sight, critical of an expansion of the remit to new media markets. This critical stance is not straightforward, however, and other observers maintain that the Commission supports a 'full participation of PSBs in the merging converged environment' (Nikolinakos, 2006, p. 398), even if within a more rigorous state aid framework.

Overall, the chronological perspective illustrates that, in spite of Arino's aspirations that European intervention in the media arena 'should not be a power struggle between MS to avoid interference' (Arino, 2004, p. 125), the issue of state aid control of public broadcasters is very often, at the very least, perceived as an 'either–or' question. The initial intervention of the Commission was perceived as a nearly automatic decrease of MS' competencies on the matter. The furious reactions of MS, which provoked reluctance of the Commission to go forward with the received complaints, show this. In addition, more recently, with regard to particular decisions (e.g. the *BBC Digital Curriculum* case) or the 2009 Broadcasting Communication, the debate is very often centred on the division of competencies between MS and the Commission. MS seem to think that every principle the Commission suggests leads to a loss of competencies on their side and a gain of competencies on the Commission's. And, although subsidiarity is a crucial principle in the order of the EU, it is very often more important to have a look at the positive or negative aspects of Commission intervention in regard to the central values of PSB.

8
'Europe Decides': Evaluating Public Broadcasting Schemes

Seen from a historical perspective, no big European 'master plan' against public service broadcasting (PSB) existed. Initially, the Commission reluctantly reacted to private sector complaints. Only from 2003 onwards did a more proactive approach develop. The Commission's approach is shaped by specific cases and decisions. In spite of several analyses of the Commission's policies (*e.g.* Humphreys, 2003; Ward, 2003, 2004a, 2008; Antoniadis, 2006; Brevini, 2010), an in-depth analysis of decision practice is largely lacking.

This chapter presents a meticulous analysis of the Commission's decision practice, focusing, firstly, on the state aid qualification of funding schemes for PSB. Subsequently, the Commission's interpretation of the three Broadcasting Communication criteria (i.e. a clear definition of the remit, independent control and proportional funding) is addressed. The chapter does not contain a chronological summary of each specific state aid decision on public broadcasting. Rather, there is a discussion clustered around themes. Some decisions will receive more attention as they touch upon all Broadcasting Communication criteria (so-called 'whole package' cases). Other cases are concerned more with the structural reorganisation of public broadcasters ('reform' cases) or specific services like thematic channels ('single issue' cases).

State aid or no state aid? That's the question

Every Commission investigation starts with the qualification of a measure as state aid. If a measure is not state aid, there is no legal ground for Commission intervention. There are over 25 Commission decisions on PSB. Only in three decisions did the Commission conclude that there was no state aid – being overruled by the General Court in one case only (CFI, 2000). Several scholars (e.g. Koenig and Haratsch, 2003; Katsirea, 2008) and public broadcasters dispute this 'easy' qualification of funding schemes to public broadcasters as state aid. Essentially, three reasons are invoked.

Firstly, some Member States (MS) (notably, the Netherlands and Flanders) have, rather symbolically, opposed the application of the state aid rules, pointing to the Amsterdam Protocol. Allegedly, the latter exempts public broadcasters from the application of the state aid rules. As the Amsterdam Protocol foresees in a balancing exercise between competition rules and public interest objectives – paraphrasing Article 106(2) TFEU – such an appreciation of the Protocol would go beyond its scope.

Secondly, several MS argue that the Commission is overly rigid in its interpretation of *Altmark*, which prevents an escape from the application of the state aid rules. In *Altmark*, the Court identified a set of four criteria that make it possible for state aids to services of general economic interest (SGEI) to escape Commission control (see also Chapter 6). However, to date no public broadcast funding scheme has complied with the *Altmark* criteria (Antoniadis, 2008). Several MS have argued that their funding schemes were in line with *Altmark*, however (EC, 2006a: §94, 2007b: §83, 2008b: §68–9). For example, in its decision on Spanish initiatives to compensate for RTVE's workforce reducations, the Commission said that one of *Altmark's* criteria was not complied with, asserting that an efficient and well-run undertaking would not have built up an excessive workforce. Subsequently, an efficient undertaking would not have required government aid (EC, 2007a: §29). Such an argument is weak, keeping in mind major restructuring of private companies in, for example, the automobile industry. Regardless of the interpretation of the *Altmark* criteria, some MS also find the use of criteria, derived from a transport case, inappropriate in the broadcasting sector (EC, 2006a: §76, 2008b: §68–9).

The Commission's rigid approach to *Altmark* has been criticised by the General Court (2008c: §227–32; see also Donders, 2009) in a ruling on Danish public broadcaster TV2. First and foremost, the Court criticised the limited analysis on the basis of which it concluded that *Altmark* was not complied with. In fact, the *Altmark* assessment of the Commission is virtually the same in all state aid decisions, repeating nearly *pro verbatim* the words of the *Altmark* ruling (CFI, 2008b: §232; Mortensen, 2008). Moreover, the Court argued that compliance with *Altmark* was possible for the Danish aid scheme, saying that a strict, *à la lettre*, interpretation of the four criteria is not desirable. Nevertheless, most funding schemes for public broadcasters would – even in case of a more flexible Commission approach – fail to meet *Altmark*. Public broadcasters do not always work like well-run undertakings; their compensations are often not determined on the basis of clear parameters, but rather the result of political negotiations, and so on.

Thirdly, it has been argued that licence fees are not state aid as they do not involve a transfer of government resources. The German Länder and the federal state have consistently argued that their licence fee is not 'imputable' to the state, as an independent body determines the level of the fee and collects it directly from German tax payers (Koenig and Kühling, 2001; Koenig and Haratsch, 2003, p. 574; Katsirea, 2008, p. 331ff). Strictly speaking, the Länder parliaments decide on an increase or decrease of the licence fee, but the frame for intervention is very narrow as the German Constitutional Court has significantly limited political action in this regard. Germany and the Länder insisted on this point until the end of the state aid procedure. Even in the final decision, although agreeing to a number of commitments, they asked for the inclusion of a paragraph stipulating that 'the German government has stressed that its agreement to amend the current financing regime for public service broadcasters cannot be understood as having accepted the Commission's qualification of the licence fee funding as State aid' (EC, 2007b: §323). For the moment, it thus remains unclear what the state aid status of a licence fee is. The Commission continues to insist that the German licence fee is a transfer of state resources. The fact that an independent body controls the collection of the licence fee does not exclude control of the Länder. The Länder have granted the independent body the right to collect and determine the licence fee. They may also withdraw this right and, in addition, may also legally enforce the collection of the licence fee (EC, 2007b: §142–50). When taking into account the purpose of state aid control, it indeed makes sense to provide for an identical treatment of aid schemes that have a similar effect. A licence fee and a direct government grant have similar effects on the market. The replacement of the licence fee in the late 1990s in the Netherlands and Flanders by a government grant, which had no observable effect at all, is a case in point. In addition, the German Länder, albeit not in charge of the procedure to determine the level and collection of the licence fee, have a final say about public broadcasters' budget and entrust the control body with its given competencies. In that sense, there is government control over the resources transferred from the collecting body to German public broadcasters. If the Commission disqualified such an aid scheme, saying it is not imputable to the state, this could stimulate MS to install licence fee schemes in order to circumvent the application of the state aid rules. The latter would hardly meet the Commission's goals of establishing an internal market in broadcasting.

Overall, most countries and public broadcasters have come to accept that there is Commission intervention. One public broadcaster representative even said that the state aid qualification question is a lost battle.

The battle for the public service remit

The most contentious aspect of Commission intervention is undeniably its possible and perceived impact on the public service remit. Many observers fear that there might be a narrowing of public broadcasters' scope of activities, in particular in the area of new media services and sports. With the exception of sports, the Commission has rarely paid particular attention to specific genres of content such as, for example, entertainment.

New media and the possibility of mission creep

For both 'old' and 'new' media, the 2001 Broadcasting Communication gives few indications of the required specificity of the definition of the public service remit,. The competence to define this are assigned to MS. The Commission is competent only to object in the event of a manifest error occurring. Concretely, this implies that MS are funding services undisputedly commercial in nature, as in the case for advertising or e-commerce. The manifest error concept is not beyond question, however, as it is difficult to assert which services are inarguably commercial in nature. MS' and Commission's opinions diverge on this point. The former stress their autonomy, while the latter is suspicious of an abuse of the flexible state aid rules, referring to the possibility of a 'mission creep' as a consequence thereof.

In particular for new media services, there are diverging opinions on the task of public broadcasters. Consequently, the balancing act between MS and Commission competencies has proved to be a very difficult one in this area. To date, the Commission has put forward four (consecutive) approaches towards the issue of definition and new media services.

1. Thematic channels fit within the remit and the remit is an MS competence.
2. New media services must be closely associated with traditional radio and television services.

3. New media services must be part of a clearly defined remit and some services are not part of that remit.
4. New media services must be part of a clearly defined remit and it is the MS' responsibility to decide on the services covered by the public service remit.

Thematic channels fit the public service remit

In 1997, private broadcasters in Germany and the UK filed complaints against the launch of thematic channels by ARD, ZDF and British Broadcasting Corporation (BBC) (EC, 1999a, 1999b). Their argument against the channels was twofold. Firstly, the channels were said to fall outside the public service remit as they were targeting niche audiences. Secondly, public intervention was considered unnecessary given the existing services of private broadcasters (EC, 1999b: pt. 4).

The Commission disagreed on all points, saying that MS define the task of public broadcasters and that the Commission is limited to checking for a manifest error only. This does not imply the Commission evaluating whether a service fits within the remit as defined by an MS. This would entail an evaluation of MS' definition, which would go beyond the competencies of the Commission (EC, 1999b: pt. 10, 2002a: §46). Besides this more generic point, the Commission counterargued several private broadcaster arguments. For example, it refuted BSkyB's allegations of market-distortive behaviour, maintaining that a level of market distortion is acceptable (EC, 1999a: §93–9).

Essentially, the Commission approached the new media issue from a rather positive angle, albeit not without preservations. By 1999 the Commission had indeed raised concerns about legal frameworks, leaving too much room for interpretation on the breadth of the public service remit (EC, 1999a: §69).

Closely associated

A case on online education services offered by the BBC breaks with the rather positive approach of the Commission. In early 2003, the UK government notified its support for an online BBC educational service, better known as the BBC Digital Curriculum. This service involved the offer of online educational content within a virtual learning environment (EC, 2003b) and was to be made available through the BBC's BBCi websites. Its budget, amounting to £135–150 million (for a period of five years), was to be paid from the overall licence fee budget. The UK government approved the service after extensive research, indicating the wide approval of teachers and pupils involved in a pilot scheme (Coe et al., 2002). Several private providers of online educational services in the UK, in particular software specialist RM, opposed the BBC Digital Curriculum, arguing against the use of licence money for free services already catered for by the private sector (Shah, 2003). In response to private sector concerns, the BBC announced its willingness to cooperate closely with its competitors wherever possible. Consequently, the UK government conditionalised the approval of the BBC Digital Curriculum, requiring it to offer distinctive and complementary services (in comparison with the private sector) and limit the duration of the project to five years (Harvey, 2010).

The Digital Curriculum was thus a contentious issue at the national level. After the private sector threatened to take matters to 'Brussels' (Gibson, 2003), the UK government notified the aid with Director General (DG) Competition. This did not prevent private companies from filing complaints.

Hence, the 'hot potato' was served on the Commission's plate. The latter argued that the Digital Curriculum was not covered by the BBC's public service remit, pointing out the lack of a 'close association' between side activities such as the Digital Curriculum and the so-called 'core' remit of the BBC. In the absence of a close association, MS need explicitly to entrust the service to the public broadcaster. The necessity thereof for an existing service catered for by the private sector was also disputed (EC, 2003b: §36). In the end, the Commission qualified the Digital Curriculum as an SGEI as no manifest error could be detected. Consequently, the general exception for these services was invoked and the Digital Curriculum was declared admissible.

The Commission's decision – although accepting the scheme under general rules for SGEIs – was heavily criticised (Wiedemann, 2004; Harvey, 2010), and undeniably for valid reasons. Firstly, the closely associated principle infringes MS' competencies to define the remit. It indeed implies that services not closely associated with existing radio and television services cannot be part of the remit and subsequently, cannot be regarded as a public broadcasting service. In that sense, the closely associated concept implicitly limits public broadcasters' remit to traditional radio and television programmes (Bardoel and Vochteloo, 2009). Secondly, the approach upheld in Digital Curriculum does not appear to be technology neutral. Education has always been a core activity of the BBC. The online nature of the Digital Curriculum should not have led the Commission to conclude that education is no longer a public broadcasting goal once it moves online.

A competition law rationale defined the proposed scheme as outside the existing public service broadcasting remit. The Commission pointed to the situation for commercial competitors, and deemed the Digital Curriculum as belonging to the market too far beyond BBC operations. The resulting decision took a restrictive approach. It introduced the criterion 'closely associated' to radio and television programmes as a measure of online activities' public service value. Only via a detour was the curriculum endorsed, uncoupled from the broadcasters' remaining service. The decision was a clear rejection of the British Government's approval of the BBC's right to include the Digital Curriculum in its existing public service remit. (Moe, 2008a, p. 221)

Certain factors explain the Commission's approach. First and foremost, this was one of the first cases in which the Commission dealt with the expansion of public broadcasters to markets in which players, other than broadcasters, are active. There was significant pressure to curb the BBC's expansion. Taking into account the lack of knowledge within DG Competition on the broadcasting sector and the uncertainty over public broadcasters' new media intentions, certain closely associated concepts were introduced to enhance legal certainty. These did not live up to that goal, however, as they went beyond the division of competencies between the MS and the Commission. Moreover, the critical stance of the UK government itself and the market impact assessment carried out inspired the Commission's stance (Harvey, 2010). Interestingly, and probably related to the former point, resistance against the Commission's decision was located outside the UK, where both the UK government and the BBC accepted the decision in a rather pragmatic way. The Commission repeated its stance in a decision on the funding of Danish public broadcaster TV2, stressing that information society services and broadcasting were not similar. Information society services were required to meet the same social, democratic and cultural needs of society (as stipulated in the Amsterdam Protocol). Some services, like chat rooms or video games, could not be considered public services (EC, 2004a: §90–2) as they were, in the Commission's opinion, similar to commercial offers and did not expose public value. Again, the Commission went beyond its competencies, essentially following the policy formulation of the Danish government. Other MS might disagree on the Danish approach, however. Hence, the Commission should refrain from generalising standpoints on the public service remit.

The most important point made by the Commission in the Digital Curriculum and TV2 decisions is that the idea that everything that public broadcasters do is public service no longer holds (if it ever did) (Ward, 2008, p. 78). Reflecting on the Commission's stance, MEP Hieronymi (2004) argued in favour of a more clearly defined remit. If MS fail to provide such a definition, a sustainable expansion of public broadcasters' remit in the digital age is off the agenda and the 'twilight zone' between public and commercial services will increase. The Commission's competencies will expand accordingly, as it is will get caught in a trial-and-error process, both staying within and going beyond its competencies.

Walking the line between the scope of the remit and its formulation

The imperfections of the Digital Curriculum and TV2 decisions were not neglected and, in its decision on the German licence fee funding of ARD and ZDF, the Commission put forward a slightly different approach (Bardoel and Vochteloo, 2008: 10). It made two core remarks on the remit.

Firstly, the Commission stated that there was no clear dividing between commercial and public services in the German public broadcasting system (EC, 2007b: §238–9). This enabled ARD and ZDF to exploit commercial services on the basis of public funding. Hence, a manifest error could occur. In focusing on the division between commercial and public services, it is emphasis on the business model rather than on the platform that determines the nature of services. Albeit more technology neutral, this appreciation was potentially problematic as well. Indeed, the Commission suggested that pay-per-view services, supported by a business model for on-demand services, were not public services (EC, 2007b: §239–40). This logic was not conclusive, as MS autonomously decide on the funding mechanisms (e.g. grant, licence fee, advertising, pay-per-view, subscription) of public broadcasting services.

Secondly, the definition of the remit is too vague. In particular, the delivery of new media services cannot be justified on the basis of imprecise cultural, educative and democratic objections. There is a need for a 'clearer circumscription, showing also the "added value" of new services in comparison with already existing services' (EC, 2007b: §227). New services 'that are not "programmes" in the traditional sense' (EC, 2007b: §222) are permissible, however, which also shows the willingness of the Commission to accept public broadcasters expanding into new media markets. At the same time it also illustrates the conceptual difficulties of framing these new activities in a technology-neutral way, remaining, moreover, within the field of application of the Broadcasting

Communication. Even though the requirement of an added value of new services is far from technology neutral, the Commission's insistence on a more clearly defined remit is legitimate, given its task to check for manifest errors.

No hands-off approach

In its decisions following the German case, the Commission tried (even) 'harder' to stay within its competencies when dealing with the public service remit. It still asked for a clear definition in order to check for so-called 'manifest error' (EC, 2008b: §166, 2008d: §89, 2009b: §138, 2010: §156). It also continued to insist on a clear demarcation between public and commercial services in order to avoid the exploitation of commercial services on the basis of public funding (EC, 2008a: §88) and to enhance legal certainty for private media companies (EC, 2008b: §169). In stressing this, the Commission also asserted that a clear remit was indispensable if MS wish to avoid the funding of commercial services. The Commission's demand for clarity should not be confused with a demand for a completely spelled-out definition, squeezing the editorial independence of public broadcasters. The Commission acknowledged the importance of independence in several of its decisions (EC, 2008b: §167, 2008d: §86, 2009b: §139).

Basically the Commission, in its decision practice following the German case, stressed that MS should clarify which new services were part of the remit and why this was the case. As the Commission made explicit in its decision on the funding of Austrian public broadcaster ORF, 'the public service remit may also include services which are not programmes in the conventional meaning' (EC, 2009b: §140; see also EC, 2008b: §168). Whereas the Commission had previously asked for a close association between old and new services, it now said (and more explicitly so than in its decision on the funding of ARD and ZDF) that such an association in itself did not legitimise all new services. On the contrary, in the Austrian case, it emphasised that the demand for a close association or a link between new and old services in national legislation was in itself not evidence of a clear-cut definition or the absence of a manifest error (EC, 2009b: §143). The Commission observed that the Austrian public broadcaster was, while the legal framework was asking for a close association between Internet services and existing television and radio offers, offering services like ring tones for mobile phones, e-cards, dating and partner websites, real estate and job postings, gambling and betting services, e-banking and online auctions. ORF has, in the course of negotiations between the Commission and the

Austrian government, stopped most of these activities. Nevertheless, in the Commission's opinion the public value of these activities' was rather dubious. In other words, the remit was not sufficiently clear as it left too much room for interpretation (EC, 2009b: §144–5).

For that reason, the Commission encouraged MS to define the remit more elaborately in legislation and, if MS preferred that option, through additional programme guidelines, charters, public service contracts or self-commitment by public broadcasters (which is the approach followed in EC, 2008b: §170, 2008d: §89–91; 134, 2009b: §142, 2010: §216ff). The Commission thus wanted MS to regulate public broadcasters more closely. Although the Commission still gave in to the temptation to question-specific services in, for example, the Austrian case, it became more prudent and stressed above all that government authorities need to ensure that not public broadcasters, but they themselves, are in charge of the scope of the public service remit (EC, 2008b: §181). The underlying idea is that not everything can be swept away under the carpet of democracy, social cohesion, universal service delivery and cultural diversity.

Hence, the evaluation of the definition criterion is captured in one single question: is there a mechanism, imposed by MS, that prevents public broadcasters from freewheeling in new media markets?

Evaluation on definition

A number of conclusions can be derived from the Commission's practice on the definition of the remit. Firstly, until the recent decisions on Austria, the Netherlands, Ireland and Flanders, the Commission favoured a link between old and new services in order for the latter to be admissible. Secondly, the Commission wanted services of public broadcasters to be distinctive. Although this demand is fed by market failure ideas (dominant in competition analysis, albeit that they are no legal basis of procedures concerning services of general economic interest), since 1998 the Commission has no longer questioned the holistic nature of PSB. Thirdly, the Commission's practice is dominated by market-oriented arguments, focusing on legal certainty of competitors and, setting out from the competition framework, looking upon public broadcasters as de facto distorters of a utopian market equilibrium. Fourthly, a clear demarcation between public and private services is indispensable for compliance with the state aid provisions. Whereas the Commission used to meddle with the actual scope of the remit in order to further such a clear demarcation and, in so doing, was overstepping its competencies, it now tries to force MS to 'clean the carpet', preventing the possibility of mission creep as much as possible. Fifthly, and related to the former point (and often overlooked in other contributions on this topic), there is a distinction between the decisions made before 2005 and the more recent decisions on Germany, Austria, Flanders, Ireland and the Netherlands. In the latter case, the Commission has modified its approach in order not to cross the thin line between analysing the possibility of manifest errors on the one hand and co-defining the remit on the other. Finally, the controversy surrounding the issue of definition is both pertinent and persistent because of the enormous uncertainty associated with it (Ward, 2008). Due to technological progress, market evolutions, changing consumer needs, developing Community law and MS' evolving regulation, state aid control of PSB is a trial-and-error process. Since the first thematic channels decisions, the Commission's assessment of the definition condition has been a learning process. Although the Commission has always emphasised the need for a clear remit and proper entrustment, different decisions have not always been consistent. Recent decisions on the Irish, Flemish, Dutch and Austrian funding of public broadcasters might create more legal certainty, as they clearly put forward a 'no hands-off' or 'responsabilisation' approach. In that sense, with regard to the issue of the definition and scope of the public service remit, the Commission's approach has become more coherent. MS have an important role to play in overcoming remaining uncertainties. The definition of the remit is crucial in order to facilitate a transfer from PSB to public service media. A more precise definition of the remit might perhaps be perceived by public broadcasters as burdensome and uncomfortable – and, indeed, one should be careful when intervening with the independence of public broadcasters. However, it is necessary to legitimise better the need for public broadcasting in a rapidly developing and far more complex media landscape.

Independent and *ex ante* control vs. the autonomy of public broadcasters

Exporting the Public Value Test

In its five whole-package decisions (i.e. Germany, Flanders, Ireland, Austria and the Netherlands), the Commission has intensified its efforts towards a more clearly defined remit through its demand for an *ex ante* evaluation. The Commission finds that new services not covered by a law or contract between government and the public broadcasters should be separately entrusted to public broadcasters. As made explicit in, for example, its decision on the Flemish public broadcaster VRT, an *ex ante* assessment of new services should precede such a specific entrustment: 'without any prior evaluation and explicit entrustment of the Flemish government, the VRT is not allowed to deliver services or perform activities that are not covered by the Beheersovereenkomst' (EC, 2008b: §239 [translated from Dutch]). An *ex ante* evaluation ideally consists of a public value and a market impact assessment of a newly proposed service (EC, 2007b: §313, 328, 2008b: §230, 2008d: §141ff, 2009b: §198ff, 2010: §234ff).

The demand for an *ex ante* evaluation was inspired by the UK Public Value Test (UK PVT). Several Commission officials indeed said that they considered the PVT as a means to settle private companies' concerns and to refer complaints back to the national level. The idea was that a PVT resembles the balancing act created by the Commission under state aid law itself and would, consequently, make the Commission's work superfluous. Putting it bluntly, the Commission thought it had found the 'golden egg' or a way out of all the complaints being filed by the private sector (these complaints resulted in a major work overload for the unit within DG Competition, which deals with media-related state aid schemes).

In order to avoid MS' frustration concerning the demand for a PVT, the Commission redubbed it the 'Amsterdam test' (Kroes, 2008). This new term did not prevent the test from meeting with much hostility, however. MS and public broadcasters still fear it will marginalise public broadcasters' activities and limit innovation and creativity. DG Competition claims that the test is a mere transposition of the Amsterdam Protocol for new media services. The Protocol consists of two legs: the first ensures MS' rights to organise and define their PSB system; the second, however, stresses that PSB should not bring about unnecessary market distortions. In that sense, an *ex ante* evaluation conducted at the national level indeed ensures MS' autonomy in the area of public broadcasting. And, at the same time, it also ensures that a balancing act between public value on the one hand (public interest) and the possibility of market distortions on the other (Community interest) is conducted.

In spite of the initial reluctance to accept a test and recognising the manifest differences between *ex ante* evaluations in Germany, Ireland,

Flanders, Austria and the Netherlands, all concerned governments have agreed to:

- define which services are considered new media services and, hence, require an *ex ante* evaluation;
- establish an *ex ante* evaluation for new media services;
- submit these services to an objective evaluation preferably carried out by an independent monitoring body;
- ensure that third parties are involved in the procedure and have time to comment on public broadcasters' new services;
- ensure the publication of the independent body's advice; and
- base their acceptance or refusal of a new service on that independent body's advice (however, often not binding) (EC, 2007b: §328ff, 2008b: §230, 2008d: §141ff, 2009b: §198ff, 2010: §234ff).

There are several valid reasons to criticise the Commission for imposing an *ex ante* evaluation. Firstly, it is uncertain whether the PVT that is embedded in a very specific public broadcasting regime can be exported successfully to countries other than the UK. The instrument, launched in 2007, goes back to earlier initiatives of the Department for Culture Media and Sport to subject new services to prior approval of the Secretary of State. By imposing a PVT-like model on other countries, the Commission might overlook the embedded character of the test. Secondly, a PVT could be too burdensome (in terms of staff and money) for public broadcasters with budget constraints. In the UK, a vast army of people work on these tests and it must be noted that not all new services are subjected to the test, and hence, it does not offer an absolute solution for all new services offered by public broadcasters. On paper, the PVT is a good idea, but in a specific broadcasting situation it will need continuous adaptation and improvement, however. Thirdly, the market impact assessment – an essential part of the Commission's demands – assumes involvement of third parties in the appraisal of new public broadcasting services. It is somewhat problematic that private companies might co-decide on the scope of activities of direct competitors. Fourthly, and perhaps most crucially, *ex ante* evaluations concern distinct services whereas public broadcasting is a holistic project. The evaluation of distinct services can introduce a market failure logic into public broadcasting regulation and lead to a marginalisation of public broadcasters. Finally, numerous MS and public broadcasters uphold the view that the Commission is not competent to ask for an *ex ante* evaluation of new media services. In these MS' and public broadcasters' opinion such a demand goes against the subsidiarity principle and its specific transposition to PSB in the Amsterdam Protocol.

Although many contest the Commission's demand and argue that there is a violation of the subsidiarity principle, it is not always clear how far Commission competences (can) go in competition policy. Given the numerous problematic aspects of *ex ante* control of new media services, MS' caution with regard to *ex ante* control is, on the whole, certainly understandable and – to some extent – justified. However, the problematic aspects of a PVT do not mean that this tool – if adapted to local circumstances – cannot be a useful exercise in strengthening public broadcasters' position within a new media environment. In light of technological and economic evolutions, public broadcasters' role is under fire. As public broadcasters are expanding activities to new markets, it is vital to illustrate the importance of their presence there. Steemers (2003, p. 133) puts her finger on the button by saying that 'failing to demonstrate both uniqueness and appeal across a broad range of output, the consensus surrounding public funding could conceivably dissolve'. In this regard, Suter (2008, p. 5) stresses that it is vital to treat the test as something more than a necessary evil. Because 'PSBs face unprecedented pressure to make, and justify, investment in new means of productions and distribution', they have to illustrate how new services deliver public value to – *ad ultimo* – citizens. PVTs should be grasped as an opportunity proactively to tackle questions on the position of public broadcasters (especially) in new media environments: Should public broadcasters offer on-demand sports content? Are pay-services public services? Are there limits to public broadcasters' presence online? Is there a justification for an 'internet licence fee'? Such questions will certainly arise and might lead to a decline in public, and also political, support for public broadcasting. However, imposing a PVT on MS will not encourage them, nor their public broadcasters, genuinely to complete an evaluation of new services:

> Accountability is not inconsistent with freedom, when it is voluntarily conducted in the form of dialogue and debate, with some mutual respect and tolerance of differences. (McQuail, 2003, p. 28)

Independent control

In relation to its demand for an objective evaluation of new media services, the Commission has also stressed the necessity of independent control. This inquiry is transposed differently in decision practice. In the Irish, Flemish and Austrian cases, the Commission has emphasised the necessity of legally external control, that is the establishment of a control body that is legally separate from the controlled public broadcaster. This prompted the Irish, admittedly in line with broader policies to reform existing monitoring bodies and centralise competences, to create the Broadcasting Authority Ireland (BAI). The latter is responsible for a constant monitoring of Irish public broadcasters' activities, and is required to carry out an annual review of the ways in which RTE and TG4 have complied with their financial commitments and a five-yearly review of the adequacy of public broadcasters' funding. In addition, the BAI is required to conduct *ex ante* evaluations when new media services are launched by public broadcasters (EC, 2008d: §151). Flanders created the Flemish Regulator for the Media in the course of its negotiations with the Commission. Again, this happened within the broader framework of rationalisation and also because of failure in enforcement of the Television without Frontiers Directive (TWF). In any case, the Commission was very interested in the Regulator's control of the Flemish public broadcaster's behaviour and appeared to be satisfied with the Flemish initiatives in this regard by the end of the state aid procedure, as the Regulator became responsible for monitoring of the VRT's market-conforming behaviour and overseeing whether the public broadcaster was meeting its contractual obligations with the Flemish government. In the Austrian case, it was also agreed to create an independent body, external to the public broadcaster. This body will evaluate ORF's performance (EC, 2009b: §210).

In the German case, the Commission has been more lenient and accepted the German Broadcasting Councils as adequate controlling bodies. In spite of the Commission's doubts about the Councils (EC, 2007b: §256), it had to accept them as the German Länder were not prepared to abandon their carefully designed system of internal control. In exchange for the Commission's flexibility in this regard, several measures were introduced to ensure the independence of the Councils *vis-à-vis* the management of public broadcasters. 'Chinese walls' had to be introduced between the two bodies, Councils are gaining more staff and resources, and, morever, most stakeholders agree that there is much attention given to the position and effective control of the Broadcasting Councils, given the Commission's intervention.

The proportionality of public broadcasters' funding

Next to a clearly spelled-out public service remit and adequate control, the Broadcasting Communication requires that funds granted to public broadcasters are proportional and transparently allocated. While the nature (i.e. public, private or both) of funding mechanisms is determined solely by the MS (Antoniadis, 2006, p. 596), the Commission requires and checks that public compensations for public service obligations amount to the net cost of these obligations. If the compensation is higher than the net cost, there is overcompensation and aid is not considered proportional. This in turn leads to the incompatibility of the aid scheme.

There are five inherent difficulties attached to the proportionality provision and the Commission's analysis thereof. Firstly, the 'net cost' concept assumes that one can establish the exact quantitative cost of PSB before the delivery of the services concerned. This is not easy given the rather qualitative nature of the public service obligations at hand (Donders and Pauwels, 2008). Secondly, for its analysis of possible overcompensation, the Commission largely relies on data provided by the recipients of the aid, that is public broadcasters. Thirdly, the proportionality assessment is an indirect indicator. Its finality lies in uncovering market distortions. However, it is conceivable that there is no market distortion while there is overcompensation, and *vice versa*. The methodological and empirical link between the proportionality provision and market distortion is, for that reason, rather weak. Fourthly, the calculation of the net cost demands a strict and clear separation between public and commercial revenues/spendings. Such a separation is meaningful only when there is a clear demarcation between public and commercial service delivery. The analysis of the Commission's decision practice concerning the definition of the public service remit (*cf. supra*) shows that such a demarcation between public and commercial service delivery has proved problematic, from the first complaints in the early 1990s until the present. Finally, an observation of overcompensation can lead to a reimbursement of the state aid when the Commission's investigation deals with new aid. Such a reimbursement from public broadcaster to state authority impinges directly on the budgets of public broadcasters, is a tangible outcome of the Commission's state aid control and, hence, is politically volatile.

The Commission has operationalised the proportionality provision. There are five specific focal points of attention or measurement indicators in the Commission's analysis of the proportionality of the funds of public broadcasters (Donders and Pauwels, 2009).

1. Is there a compensation of the net cost of the public service delivery?
2. Is the structural and financial organisation of the public broadcaster transparent?

3. Are there mechanisms in place that allow governments or monitoring bodies to discover possible overcompensation and prevent it from happening?
4. Are there any reserves and are they earmarked?
5. Is there market distortion?

The above questions have been addressed in numerous cases. Decisions reveal similarities, but also differences. Three groups of cases can be discerned. Firstly, in two decisions, concerning the funding of the Dutch public broadcasters and Danish TV2, the Commission asked for a reimbursement of government money. These decisions focused on the mathematics, attempting to establish overcompensation. Secondly, several decisions tackled the reorganisation of funding schemes in Spain, Portugal, Italy and France. Thirdly, the whole-package decisions on Germany, Flanders, Ireland, Austria and the Netherlands fine-tuned the funding schemes of the public broadcasters involved.

Establishing overcompensation and its link with market distortion

In their complaints against the funding of Danish TV2 and the Dutch public broadcasters, private broadcasters claimed that the aid schemes in question were not proportional and, hence, induced market distortion. In the Danish case, licence fee revenues, ad hoc funds and loans of TV2 were investigated. These were all considered as new aid, given the creation of TV2 in 1989 after the accession of Denmark to the EU. In its assessment, DG Competition added the gross public service cost and commercial revenues. The net public service cost is the outcome of this sum and amounted to €498.29 million, while the public service compensation totalled €582.56 million. This means that there was, *strictu sensu*, an overcompensation of €84.27 million (EC, 2004a: §24–5, 57–68, 78). In spite of its finding of overcompensation and its subsequent demand for a reimbursement, the Commission (EC, 2004a: §62) was not able to establish a link between its findings of overcompensation and the alleged market distortion.

The Danish authorities criticised the Commission's findings, arguing that the existence of the surplus was justifiable, referring to the anticipation of fluctuating advertising revenues and the right to a reasonable profit. The Commission firmly disagreed, arguing that surpluses were not earmarked and, therefore, uncontrolled. Moreover, the surpluses remained unused and were, for that reason, unnecessary (EC, 2004a: §111–14). The General Court overruled the Commission on this, concluding that an accumulation of surplus revenues is not sufficient to assume a lack of control. In addition, the Court (CFI, 2008b: §197–9) also stated that a lack of earmarked reserves is no valid reason to conclude that there is an overcompensation of the public service remit. The fact that the reserves were not yet used at the time of the investigation was irrelevant in this respect. The entire idea of reserves, so the Court claimed, is to anticipate situations that, perhaps, do not occur.

The decision concerning the Dutch public broadcasting system was somewhat more complicated than the Danish case. The Commission investigated several ad hoc payments and reserves – all created in the 1990s and, hence, new aid (EC, 2006a: §37–51) – held by several public broadcasters in the Netherlands. The Commission considered these mechanisms independent from the the annual compensation the Dutch public broadcasters receive. The annual grant was subject to a separate procedure.

In spite of the separation of the two procedures, the Commission assessed the proportionality of the ad hoc funds, also including the annual grant in its calculation. Whereas the requirement for public funding (i.e. the theoretical net cost) is €799 million, the actual annual grant amounts to €819.6 million, meaning that there is a surplus of €20.6 million for the existing annual grant (for which no reimbursement can be asked). The new aid mechanisms amount to €77.7 million, resulting in an overall surplus or overcompensation of €98.3 million, which had to be reimbursed to the Dutch authorities. As in the case of the Danish decision, the Commission gave no evidence on possible market distortions resulting from the observed overcompensation. It should be mentioned that the Danish government compensated TV2/Danmark after the reimbursement of the aid in order to prevent the company from going into debt. This compensation was accepted by the Commission, recognising it as a measure to ensure the financial health of public broadcasters and allowing it to fulfil its public service objectives (EC, 2004b).

The Dutch decision is problematic for two reasons. Firstly, the calculation of the Commission is flawed. The proportionality assessment of the ad hoc funds included not only a cost/revenue assessment of the funds in question, but it also took into account the entire annual funding scheme. The new aid schemes were *a priori* overcompensating Dutch public broadcasters, as analysis of the annual funds revealed a surplus of over €20 million. Leaving aside the impossibility of conducting another mathematical exercise, assessment of the proportionality of the new aids (that added new aid mechanisms and the annual public revenues) could not determine to what extent the new aid mechanisms as such exceeded the net cost of the public service delivery for which they were intended. The new aid mechanisms under scrutiny had specific public service obligations to live up to. Secondly, and this also applies to the Danish decision, the Commission was not able to proove the alleged market-distortive behaviour.

Because of the lack of evidence supporting the claim that overcompensation leads to market distortions, the Dutch authorities argued that the Commission was wrong to declare that the state aid measures were incompatible with the state aid provisions. In that respect, the Netherlands, moreover, pointed to the Amsterdam Protocol, which explicitly states that funding of PSB is acceptable 'insofar [as] such funding does not affect trading conditions and competition in the Community to an extent which would be contrary to the common interest'. Since the Commission could not verify that there was indeed a negative impact of the behaviour of the Dutch public broadcasters on overall competition in the media market, it should not have reached its negative conclusion on overcompensation.

Discussion of the Dutch and Danish cases might appear rather technical and, perhaps, insignificant for that reason. However, these are important as they illustrate very clearly that mathematics, although objective, is not flawless. Nevertheless, 'simple' mathematical exercises can have very real consequences for public broadcasters compelled to reimburse aid which they thought had been legitimately granted by their national governments.

Reform strategies for Southern Europe

Other decisions illustrate more clearly the intrinsic value of the Commission's proportionality assessment. These concern the annual funding and other support mechanisms for public broadcasters in Spain, Portugal, France and Italy. Several action points characterise the decisions on Southern European public broadcasters.

Firstly, Spain, Italy and France were compelled to introduce separate accounting systems for commercial revenues and costs (EC, 2003d: §81, 2005b: §67–70, 2005c: §58–9). There were no penalties for breaching the state aid rules. Rather, a future-oriented approach, asking MS structurally to reform the accounting systems of their public broadcasters, was followed.

Secondly, all involved countries agreed to introduce safeguards against overcompensation (EC, 2005e: §60, 2006c: §100). In fact, there was no net cost calculation of public broadcasters' service delivery. This, as the Commission discovered in its investigation of Portuguese RTP and

French France 2 and France 3, also masked the undercompensation of certain public broadcasters (EC, 2003a: §189, 2003d: §89).

Thirdly, government guarantees, enabling public broadcasters to accumulate deficits without the possibility of going bankrupt (while broadcasters like RTVE were virtually bankrupt), had to be abolished (EC, 2005b: §67; Pérez Gomez, 2006). The Commission demanded the abolishment of these guarantees, claiming they constituted an unfair advantage *vis-à-vis* competitors. However, these mechanisms also gravely undermined the financial health of public broadcasters in Southern Europe, adding to their political dependence.

Finally, acts and media laws were adapted in order to ensure that public broadcasters behaved in a market-conforming way, charging market prices for programme rights and advertising. Moreover, the 'arm's length' principle was introduced and operationalised in order to ensure that public broadcasters did not act unfavourably with subsidiary companies (EC, 2005b: §71, 2005c: §60ff, 2005e: §69ff, 2006c: §101ff).

It deserves mention that, among all these action points, efficiency was not mentioned in the Commission's assessments. Although private broadcasters have consistently asked for benchmarks in order to expose the allegedly inefficient behaviour of public broadcasters, the Commission has refrained from repeating this question as it is not competent to meddle in the efficiency of public broadcasters' corporate conduct. The Commission has only once mentioned efficiency: in a decision on Spanish workforce reductions involving RTVE, it applauded the measure announced for 'ensuring that the future RTVE can carry out its public service obligations in a more efficient way, while reducing the overall State financing' (EC, 2007a: §56).

Southern European countries are known for their highly politicised, bureaucratic and inefficient public broadcasters (Papathanassopoulos, 2007b). Commission intervention in these countries can be evaluated in two ways. On the negative side, the length of the procedures in which Spain, Portugal, Italy and France were involved was excessive. The decisions discussed above go back to complaints filed in the early to mid-1990s. Hence, complainants had to wait for more transparency and legally enshrined principles of market-conforming behaviour for more than ten years. In addition, the Commission concentrated its efforts on enforcing legal changes. Regulatory reform, so the Commission hoped, would rule out unwarranted behaviour in the Southern European broadcasting markets (Ward, 2008: pp. 64–5). However, adaptations of legal frameworks do not automatically and necessarily give rise to de facto changes in the media sector. Changes are embedded in a political climate that is, with regard to the countries concerned, rather unaccommodating of PSB and, in addition, still concerned mostly with the political control of public broadcasters. On the positive side, it cannot be ignored that many changes were made in media legislation as a consequence of the European state aid procedures. As such, the Commission – albeit not solely responsible – has contributed to a process of change. Indeed, reforms were absolutely necessary to restore the structural and financial dysfunction of, for example, the Spanish public broadcaster RTVE. Overall, the Commission's intervention in the Mediterranean countries has not been a panacea for all problems associated with their public broadcasters. However, it has resulted in a renewed organisation of public broadcasters in these countries and, leaving aside the empirical flaws in the Commission's proportionality assessment, indicated the real and intrinsic value of this assessment for PSB.

Superficial harmonisation and good governance

In all five whole-package decisions, the Commission asked for the further strengthening of proportionality and transparency-related mechanisms. Whereas demands for reform were more structural in Southern European countries, the countries involved in the whole-package cases were confronted with more detailed demands. A distinction between four demands can be made. Firstly, in the German case the Commission asked for the legal entrenchment of transparency principles in the German Länder's public broadcasting legislation. Although transparency principles were, in the opinion of most stakeholders, followed in practice, their legal entrenchment was not a fact before the state aid procedure and, as such, the transparency principles could not be legally enforced (EC, 2007b: §266–7). Secondly, the Commission asked for a better monitoring of market-conforming behaviour. For example, it required that the participation of German public broadcasters in other companies ought to be better monitored (EC, 2007b: §287). Reference can also be made to the Irish case, where the Irish government promised to ensure that public broadcasters' commercial activities were performed on an 'arm's length' basis and that objective, predictable and pre-set arrangements would be made with third parties concerning the use of the public broadcasters' archive (EC, 2008d: §161ff). And, in the Flemish case, the government authorities promised to publish an existing framework in which the guidelines for VRT's commercial behaviour are outlined (the so-called framework for merchandising and side activities) (EC, 2008b: §229). Even the structural separation between public and commercial activities has been suggested as a measure to ensure market-conforming behaviour. In the Austrian case, for example, it has been specified that all ORF's commercial activities must be outsourced into ORF's own commercial subsidiaries (EC, 2009b: §220). Thirdly, the Commission required more/other mechanisms to ensure that compensation to public broadcasters is limited to the net cost of the public services discharged (EC, 2007b: §182, 2008b: §234–5, 2008d: §158, 2009b: §218). Finally, the Commission asked Germany, Ireland, Flanders, Austria and the Netherlands to impose a 10 per cent limitation on the accumulation of reserves by public broadcasters. Although public broadcasters and MS have consistently argued that this 10 per cent norm is overly rigid, as it prevents public broadcasters from anticipating the ups and downs in media markets (EBU, 2008, p. 24), all five countries (EC, 2007b: §281, 2008d: §158, 2009b: §219, 2010: §232–3) have agreed to implement a 10 per cent limitation on reserves. As the Commission has introduced this rule in its soft law guidelines for state aid to PSB, other countries are following suit.

Europe decides ... is Europe deciding?

Summarising remarks

European decision practice is moving constantly, as shown by two more recent decisions dealing with the compensation of the removal of advertising revenues from public television in France and Spain (EC, 2009c; Donders and Lamensch, 2010). The decisions issued by the Commission since the late 1990s deal with a variety of subjects such as annual funding and licence fee schemes, thematic channels, side activities of public broadcasters, ad hoc funds, restructuring aid and so on. Nearly all public funding methods of public broadcasters have been scrutinised (Antoniadis, 2008: pp. 1296–302). The Commission, therefore, does not differentiate between the form of a subsidy or support scheme. The analysis shows that (only) two negative state aid decisions have been taken to date. Both the Danish public broadcaster TV2 and Dutch public broadcasters have been asked to reimburse illegal aid to their respective governments. In all other decisions, the Commission concluded that there was no aid or, more often, that the state aid was compatible with the internal market provisions. In most decisions compatibility is obtained through MS commitments (and not penalties!) to alter certain aspects of the funding of public broadcasters. These commitments provide evidence for the claim that European state aid law enforcement results in a superficial harmonisation of public broadcasting law, since the Commission has a set of similar principles that it seeks to introduce in all MS' regulatory frameworks for PSB.

Furthermore, the analysis of decision practice illustrates that the Commission has become more active in taking decisions with regard to the funding of PSB. This remark needs to be nuanced, however. Several decisions – for example, those relating to public broadcasting in France, Spain, Portugal and Italy – in 2003, 2004 and 2005 refer back to complaints from the the early 1990s. It would not be entirely correct to claim that negotiations in the latter cases took much longer than more recent cases concerning the funding of Flemish public broadcaster VRT or German public broadcasters ARD and ZDF. In fact, negotiations in these cases were not really begun during the first five years that they were pending. Also, note that existing aid procedures take more time to conclude; given the scope of the procedure (which is greater than in procedures dealing with ad hoc measures or thematic channels), this is not surprising.

The analysis in this chapter does not support a fully negative appraisal of the Commission's intervention in the field of public broadcasting, nor does it absolve DG Competition from all criticism. The Commission decides on the compliance of funding schemes with the Treaty, and sometimes it decides on the future of PSB overstepping its competencies. These indiscretions are rare, however, and should, hence, not be taken as typical examples of the Commission's behaviour.

The long road to technology neutrality

Reiterating the criteria of the analytical framework (i.e. cross-media, core, clarity, cost control and command, checks and balances) (see Chapter 4), it will be observed first of all that the Commission has become more technology neutral in its approach; it remains highly critical of online services. However, it accepts that platform independence is a legitimate departure point for definitions of public broadcasters' remit. This has resulted in an approach following which thematic channels or the online streaming of news broadcasts are acceptable, whereas other online services are explicitly stated as not automatically fitting the public service remit.

From closely associated to *ex ante* test

Secondly, in order to come to a sustainable public service media policy, a precisely defined remit is indispensable. This remit should be defined in terms of specific goals, not in terms of genres of platforms.

The Commission has not always met this criterion, arguing in some cases in favour of a so-called 'closely associated' approach following which services are admissible only insofar as they are linked to existing radio and television services. Such an approach demonstrates that the Commission's competencies are limited to checking for a manifest error only and are, moreover, outdated. Public broadcasters should be active in those domains where their relevance is highest. This is also the case for new services, which should be evaluated on the basis of their link to the public service remit. Gradually, the Commission has evolved from the closely associated approach to the latter strategy. Its demand for an *ex ante* evaluation, in which a service's fit with the public service remit and its possible market impact are scrutinised, is a case in point. It also shows the Commission's attempts to stay within the boundaries of its competencies.

A marginal effect on funding

With regard to the funding of public broadcasters, one can be brief. The Commission has virtually no influence on the level of financing as such. Admittedly, in the Danish and Dutch decisions reimbursements were requested. One could argue that overcompensated (or unnecessary) aid was simply recovered in order to reverse market distortions. It is doubtful whether such an *ex post* recovery can actually do this, yet it is also unclear whether a reimbursement damages public broadcasters in practice. In both countries, government compensated the public broadcasters concerned for the reimbursement made. Setting out from the perspective of the state aid control policy's effectiveness, this obviously leads to the questioning of the reimbursement mechanism. Nonetheless, the fact that the Commission can ask for a reimbursement of aid is of major political importance and is one of the most visible (but not necessarily most concrete) outcomes of a state aid procedure. A second element that could be used to indicate the Commission's impact on public broadcasters' funding is its demand for a 10 per cent cap on the accumulation of reserves. This demand seems to be somewhat more controversial. In theory, and the Commission has emphasised this point, the proportionality condition in the 2001 Broadcasting Communication prohibits the accumulation of reserves as this states that public broadcasters can only be compensated for the public costs of public service delivery. Every surplus is, in that sense, evidence of overcompensation. However, public broadcasters argued that they need reserves in order to cope with fluctuations in the audiovisual market, and MS often supported their public broadcasters' claims in this respect. In order to reach a consensus on this issue, the Commission invented the 10 per cent cap. This allows public broadcasters to have some reserves while preventing them from building up excessive amounts that could lead to distortion of the market (by, for example, overbidding on sports rights).

Hence, it is difficult to argue that the Commission has pleaded in favour of sustainable financing of public broadcasters. It is equally difficult to argue that the Commission has fought against it. Essentially, the Commission is not concerned about the level of funding or the funding mix. Given the fact that state aid is concerned with the investigation of funding schemes and that the aim of state aid control (i.e. realising less aid and more effective state aid), this is rather surprising. However, this finding is completely in line with the legal framework that is applied by the Commission in its decisions (see Chapter 6).

Transparency as the cornerstone of Commission intervention

With regard to the clarity criterion, the decisions made show that the Commission has been very much concerned with the issue of financial and organisational transparency. Although this issue is not touched upon in single-issue decisions (i.e. decisions that deal only with one single aspect of public broadcasting regulation), it has been a focal point of attention in the reform decisions concerning the funding of public broadcasters in Spain, Italy, Portugal and France, and in the whole-package decision concerning the funding of the German public broadcasters ARD and ZDF. It can be inferred from these decisions that the Commission insists on compliance with the Transparency Directive. In the decisions concerning Spain, Italy, Portugal and France, the Commission's investigations have been key; the financial and organisational structure of public broadcasters in these countries was far from transparent. This also resulted in major financial problems and, moreover (although not stressed by the Commission), prevented public broadcasters from sourcing efficiency gains. Hence, from a public broadcasting point of view and also in the light of public broadcasters evolvement into public media services providers (offering an increasing array of services in a complex media ecology), the Commission's decisions have come to emphasise the importance of a good governance principle (i.e. transparency) that is at the core of public broadcasters' evolution into public multimedia entrepreneurs. No evidence suggests that the Commission requires public broadcasters to disclose information that would be of a confidential nature. Overall, a majority of interviewed experts seemed to agree that an increased level of transparency is beneficial for public broadcasters and the citizens they serve. It is, moreover, also indispensable if one wants to ensure both internal and external accountability.

The *ex ante* test to deal with public broadcasters' expansion into new media markets

The fifth criterion, that is control and command, has provoked more controversy than the issue of transparency. The issue of external control and the *ex ante* evaluation of new media services has been discussed widely by the Commission in its whole-package decisions concerning the funding of the German, Irish, Flemish, Dutch and Austrian public broadcasters. In the section dealing with these issues, a number of advantages and disadvantages of external control and the Commission's demand for an *ex ante* evaluation of new media services have been listed. The discussion showed that the demand for external control is not necessarily problematic from a 'middle-range' public service media perspective (the choice for external control is very much embedded in the specific national public broadcasting system): the demand for an *ex ante* evaluation poses problems. On the one hand, one could argue that the *ex ante* test embodies the balance sought in the control and command criterion as defined in the public service media policy approach. Indeed, the analytical framework puts forward a system in which the regulation of public broadcasters is oriented at ensuring an adequate level of control (both with regard to performance and the position of public broadcasters in the market) and the necessary level of editorial independence. It also formalises this balancing act and makes it more transparent. This is desirable from both a clarity and checks-and-balances (*cf. infra*) point of view. In theory, it ought to make decision making more transparent. It should also ensure, again in theory, that different stakeholders can engage in this formalised process and prevent them, as much as possible, from dominating informal lobbying with policy makers. On the other hand, the *ex ante* test could also result in an overly rigid control of public broadcasters' activities. If one conducted an *ex ante* test for every separate service a public broadcaster wished to launch, the latter would be buried beneath bureaucratic processes and deprived of the flexibility to innovate and, as such, to contribute to both public interest objectives and economic welfare. When private companies become overly involved in the process, the *ex ante* test could evolve into a bureaucratic monster not aimed at controlling, but rather at constraining, public broadcasters. Hence, it seems crucial to discover how the *ex ante* test is implemented at the national level. From the five decisions in which the *ex ante* test was discussed and identified as an appropriate measure, one can indeed conclude that the Commission stresses the importance of the involvement of third parties and the execution of a market impact assessment for a new service.

Consultation- or confrontation-based regulation?

This, finally, is also linked to the checks-and-balances criterion that is defined in the analytical framework. Indeed, a majority of the Commission's decisions have been initiated by private sector complaints. Whereas private broadcasters and other commercial companies were sometimes not heard, the state aid rules offer them an additional platform to express their grievances. This in itself results in a change in the checks and balances between public and private players in the new media ecology. Leaving that aside, it is difficult to conclude from decision practice that the Commission would involve private actors more than public broadcasters. Most interviewees acknowledge that both private parties and public broadcasters are consulted by the Commission throughout investigations. Whether this and the Commission's demand for an *ex ante* test, more transparency, adequate control, and so on results in regulation that is consultation- and not confrontation-based is less clear. The impression exists that the emergence of consultation-based regulation is dependent more on domestic factors and less on the Commission's intervention by means of the state aid rules. Some interviewees even indicated that a European state aid procedure further opposes public broadcasters and their competitors.

Overall, the analysis of the Commission's decision practice illustrates that some issues are prioritised in the Commission's decision practice. In line with soft law specifications, a clear demarcation between public and commercial services, transparent accounts in which this demarcation is reflected and independent control are central concerns in most decisions.

The ways in which certain principles are being enforced differ, which indicates a lack of coherence in decision practice. With regard to the definition of the public service remit, it will be observed that the Commission's approach has not always been coherent; in earlier decisions on thematic channels, the Commission's approach with regard to new media services was rather lenient. Other decisions (for example, the *BBC Digital Curriculum* decision), however, were more rigid. More recent decisions on annual funding systems in Germany, Flanders and Ireland attempt to walk the line between the scope and definition of the remit, and exemplify Commission attempts to reach a coherent approach on the issue. In addition, with regard to independent control, it is notewor-thy that the Commission asks for legally external control in some MS but, nevertheless, accepts internal controlling bodies in others.

To summarise, decision practice does not reveal a negative precon-ception of PSB. It shows the Commission's struggle to implement the provisions of the 2001 (and later the 2009) Broadcasting Commu-nication without crossing the thin line of subsidiarity. Some of the Commission's initiatives go against the public service media approach put forward in Chapter 4 of this book. Other requirements, ideas, con-cepts and so on are more in line with some of the analytical framework's criteria. This should not lead to the conclusion that the Commission aims to create 'better' public service media regulation, however. Nor should it lead to the conclusion that its decision practice affects MS' regulation of public broadcasters in a sustainable public service media-oriented way. The latter aspect is discussed and analysed in the following chapters.

9
Germany

Over the course of 2003, the Commission started an investigation into the licence fee funding of broadcasting organisations ARD and ZDF. The investigation and the subsequent negotiations between 2003 and 2007 are said to have been a particularly difficult process, which resulted eventually in an extensive list of commitments significantly altering the regulation of public broadcasting.

On the one hand, this chapter will provide a chronological narrative of the German state aid procedure. Keeping in mind some of the basic features of the German public broadcasting regime, its distinctive elements will be assessed. On the other hand, the chapter analyses the implementation of commitments and evaluates whether European intervention has contributed to a transfer from public broadcasting to public service media in Germany. Note that there is a difference between the analysis of the state aid procedure and its outcome. The narrative is focused on the sequence of events, the dynamics between different actors and the bottlenecks that appear throughout negotiations. The assessment of impact and evaluation aims to discover the actual outcome of Commission interference. This chapter will not cover in detail all issues that are relevant to public broadcasting policy in Germany. There is neither an in-depth discussion of the historical development of German public broadcasting nor a systematic assessment of all new media services offered by ARD and ZDF. That is not to say that these issues do not merit discussion; however, the main interest here is to dissect these elements that are relevant to the study of the impact of European state aid control on Germany's regulation for ARD and ZDF. The relevance of this case study lies, consequently, in enhancing the understanding of a state aid procedure and its impact on national policy frameworks for public broadcasting.

Distinctive features of public broadcasting policy in Germany

After the Second World War, Germany departed from a centralist and government-controlled policy for broadcasting. The Allies supported a new broadcasting regime that was, according to Dörr (2009c, p. 135), based on three main principles: independence from the state (*Staatsferne*), federalism (*Föderalismus*) and pluralism (*Pluralität*).

Independence from the state

A focal point of attention in the Western Allies' policies was the establishment of free press and broadcasting systems for the 're-education of the Germans towards liberal democracy' (Humphreys, 1994, p. 128; Schüller-Keber, 2009, p. 67). For the press a free market model was followed, whereas broadcasting became organised as a public (not state!) monopoly at the Länder level. Initially, six regional broadcasters (some of which were shared between different Länder) were created. In 1950, these regional broadcasters created ARD, which broadcasts nationwide. Regional broadcasters remained independent and still operate their own channels, however. Decentralisation of public broadcasting and application of policies was, consequently, a means to an end in ensuring public broadcasters' independence from the state.

Several legal safeguards were created in order to further the independence of public broadcasting from both market and political influence (Holznagel et al., 2008, p. 170). Compared with other public broadcasting regimes in Europe, these were fairly unique (Hoffmann-Riem, 1991, p. 21). The first, and most important, safeguard can be found in the German constitution (1949), which provides in its Article 5(1):

Jeder hat das Recht, seine Meinung in Wort, Schrift und Bild frei zu äußern und zu verbreiten und sich aus allgemein zugänglichen Quellen ungehindert zu unterrichten. Die Pressefreiheit und die Freiheit der Berichterstattung durch Rundfunk und Film werden gewährleistet. Eine Zensur findet nicht statt. [Everyone has the right to express himself freely and to disseminate his opinion by speech, writing and pictures and to inform himself without hindrance from generally accessible sources. The press freedom and freedom of reporting by radio and motion pictures are guaranteed. Censorship is not].

The German constitution firmly recognised the importance of the freedom of press, broadcasting and film (Fechner, 2009, p. 48), to be ensured at both the individual and institutional level. State authorities were obliged to ensure citizens' participation right, the right to broadcast and the independence of broadcasters. The constitutional protection of public broadcasting in Germany is elaborate and is, in fact, determined by a legalistic political culture in which the role of the Constitutional Court is key (Dyson and Humphreys, 1988a, p. 92). Another safeguard is the freedom of programmation enjoyed by public broadcasters. The latter are public, but not state owned and can, for that reason, develop their programme schedules independent from any state influence. This does not mean that there is no control of public broadcasters. A complex web of control bodies in combination with self-commitments, some of which need the approval of the Länder governments (Hoffmann-Riem, 1991, p. 41), has been developed over the years. For the purpose of this book, self-commitments are defined here in a semantic way. The use of the concept is not limited to the self-commitments in which public broadcasters clarify the fulfilment of the public service remit. All other documents in which public broadcasters clarify aspects of the remit or even specific activities are also regarded as self-commitments.

A final safeguard to ensuring public broadcasters' independence from government authorities is the so-called continuance and development guarantee (*Bestands- und Entwicklungsgarantie*). This principle, which was introduced by the Constitutional Court, implies that the Länder governments ensure that public broadcasters can actually fulfil their remit and can, moreover, further develop their activities towards that aim (Hoffmann-Riem, 1991, p. 39). This has been elaborated upon on multiple occasions by the Court, which has stressed that the guarantee refers to a holistic public service remit. Public broadcasters have to be active in all genres and on all platforms. Only if public broadcasters provide a basic service are private broadcasters' activities permissible, as pluralism is safeguarded. Basically, the Court has consistently put forward a functional and dynamic concept of public broadcasting. It prevents the marginalisation of public broadcasting, although it is admittedly less clear on how far the idea of basic service extends now that public broadcasters are moving into the online realm (Hoffmann-Riem, 2000, p. 15). The continuance and development guarantee is, moreover, related to the funding of German public broadcasters. The latter are financed by a licence fee, which ensures independence from the state (Hesse, 2003, p. 178). The level of the licence fee is determined by an independent commission, that is the KEF, which also controls the cost-efficient behaviour of public broadcasters (Dörr, 2009c, pp. 168–73). Interestingly, the licence fee has to be paid by all owners of radio, television or new media equipment, from €5.76 for a personal computer to €17.98 for radio and television. The extension of the licence fee to new media ('pc-fee') in 2007 was rather controversial and widely covered in the written press. It proved, however, that the functional and dynamic conceptualisation of the remit in Germany is not only about paying lip service to public broadcasting.

Federalism

Federalism is another pillar of public broadcasting in Germany. Competencies over broadcasting are with the German Länder (Humphreys, 1994; Fell, 2005; Cole, 2009, p. 90). They have, since the 1950s, successfully cooperated, agreeing – albeit sometimes with great difficulty – to interstate treaties that cover several aspects of broadcasting regulation. This type of cooperation, which does not prevent the Länder from remaining fully competent in the area, is termed cooperative federalism (Erk, 2003, p. 107; Hesse, 2003, pp. 15–16).

Cooperation and conflict between Länder go hand in hand. The Länder have diverging economic and political interests. Social Democrat Party (SPD) is, in general, more favourable to public broadcasting, whereas Christian Democrat Party (CDU) has traditionally supported the free press and also advocated strongly for the liberalisation of the broadcasting sector in the 1970s and 1980s. These divisions are still apparent today, as CDU is more critical of public broadcasters' expansion to new media markets. This is not to say that SPD has always been a supporter of public broadcasting. Very often, the stances of the socialist and Christian democratic parties have aligned with the economic interests of the Länder. This is termed *Standortpolitik* and is a phenomenon that has, as Humphreys (1994) meticulously illustrates, driven public broadcasting policy in Germany since its inception after the Second World War. It can be expected that *Standortpolitik* has also affected the outcome of the European state aid procedure (see later in this chapter).

Pluralism

Finally, broadcasting regulation aims to ensure and enhance the diversity of opinions being covered. For obvious historical reasons, the Allies strongly advocated for a broadcasting system reflecting the pluralism and heterogeneity of society (Humphreys, 1999, p. 24; Hoffmann-Riem, 2006, p. 98). For that purpose, pluralistic programme schedules have to be developed and, moreover, public broadcasters' controlling bodies (Broadcasting Councils) represent different groups in society.

Pluralism is thus not only a matter of content, but also of the internal organisation. Pluralism is strongly linked to the idea of diversity of voice rather than only diversity of (quantitative) choice. For that reason, competition in the broadcasting sector is always viewed from the angle of competition for quality (*Publizistischer Wettbewerb*). In addition, this cornerstone of German regulation for public broadcasting appears important in the negotiations with the Commission and their final outcome (see later in this chapter).

Principles in practice

Today, there are nine regional public broadcasters in Germany. Some of these operate in several Länder that jointly agree on a specific set of rules for the regional broadcaster concerned. All regional broadcasters are members of ARD. After ARD, there is a second nationwide television broadcaster, ZDF, created by the Länder in the 1960s. German public broadcasters are usually structured as follows. There is a Broadcasting Council that consists of so-called socially relevant groups (Humphreys, 2008b, p. 2). The composition of the Council and the way in which its members are chosen differ. Humphreys (1994, p. 143ff) describes how the Broadcasting Councils in Germany have been subject to processes of politicisation and the dominance of CDU vs. SPD. The Councils can be seen as the internal parliaments of the public broadcaster, and their competencies are extensive. They have a supervisory function and aim to ensure that public broadcasters provide a diversity of opinions and contribute to formation of opinion. They have a say in editorial policy, programming regulation, complaints concerning public broadcasters and elect its Director-General (DG). They often oversee the financial decisions of the public broadcaster. Some members of the Broadcasting Council make up the Administrative Council; this Council is occupied with the daily functioning of the public broadcaster. This structure of the public broadcasters emphasises the importance of internal control and internally organised accountability (Humphreys, 1994, p. 141). It is based on the twofold assumption that internal control, firstly, ensures that public broadcasters fulfil the remit better than state control and, secondly, results in pluralism as the composition of the bodies aims to reflect all groups in society.

Given the central role of the Broadcasting Councils, the competencies of the Länder to control public broadcasters are rather limited (Meier, 2006, p. 264). They draft, approve and ensure the implementation of the so-called Interstate Treaty for Broadcasting, which defines the main rules for (public and private) broadcasting in Germany. They are not allowed to intervene in the day-to-day operation and editorial decisions of public broadcasters, however. The licence fee has to be approved by the Länder, albeit that this approval is of a more formal nature (Dörr, 2009c, p. 134ff).

All public broadcasters have to meet the provisions of the Interstate Treaty on Broadcasting and Telemedia. Since its entry into force, this Treaty has been amended 12 times. The revision of the 11th Interstate Treaty on Broadcasting and Telemedia, which resulted in the 12th Interstate Treaty (coming into force on 1 June 2009), was entirely the consequence of the Commission's state aid procedure. The Treaty aims to reflect the main pillars of German public broadcasting policy and was the basis of negotiation between the Commission and the Länder.

Länder and Commission interests at stake

Instrumentalising state aid control

Well-known frustrations in the private sector concerning German public broadcasters have dominated the public and political debate on public broadcasting in the Länder since the 1950s. Initially, publishers argued against advertising on public broadcasting channels. In the 1960s, they resisted the creation of ZDF and, later on, that of teletext. In the 1990s, the launch of thematic channels provoked private sector frustration. Private broadcasters explored for the first time in what way European state aid policy might further their interests, challenging the funding of thematic channels Phoenix and Kinderkanal (Kleist, 2003). In 2003, the new media activities of the German public broadcasters in particular provoked concerns, and matters were taken to 'Brussels' once again.

The complaints of the private sector were no surprise. On many occasions, German private media companies addressed the Länder about their concerns. Sometimes, the Länder governments were receptive, but very often they were caught between their own diverging interests and the extensive programmation autonomy of the public broadcasters. As private media companies perceived the Constitutional Court and the Broadcasting Councils as supporters of a catch-all public service remit, they decided to 'use' the Commission in order to move things forward at the Länder level. As illustrated by the broadcaster VPRT's position in the 1990s, these procedures do not necessarily need to be concluded at the European level; rather, they need to produce changes at the Länder level. In December 1998, VPRT chairman Jürgen Doetz even suggested dropping the complaint about thematic channels if ARD and ZDF postponed the introduction of additional channels for another five years. The public broadcasters disagreed, underlining the legitimacy of thematic channels (Herrgesell and Kotsch, 1999). The clearance of thematic channels by the Commission did not prevent private companies from filing another set of complaints in 2003. These complaints (preceded by some informal talks between the German newspaper publishers and the Commission in 2002) quintessentially dealt with the same issue. Again, the scope of public broadcasters' activities was questioned. The complaints in 2003 were the starting point of a series of complaints from private media companies. In these complaints, above all they questioned the expansion of public broadcasters' activities into online and mobile services, arguing that these domains were not covered by the remit and stifled competition (e.g. Burda, 2007). Admittedly, there is little evidence sustaining the latter claim. Public broadcasters counterargued that their new media investments did not and could not outweigh publishers' investments. Moreover, there was no commercial communication on their websites, which prevented any effects on private actors' business models. Public broadcasters' arguments are flawed in two respects. Firstly, services – even if free of commercial communication – can have an effect on competing services, as there is always a competition for audiences. Moreover, as indicated by the KEF (the independent body responsible for the licence fee) (KEF, 2008), the cost allocation of German public broadcasters' new media activities was far from transparent.

The ambiguity of Länder positions

Complainants aimed to provoke regulatory reform at the Länder level (VPRT, 2003). In instrumentalising European state aid control, German publishers and private broadcasters were not alone. Albeit less explicit, several Länder also used the state aid procedure to push through reforms. Officially, all Länder opposed Commission intervention, claiming it was not legitimate. Even the federal government was stunned when receiving questions from the Commission about the public broadcasting system, wondering how 'Brussels' could intervene with such an internal competence. However, the Commission's Article 17 letter (formally containing certain European concerns with the public service broadcasting system (PSB), see EC, 2005a) made the factuality of Commission intervention abundantly clear.

Opposition to Commission intervention, which few Member States (MS) welcomed, is not exceptional. Public broadcasters and most Länder were of the opinion that the public broadcaster was simply not a matter for the Commission to deal with. In all replies from the Länder to Commission questions it was repeatedly stated that the licence fee was not state aid and, consequently, not covered by state aid control. At the beginning of the state aid procedure, the Länder considered filing an action for the Court of Justice of the EU. Eventually, they refrained from such action, as success in such endeavours is never certain, negative precedents could be set and a consensus was privileged over a lasting conflict with the Commission. It should be stressed that some Länder, aspiring to make public broadcasting regulation more stringent, were not supportive of a 'Luxembourg' scenario.

During the Commission's investigation, four Länder negotiated on behalf of all other Länder with DG Competition. Rhineland-Palatinate was very supportive of public broadcasting, being loyal to ZDF, which is located in its capital, Mainz. Bavaria, the basis of the Kirch Group, was considerably more supportive of Commission intervention, as was North Rhine Westphalia where the Bertelsmann group is sited. Saxony-Anhalt was situated somewhere between these positions. *Standortpolitik* thus played a role in this procedure. It, together with other factors, prevented a legal procedure, questioning the state aid status of the German licence fee and would eventually result in rather far-reaching commitments by the German Länder towards the Commission.

Bottlenecks

In particular, the demand for an *ex ante* evaluation of new media services and the establishment of a control body legally external to the public broadcasters were particularly difficult nuts to crack in the state aid procedure. With regard to *ex ante* evaluation, several interviewees asserted that such an instrument would go against the sacrosanct independence of public broadcasters from the state. Private media companies disagreed, saying the test of a new service is evident should one wish to ensure that it fits the public service remit. The discussion on this issue was far from trivial, and produced two opposing views on public broadcasting. Private media companies and, to some extent, the Commission talked about new markets. Public broadcasters and most Länder upheld a functional approach, following which public broadcasters did not enter 'new markets' but explored new opportunities better to fulfil their remit. The Länder did not oppose a compromise on the matter, and a pragmatic settlement between the two traditions was reached (Schultz, 2009). It was agreed that a test would be implemented, grounded in public broadcasters' contributions to competition for quality, and firmly rejecting a market failure approach.

In exchange for the 'leniency' about *ex ante* evaluation, the Länder insisted on retaining the Broadcasting Councils. The Commission questioned their role and, in particular, the independence of the latter. This provoked fierce reactions, with several Länder politicians and public broadcasters accusing the Commission of not sufficiently grasping the complexity of the equilibrium sought in the German system. It should not be underestimated how the Weimar Republic and the Second World War heritage have made all actions in public broadcasting very sensitive towards the possibility of government intervention. Given the sensitivity of the issue, the parties had agreed by the start of 2006 to leave the system of Broadcasting Councils relatively untouched, provided some mechanisms ensuring the transparency and independence of the Councils from public broadcasters' management were introduced.

Basic bargaining resulted in an agreement in principle in the autumn of 2006, and a decision was issued on 24 April 2007. Although most demands of the Commission had also been on the political agenda of the Länder, intervention met fierce opposition from the start of negotiations. Tough bargaining characterised the negotiations, in which all stakeholders tried to maintain as much of their initial offer as possible. On the one hand, the Länder authorities, with their own agenda on public broadcasting in mind, acknowledged that their attachment to holistic and independent public broadcasters did not *a priori* exclude the possibility of more precise regulation. On the other hand, the Commission had to accept the specific set-up of German policy in the field of public broadcasting.

Commitments

The German Länder promised to implement a number of commitments within 24 months, starting from the adoption date of the Commission's decision (24 April 2007). With regard to the definition of the public service remit, the Länder agreed to further substantiate the remit and, in particular, the concept of 'telemedia', which is used as a container concept for new media services. Telemedia are limited to 'editorially arranged' content. This basically means that public broadcasters cannot evolve into new YouTubes, acting as a mere platform for video. Public broadcasters are responsible for the further substantiation of the public service remit. They will develop an explanatory memorandum concerning the definition of telemedia and will, moreover, compile a list including telemedia that cannot be considered legitimately to fall within the scope of the activities of a public broadcaster. For digital channels, public broadcasters will develop programme concepts, specifying the aims of these channels and specific programme categories catered for by them. Far-reaching adaptations will require the approval of the Länder parliaments.

Besides a more clearly spelled-out definition, an *ex ante* evaluation for new media services was introduced (EC, 2007b: §328). Public broadcasters define what new services are, considering, *inter alia*, the importance of a new project for editorial competition, its financial impact and its duration. The Broadcasting Councils are in charge of the evaluation of new services, dubbed *Drei-Stufen-Test*. In the three-step-test, three questions are successively answered.

1. Is the proposed service covered by the public service remit and does it, as such, serve the democratic, social and cultural needs of society?
2. Does the service contribute in a qualitative manner to editorial competition?
3. What is the financial impact of the proposed service on the overall budget of the public broadcaster?

Public broadcasters have to present a concept of each new service. The opinion of third parties, of an advisory and informative nature only, is also taken into account.

Finally, there are a number of commitments that relate to the funding mechanisms of the German public broadcasters.

- Public broadcasters do not put direct links to commercial offers on their websites.
- Commercial activities will be better regulated.
- Commercial activities are performed under market conditions.
- A separate accounting system is introduced.
- A 10% limitation on reserves is introduced.
- Market conformity and 'arm's length' principles are introduced (in particular, this should ensure transparency of relations between public broadcasters and their subsidiaries).
- Commercial activities fall within the scope of the activities of subsidiaries.
- The control competencies of both the KEF and the Courts of Auditors are strengthened.
- Annual broadcast time in the main programme schedules of sports is not to exceed 10% under normal conditions (it may be higher when several major sports events occur at the same time; sports broadcasts

on digital channels are still possible provided this does not change the focus of the channel).

- Sports rights that remain unused are to be sub-licensed under clear (European Broadcasting Union (EBU)-defined) and transparent conditions.
- No dedicated sports channel can be created without prior approval of the Länder.

The list of commitments is substantial. However, it should be borne in mind that the extensive list of commitments is not solely based on Commission demands. State aid procedures are a give-and-take process. The Länder suggested several commitments in order to ease certain concerns of the Commission. In this regard, one should not overlook certain Länder economic incentives to curb public broadcasters' new media activities.

A new Interstate Treaty

The implementation of all commitments is by no means a straightforward exercise. Changes in the Interstate Treaty on Broadcasting and Telemedia and the implementation of the new rules in practice are the consequence of dynamics between various stakeholders – as was the case with the negotiations in the European state aid procedure. In these dynamics, the Länder attempted to strike a balance between their own political and economic interests and the constitutional protection of public broadcasters' independence. This complex exercise eventually resulted in the adoption of a new Interstate Treaty in late 2008 and its entry into force in June 2009.

Broadening the public service remit

The new Interstate Treaty specifies that public broadcasters can offer both broadcasting and telemedia services (Article 11). The latter are all considered new media services provided they are editorially arranged and fall within the scope of the public service remit. Admittedly, some limits to the remit were also introduced. For example, print services can only be offered when they are linked to a specific radio or television programme (or a part thereof). Several press-like services did not fit this qualification and were removed from websites ('depublishing') by German public broadcasters. Furthermore, public broadcasters have developed digital concepts for their digital channels. These concepts are annexed to the Interstate Treaty – significant alterations require Länder approval. Legally speaking, the digital channels do not require an *ex ante* evaluation. The introduction of the concepts in the Interstate Treaty was, in that sense, a compromise between the interests of the public and private broadcasters.

Remarkably, the remit was broadened as the previous Interstate Treaty allowed only for telemedia services linked to existing radio and television services (Kops et al., 2009, p. 14). In that sense, one of the consequences of the state aid procedure ran counter to the corporate interests of the private sector. Marginalisation of public broadcasters' activities did thus not occur. Instead, the remit was re-conceptualised beyond traditional notions like broadcasting, programmes and so on and now embodies the recognition that public broadcasters deliver public service media (Holznagel, 2009; Moe, 2009b, p. 192).

Defining telemedia

Public service media is still divided into two types of services, that is 'traditional' broadcasting services and telemedia. For telemedia services in particular, several restrictions have been introduced. Although all telemedia falling within the public service remit are permissible, they are only automatically considered legitimate when they comply with the following conditions (see also Article 11 of the 12th Interstate Treaty).

- The offer of programmes online is restricted to seven days after the first broadcast of the programme (Koehler, 2008, p. 8), and for sports the time limit is 24 hours.
- The offer of telemedia services linked to radio and television programmes is restricted to seven days after the first broadcast of the concerned programme, and for sports the time limit is 24 hours.
- Press-like services not linked to a specific programme are not permissible.
- Archives with cultural or historical content can be offered without any time constraint.
- There must always be a clear temporal and content-wise link between a telemedia service and a real programme. Previously, a link was required between telemedia services and the complete programmation schedule (which was a broader categorisation).
- Telemedia services cannot be accompanied by advertising and sponsoring.
- A number of telemedia services are not permissible under any circumstances. These services are included in a 'negative' list that mentions directories, websites offering price comparisons between

services/products, route planners, music downloads, commercial services, contact websites, social networking websites, online games, photo album programmes, etc.

With regard to these conditions several points of criticism have been made. Firstly, the time limits on online offers have been criticised for not serving citizens. Public broadcasters have argued against the time limits, whereas private broadcasters have claimed that the time limits are de facto extended after *ex ante* procedures, and this for up to 90% of the telemedia offer. Although this claim is somewhat exaggerated, it is correct that time limits can be extended provided this is approved through an *ex ante* procedure. Some public broadcasters also criticised the time limits for being arbitrary – obviously influenced by the practices of the BBC. It is unclear who enforced the idea of time limits. Some interviewees suggested that the Länder came up with the seven-day limit in order to meet some of the Commission's concerns, but that the Commission itself rarely suggests specific proposals as the MS are in charge of the organisation of their public broadcasting systems. In practice, this again resulted, in the opinion of some experts interviewed for the purpose of this study, in commitments that went beyond what was necessary to make the German public broadcasting regimes compatible with the state aid provisions. The specifics of, for example, the time limits were due more to the internal dynamics in the Länder. They were introduced for emotional rather than for rational reasons. The practices of the BBC were also created to offset possible market distortions but also, and more importantly, to balance high copyright costs with disclosure of services to licence fee payers in a universal way. The time limits in Germany are not of an enabling, but rather of a constraining nature (Donders and Pauwels, 2010a). Also, the 'negative' list has been attacked for harming the independence of German public broadcasters. Indeed, it is a rather intrusive instrument. Yet, when you look at the services listed, even public broadcasting representatives admitted that most of the services in this list not fit within the public service remit. A final point of criticism concerns the definition of press-like services, for which no time limit applies, as they are totally prohibited. It is not clear what press-like means. It also remains to be seen how the required link between a press-like service and an existing radio or television programme will be interpreted. Many representatives of public broadcasters considered the introduction of this provision a victory for the publishing sector, which had lobbied ferociously for a limitation of the public service remit. They feared that the adoption of the list might have induced an approach involving the listing of specific services that public broadcasters could or could not offer.

Introducing the three-step test

The most intrusive alteration of the Interstate Treaty is undeniably the introduction of an *ex ante* evaluation for certain telemedia services, known as the three-step test. This consecutively evaluates to the extent to which a new offer meets the democratic, cultural and social needs of society; to what extent a new offer contributes to competition in a qualitative way; and the level of financial resources required to fund the new offer (Schultz, 2008). The Broadcasting Councils are responsible for answering these questions and, consequently, for clearing the service. They do so on the basis of a telemedia concept, which is to be developed by the public broadcaster, and is required to into account the opinion of third parties. The test is also published (Holznagel, 2009; Peeters, 2009, p. 33).

The Interstate Treaty makes a distinction between four types of services, of which two require an *ex ante* test:

1. Programmes on demand can be offered up to seven days after the initial broadcast without the requirement for a three-step test.
2. Telemedia services that are linked to a specific radio or television programme can be offered up to seven days after the initial broadcast without the requirement for a three-step test.
3. Telemedia services that do not refer to a specific radio or television programme require a three-step test.
4. Telemedia services that refer to a specific radio or television programme, but are offered beyond the seven-day time limit, require a three-step test (Holznagel, 2009).

This distinction between different types of services implies that there are two regimes for services that fall within the same public service remit. One regime is fixed and included in the Interstate Treaty, with the other flexible and needing further implementation beyond the static rules in the Interstate Treaty. Remarkably, in practice most telemedia services have been tested to date. It seemed more pragmatic to test services that are closely linked even if classified differently according to the typology above. In addition, all existing telemedia services were tested. Normally, only 'new' services require a three-step test prior to their delivery. In principle, the Broadcasting Councils use a set of positive and negative criteria to determine whether a service is new and requires a test. Positive criteria relate to possible significant alterations in the programme mix, changes in target groups or the budgetary requirements of a new service. Negative criteria such as changes in the design of a service or usability aspects 'disqualify' services from being a new service (Peeters, 2009, p. 26). Since German public broadcasters launched a number of telemedia services during the state aid procedure, an agreement was reached between the Commission and the Länder to submit these services to a test too – this in order to prevent escape behaviour from public broadcasters. Many public broadcasters found this an unfair compromise that was, first of all, not required in other MS (which again strengthened the impression that many alterations of the legal framework were provoked more by certain Länder than by the Commission) and, moreover, found to meet private interests disproportionally.

The question is whether the three-step test, as outlined above, furthers a rethinking of the public service media project of the German public broadcasters in practice. The answer is to be found in the numerous tests that were conducted. Over 40 tests, representing a major bureaucratic burden to all stakeholders, were begun in 2008/2009. Several weaknesses appeared throughout the testing process.

Firstly, most telemedia concepts seemed to lack direction. The telemedia concept is at the core of the entire three-step test process. It contains the public broadcasters' description of the various public, financial and market-related aspects of the service. Although the Interstate Treaty specifies that concepts must be clear, the notion of clarity can be interpreted in different ways. As a result thereof, lengthy, but not always clarifying, documents are submitted (e.g. SWR, 2009; WDR, 2009). These document cover a variety of services, referring to general public broadcasting values and the advertising-free nature of the evaluated services (ZDF, 2009). With regard to the latter, it should be stressed that the financing method (public or commercial) underlying a service cannot qualify it as a public or commercial service. Public broadcasters themselves have emphasised this on multiple occassions when the Commission doubted whether pay-per-view services could be public in nature (EBU, 2008).

A second problem that has become apparent relates to the rights of third parties. The latter allege that there are insufficient guarantees to ensure confidentiality. The role of the Broadcasting Councils is most problematic in this regard. Theoretically, the Councils represent the German population and can in that capacity decide on the desirability of a service. Yet, politicisation and a close relationship with public broadcasters' management has always characterised the Councils.

The lack of professionalism of the Councils and the close links with the management of public broadcasters has provoked concerns about the disclosure of information (Dörr, 2009a; Holznagel, 2009).

The perception that public broadcasters and Councils sort things out together has been strengthened, as it appears that the Broadcasting Council's provisional conclusions about a service can be adapted after the public broadcasters' management comments on this provisional conclusion. In the UK there exists the potential for public broadcasters to comment on provisional conclusions, yet other parties can do likewise. In Germany, this is not the case (Dörr, 2009a). This is discriminatory in nature and hampers the development of a procedure in which stakeholders are oriented at a workable consensus for all players in the field. The conclusions of the Broadcasting Councils are an additional problem in this respect; these are rather short and abstract in explaining why services were approved. Overall, most services are approved provided some additional conditions are complied with.

A final problematic aspect relates to the bureaucratic burden of the entire exercise. Over 40 tests were begun in 2008/2009. All these tests are attributed to one public broadcaster – most often the one that takes the lead in the production of the service in question. SWR executes the most tests (eight), with MDR, WDR and NDR being responsible for seven, five and four tests, respectively. For 34 of the tests, the Broadcasting Councils invoked the assistance of external experts from a consultancy agency. These were appointed after a public tender procedure and were responsible for the economic analysis of the likely impact of the proposed service. The budgets thereof are not entirely transparent, as public broadcasters do not disclose the costs of single economic assessments. SWR has, however, said it foresaw a budget of €1.2 million for eight tests. ZDF paid over €200,000 for three tests. For small MS a bureaucratic and costly exercise such as that in Germany is impossible. This is not intrinsic to the principle of performing an *ex ante* evaluation, however.

In spite of the problematic aspects of the three-step test, most interviewed experts agreed that it is a tool for public broadcasters to illustrate their importance in digital media markets that are characterised by abundance rather than scarcity. It stimulates public broadcasters to reflect upon the need for specific services in a formalised way. Several scholars have stressed that this is indispensable to securing the future of public broadcasters in a digital age (e.g. Steemers, 2003, p. 133; Tambini and Cowling, 2004, p. 4; Bardoel and Ferrell Lowe, 2007). Even if the first tests are far from perfect in this respect, consultation with third parties and insights from scholars will most likely optimise the entire three-step test process.

Outlining rules for market-conforming behaviour

The three-step test aims to ensure a transparent process of entrusting services to German public broadcasters. Transparency is also furthered through a number of other alterations in the Interstate Treaty. Article 16 of the 12th Interstate Treaty, for example, provides that commercial activities are to be delivered under market-conforming conditions, and this by subsidiaries structurally separated from public broadcasters. The relations between subsidiaries and public broadcasters must be transparent and market-conforming as well. Only in cases where the economic relevance of a commercial service is limited can the public broadcaster deliver it itself. It is self-evident that the division between public broadcasters and their subsidiaries also involves a complete separation of costs and revenues. These alterations were already required by other European provisions on transparency in public undertakings, but were introduced only after the state aid decision of the Commission. Moreover, the Interstate Treaty also provides that German public broadcasters can participate in commercial undertakings. Again, it must be crystal clear in which companies they have a stake, participation should add to the fulfilment of the public service remit and the Broadcasting Councils can control the level of participation. In fact, the director-general of each public broadcaster is obliged to inform the Councils at least yearly about participations – and their financial consequences in particular. Finally, the competencies of the body collecting the licence fee (and establishing the level thereof) and the Court of Auditors are strengthened.

Conclusion

Before the European state aid procedure, German public broadcasting law set out from the assumption that public broadcasting had to be as independent from government control as possible. For that reason, broadcasting law contained only a general description of the public service remit (Dörr, 2009c). In addition, it specified that new media services (telemedia) could be offered if they were closely associated with public broadcasters' radio and/or television programmes. Hence, telemedia did not have a separate status *vis-à-vis* the public service remit. Their legitimacy depended on their relationship with other services that were presumably at the core of public broadcasters' activities

(Holznagel, 2009). Regardless of this approach, public broadcasters' expansion strategies into new media were elaborate. It was difficult to determine what a close association meant. Moreover, the control system in Germany seemed to be inadequate as the internal Broadcasting Councils were accused of partial behaviour (to the benefit of public broadcasters) and a lack of professionalism (Lilienthal, 2009). European transparency requirements were not implemented given the Länder's resistance (at least at the rhetorical level) to any European intervention in the broadcasting sector.

Are the changes made in German broadcasting regulation significant after the state aid procedure?

The changes that were introduced after the European state aid procedure altered some of the characteristics of German broadcasting regulation and, even more so, its deficiencies. In particular the rules on telemedia and market-conforming behaviour are noteworthy. The provisions on telemedia are important in three ways. Firstly, they indicate that the public service remit is not limitless. The particular delineation between broadcasting and 'other' services has resulted in two regulatory regimes, of which that of telemedia is stricter. This exemplifies a political consensus that telemedia are not broadcasting and can, hence, not be treated as such. Secondly, the rules on telemedia also allow for the delivery of telemedia and this regardless of their link with existing radio and television services. This allows for a more public service-oriented exploration of telemedia services. Thirdly, the provisions for telemedia services (e.g. time limits, not press-like, the *ex ante* evaluation) are already somewhat specific, and entrench the idea of implementing additional and more flexible procedures in a rapidly changing media environment. With regard to market-conforming behaviour, the legal implementation of transparency principles is fundamentally important. Indeed, a number of public broadcasters were already applying these principles in practice. However, there was no legal basis for challenging a breach of the principles. Changes in this respect have hence fostered legal certainty for stakeholders.

Towards public service media?

Did the changes in the Interstate Treaty foster the emergence of a public service media policy project? In several respects the answer to this question is negative. Firstly, some concepts such as, for example, press-like are still unclear and will most likely provoke discussions in the future. Secondly, some provisions exemplify an intention of some Länder to limit the public service remit. The prohibition of press-like services that are not linked to existing radio and television programmes indeed narrows the public service remit or will, alternatively, lead to legal spin on the side of public broadcasters (Moe, 2009b, p. 196). It seems more useful, in line with the other provisions of the Interstate Treaty, to require a clear link between all services and the public service remit.

Several positive evolutions can be observed that validate the thesis that a move towards public service media can be observed after a state aid procedure. Firstly, the public service remit has been made technology neutral and has been widened (Sokoll, 2009, p. 885). The previous Interstate Treaty considered Internet services as auxiliary services, whereas they now enjoy a 'full' status *vis-à-vis* the public service remit (Holznagel, 2009). Secondly, the public service remit is more precisely defined as provisions on analogue channels, digital channels and telemedia have been added. Thirdly, the new system creates more accountability on the side of public broadcasters and is an opportunity for them to take accountability into their own hands (Dörr, 2009b). Several public broadcasting representatives said that they agreed there were some issues in this respect, as public broadcasters in the past were never required to justify in a formalised way why certain activities were legitimate in the light of their public tasks. Fourthly, the introduction of a two-track regulatory approach fits the rapidly changing media environment better than a fixed set of rules for all services delivered by public broadcasters. Such a fixed set of rules is difficult to change, as it requires the approval of all Länder governments. With a more flexible approach for new services, burdensome procedures are avoided and Länder intervention remains minimal, as the Broadcasting Councils are in charge of the *ex ante* procedure. Fifthly, the three-step test – in spite of some weaknesses – approaches public broadcasting as a holistic project focusing not on the 'pure' substitutability of services, but rather on their contribution to the competition for quality. In so doing, an offer is evaluated in the light of the offers of private media companies and the public broadcasters' own services portfolio (Kops et al., 2009). Sixthly, the three-step test procedure allows third party involvement, provided it is sustained by solid argumentation. This does not prevent private media companies from informal lobbying. However, at the same time it also obliges them to further their emotional claims with evidence. The latter should be expected, certainly from stakeholders that claim to support evidence-based policies. Finally, the enhancement of transparency in public broadcasters themselves and the various controlling mechanisms in place will further the legitimacy of the public broadcasting system in place (Hoffmann-Riem, 2006, p. 104).

Are the changes in German broadcasting policies a consequence of European intervention?

All changes made to the Interstate Treaty are in line with the appropriate measures the German Länder agreed to in the Commission's state aid decision. The question arises as to whether the changes, although seemingly flowing from Commission intervention, are indeed a consequence of the state aid procedure and were not on the political agenda of the Länder. Who has taken the lead in the process of reforming public broadcasting policies in the German Länder? Different answers are possible depending on the perspective one takes. Public broadcasters and some academics would argue that the private sector took the lead in provoking Commission attention for public broadcasting in Germany. Others suggest that reform in the public broadcasting policies of the Länder would have been very difficult, if not impossible, without the Commission pushing for it as the constitutional safeguards in place and the lack of consensus among the Länder inhibit far-reaching reforms without an external trigger. In this respect, one should also not underestimate the agenda of the Commission itself. Although it is often said by Commission officials that they 'merely' apply the state aid provisions, the case of the German public broadcasters was intended and eventually served as an example to other cases relating to public broadcasting in Austria, Ireland, Flanders and the Netherlands. The size of the market was also important in ranking it as a priority for the Commission – something that was less the case for Flanders or Austria. In some respects, some Länder took the lead in using both private sector lobbies and the Commission for their own political and economic interests. Meier (2006, p. 258) argues that the fundamental deficiencies of broadcasting regulation in the Länder made a substantial revision unavoidable.

Hence, in some ways, all stakeholders simultaneously took the lead and followed. The complexity of the state aid procedure and its outcome embodies the complexity of the German Länder's ambiguous stance on public broadcasting. On the one hand, constitutional safeguards and the highly politicised control of public broadcasters through the Broadcasting Councils bind them. On the other hand, they want to regulate the system more – be it in a more restrictive or enabling way. So, in other words, although the Länders' role is limited with respect to the organisation and funding of public broadcasting in Germany, they still have the prime responsibility for shaping the transfer from public broadcasting to public service media. The Commission procedure forced them to take this responsibility. Of course, the entire undertaking did not work out perfectly as different Länder have diverging interests, which sometimes relate to a genuine interest in designing a public service media project, but more often are determined by power politics (Holznagel, 2009). As a consequence thereof, the new framework is partly oriented at strengthening public service media, partly private sector interests. Without the intervention of the Commission, it is fair to say that most Länder would have preferred a standstill situation over the tricky reforms.

10
Flanders

In June 2004, complaints by several private broadcasters provoked a Commission investigation into the financing of the Flemish public broadcaster VRT (Vlaamse Radio- en Televisieomroep). The investigation was closed in February 2008 after commitments relating first and foremost to the new media activities of the VRT. Sports and advertising, at the core of the private sector complaints, received considerably less attention in the Commission's decision. As in Germany, negotiations between the Commission and the Flemish government were rather difficult as Flanders questioned the competencies of the Commission to intervene in the area of public service broadcasting (PSB). In its position it was supported by the Netherlands. Together, the two Member States (MS) opposed Commission intervention as long as possible, until Flanders eventually opted for a pragmatic solution – that is a decision with rather modest commitments (see later in this chapter). Former Minister of Media Geert Bourgeois (Vlaamse Regering, 2008) evaluated the decision by saying that the commitments made by the Flemish government were 'easy to execute, they do not hurt anyone and they do not cost anything'. The Dutch were firmer in their principles and 'paid the price', with a somewhat far-reaching agreement reached with the Commission only in January 2010.

In this chapter the nature and impact of the commitments made by Flanders within the framework of the European state aid procedure are analysed. The structure followed is identical to that in the previous chapter on Germany. Firstly, the basic characteristics of PSB policy in Flanders are portrayed. Secondly, the negotiation process between the Commission and the Flemish government is scrutinised. Thirdly, the commitments in the Commission's decision are listed. Fourthly, the implementation of these commitments is critically assessed and, fifthly, evaluated.

Flemish public broadcasting policies: Strategies without vision

Scientific research into the history and policy aspects of PSB in Flanders is rather limited (Perceval, 1995; Dhoest and Van den Bulck, 2003, p. 279). Some scholars argue that the focus of research is above all on the legalistic aspects of PSB (Dhoest and Van den Bulck, 2007, p. 8), but this is not entirely the case. Indeed, several publications focus on the politicisation of PSB in Flanders and the main shifts in public broadcasting policy between the 1970s and 1990s, but few up-to-date accounts of public broadcasting policy exist. In addition – and this is not surprising given the small size of Flanders – the diversity of contributors on the topic of public broadcasting is rather limited (and in contrast to the literature on public broadcasting in Germany, the UK or France).

Broadcasting as a regional competency

Essentially, there are four main characteristics of PSB policy in Flanders. Firstly, public broadcasting is a completely regionalised policy competency in Belgium. Belgium is indeed a federal state in which competencies are assigned to different governments (including regions, communities and the federal state itself). Culture is a competency of the communities, as is broadcasting (Voorhoof, 1995, p. 198). This division of competencies also reflects market reality because, as Coppens asserts (2003, p. 148), 'there are no such things as Belgian media ... newspapers, magazines, radio and television stations are either Flemish or Walloon'.

Continuous reform

Secondly, the history of public broadcasting in Flanders is characterised by continuous reform strongly linked to the political constellation. For that reason, it has always been difficult to develop a set of consistent and long-term objectives in broadcasting policy. In the early days of PSB, political interference and even censorship were institutionalised (Goossens, 1998, p. 44ff). Politicisation remained a problem until the 1980s, and was also reflected in the increase in staff – all appointed according to the political equilibrium of that time, between 1975 and 1980 (1900–2500 employees) (Verhofstadt, 1982, p. 29). Politicisation was thus not only situated at management levels, but spread throughout all levels of the public broadcaster. This hampered creativity stimulated overly buraucratic processes and rendered the public broadcaster ill-adapted to the challenges brought about by commercial television. When Flanders' new commercial broadcaster, which benefited from a monopoly on television advertising, was launched in 1989, it became an immediate success, achieving a market share of 38.3 per cent by 1993. At the same time, the public broadcaster's share dropped to a dramatic 23 per cent (Coppens, 2003, p. 148). The public broadcaster was in crisis (Saeys and Antoine, 2007, p. 108). A need for reform was apparent, and several legislative initiatives were taken to adopt management structures and allow for programming strategies much more suitable for the public broadcaster to fulfil its tasks in a liberalised market. The VRT was transformed into a more autonomous company working on the basis of a management contract, clarifying the more general Media Decree provisions on the public broadcaster. The first management contract was agreed in 1997, and every five years it is renewed. Both the Media Decree (which was revised in 2009 and brought into line with the Audiovisual Media Services Directive (AVMS)) and the management contract provide for a qualitative and broad description of VRT's tasks. The public broadcaster has to reach as many citizens as possible with high-quality programmes and services spanning different genres, including information, culture, education, sports and entertainment.

The action plan reforming VRT in the 1990s had three goals. Firstly, political interference was to be minimised through the introduction of a clear division of competencies between the Board of Governors (politically appointed) and the management. Secondly, a more management-oriented style was also introduced. Several managers from the private sector were attracted to 'run' the public broadcaster. Thirdly, the tasks of the public broadcaster were made more explicit in the management contract and coupled to performance indicators. The latter envisage, first and foremost, audience reach as a determining factor of VRT's relevance to society.

In short, VRT was gradually conceptualised as a modern media undertaking in which audience reach, in combination with high-quality offers, was at the core of its mission. The reform paid off. The downward trend stopped and was eventually reversed. In 2010, VRT achieved a market share of over 40 per cent. This does not mean that reform and discussions on the public broadcaster ended; discussions on an overly broad remit, commercialisation and political interference continued to dominate before the renewal of the management contract every five years.

Chasing ratings

After the fundamental reforms of PSB in the 1980s, the activities of VRT were focused on regaining its audiences. The management contract also required this, identifying a number of performance indicators related to the reach of particular genres of programmes. For new and current affairs programmes it was, for example, stipulated that VRT should reach 1.5 million Flemish people on a daily basis (Coppens, 2003, pp. 150–1).

Performance indicators should be seen in the light of the context in which they were introduced. As already stated, the market share of VRT had dropped sharply after the launch of the commercial channel VTM. In order to retain its relevance, VRT had to reinvent itself. Performance indicators were, in fact, a solution to end the overly paternalistic programming strategies (Van den Bulck, 2007, p. 76). Arguably, it was indeed necessary to reconnect citizens with VRT. However, some observers argued that the new VRT strategies risked jeopardising the public broadcaster's legitimacy if it excessively followed the economic logic of reach (Saeys and Coppens, 2003; Goossens, 2009, pp. 167, 197).

VRT has attempted to remedy concerns in regard to commercialisation, introducing quality measurements and its triple-track policy, which essentially aims to balance the offer of deepening and broadening content. Following this policy, VRT services are to be offered at three levels or 'tracks', that is specialised content (1) in general programmes, (2) in specialist programmes and (3) on digital specialist channels/websites (Van den Bulck, 2008, p. 335). In spite of these adaptations new reforms are at the doorstep VRT, with private broadcasters and publishers complaining about VRT's new media activities and several political parties arguing against what they perceive as over-commercialisation of the public broadcaster's offer.

Pax media

A fourth characteristic of Flemish broadcasting policy that merits attention for the purposes of this work is the so-called *pax media*. Basically, policy makers aim to maintain a 'peace' between the public broadcaster and its main competitor, VMMa (owner of the commercial channel VTM). This peace is always under pressure, and both the disruptions and their corrections are the cornerstone of the development of broadcasting policy in Flanders.

As competition increased in the 1990s, it became difficult to maintain the *pax media*. VMMa and VRT battled on a number of issues.

The former CEO of the VRT, Tony Mary, blamed VMMa for acquiring the rights to the football Champions League in 2004. VMMa, in turn, opposed the creation of a separate sports channel by VRT and consistently asked for a more clearly defined remit before every renewal of the management contract. Several of VMMa's shareholders advocated their positions in the written press, going as far even as to question the relevance of the public broadcaster (Van Thillo in Bonte, 2005). They were extremely worried about Tony Mary's intentions in launching a range of new digital channels requiring an additional government subsidy of €200 million. For obvious reasons, the private sector disagreed, lobbying for a more restrictive approach for new media services and, in addition, pleading for a more stringent regulation of the commercial communication activities of VRT. However, it is the Flemish government itself that obliges VRT to maximise its commercial revenues (to up to 38 per cent of its total revenues). These two issues, that is the new media activities of the VRT and its commercial activities, remain a thorn in the side of Flemish private media companies. The Flemish government has consistently tried to settle these conflicts in an ad hoc fashion by attempting to please different parties on different occasions.

Since 2010, the *pax media* between the VRT and VMMa has been restored. There will always be some minor, marginal conflicts and, with the management contract of 2012 in sight, the private sector will once again lobby for a more stringent regulation of VRT.

The state aid procedure: 'Team Flanders–VRT' vs. Commission

The private sector arguments for more stringent public broadcasting policies

On 30 June 2004 several private broadcasters filed a joint complaint against the allegedly unfair behaviour of VRT in the market for radio advertising. These activities were not opposed as such; rather, private broadcasters suggested that VRT had engaged in unfair pricing strategies. Two weeks after this complaint on radio advertising, private broadcaster VMMa filed a separate complaint. It argued that the remit of VRT was not sufficiently clear and did not significantly differ from the scope of activities of private broadcasters. Moreover, VMMa was of the opinion that the control of VRT was deficient – and even impossible – in the absence of transparent proportionality mechanisms. One of the main triggers of the complaint was undeniably the creation of the dedicated sports channels Sporza by VRT. This channel was launched without prior government approval (Donders et al., 2008, p. 17) and was considered evidence of the alleged overcompensation of VRT. Indeed, VRT's main competitors in the television market questioned the acquisition policies of VRT in the light of the apparent necessity of a new channel. They regarded Sporza as a tangible evidence of the overcompensation by VRT, asserting that VRT had simply bought too many rights as its regular broadcasting channels no longer sufficed.

It is noticeable that the complaints filed in 2004 did not concern new media activities. In addition, the initial lists of questions sent by the Commission to the Flemish government did not extensively cover this topic. Some discussions on new media services offered by VRT emerged in 2006. Yet, it is only since 2009 that more contentious debates have taken place in regard to the role of VRT in new media markets. In particular, Flemish publishers have criticised the use of taxpayers' money for 'copying the websites of newspapers' (Vandermeersch, 2009). The criticism of the publishing sector was at first somewhat disorganised, but became more centrally oriented by their interest group (the *Vlaamse Dagbladpers*). Hence, and this in contrast to other countries, during the state aid procedure itself the Flemish publishing sector was not involved.

The Commission itself set the agenda of new media issues. Obviously, the private sector complainants involved in the procedure picked up on this as they were of the opinion that VRT had 'freewheeled' throughout the Flemish media landscape. The perception that VRT leads and the Flemish government follows was, and remains, valid.

Flemish objections to a Public Value Test

The negotiation process between the Flemish government and the Commission was far from a smooth process; it was also influenced by external factors such as the difficulties in the Dutch case and the desire of the Commission to conclude the German, Irish, Flemish and Dutch cases simultaneously. Besides these external factors, most interviewees indicated that negotiations were particularly difficult. The Commission even considered unilaterally listing appropriate measures – which would have been an unusual outcome of a state aid procedure on public broadcasting. In the end, the Commission was forced to take into account the specificities of public broadcasting in smaller MS. It accepted rather minimal commitments on the side of the Flemish government, which had already renewed the management contract with the VRT on 20 July 2006 during negotiations with the Commission. In the management contract, it was specified that new channels require prior government approval, control of VRT would be strengthened and commercial activities more strictly regulated. Referring to these adaptations, the Flemish government and VRT were of the opinion that they met most of the Commission's concerns. In a press release on 20 July 2006, the public broadcaster (VRT, 2006) even stressed that it was 'convinced that the new management contract would take away concerns of the Commission with regard to the financing of the public broadcaster'. The Commission firmly disagreed, however. Displeased with the approach of the Flemish government, the Commission, therefore, wrote to the Flemish government (EC, 2006b) on the same day that the management contract was approved, specifying that there was still a need for adaptations in Flemish PSB legislation. The fact that both the Commission's letter and the new management contract were published on the same day was not accidental. On the one hand, the Commission was not pleased with the proactive attitude of the Flemish government in updating the management contract without consulting its competition services. On the other, the Flemish government argued that it did not require the Commission's approval of the new management contract, falling within its own autonomous competence. Moreover, it stressed the new management contract already took into account the concerns of the Commission. This stalemate situation complicated matters somewhat. On the one hand, the Commission still had demands on its list; on the other, the Flemish government had in its own opinion already delivered.

There were three main discussion points between the Flemish government and the Commission. Firstly, at the meta level, the Flemish government was of the opinion that the Amsterdam Protocol justified an exceptional treatment of public broadcasting. This issue was settled fairly soon as the Flemish government decided to cooperate, rather than to continue opposing, Commission interference (this in contrast with the Dutch strategy). Still, the Flemish government insisted that the Protocol was in fact a *lex specialis* for PSB. Its position in this respect is not surprising, as the Flemish government was one of the initiative-takers of the Protocol. It is fair to suggest that the more pragmatic stance eventually taken by the Flemish government on this issue was the only point of divergence in 'team Flanders–VRT'. Inspired by the Dutch stance, VRT preferred adherence to the *lex specialis* approach.

Secondly, the Commission asked for the introduction of a Public Value Test (PVT) for new media services. The Flemish government was not very willing to go along with these demands opposing the bureaucratic nature of the test, certainly in small markets like Flanders, and the involvement of third parties. One of the main stumbling blocks to reaching a consensus concerned the Commission's appreciation of certain new services. One of the interviewees stressed that the Commission wrongly assumed that a broadcast on a mobile platform was no longer 'broadcast'. The Flemish government and VRT, who pleaded for a genuine technology-neutral approach, disputed this.

Thirdly, in order to ensure proportionality of funding, the Commission asked to introduce a 10 per cent cap on reserves and to specify more clearly the rules of commercial activities in a separate framework. The 10 per cent cap seemed problematic to operationalise, as the basis on which to calculate the cap was disputed (limited to direct government subsidies only or also to include VRT's commercial revenues). For commercial activities, a framework on side activities and merchandising already existed, but remained unpublished. After the agreement with the Commission, the publication of the framework still took a year to complete.

The triumph of pragmatism

It might seem that the Commission and the Flemish government had reached a conclusion rather easily. Admittedly, discussion points were rather minimal; however, the positions were much more diverging. On the one hand, the Flemish government and the public broadcaster continued to question the Commission's competencies in this field and, in particular, resisted all overly meticulous demands of the Commission. Their concern was fuelled by continuous questions from the Commission in regard to alteration of certain aspects of the Media Decree. This working method of asking for other changes as soon as previous demands had been implemented was not appreciated. The Commission, on the other hand, was not always sure about with whom it was negotiating. The Flemish government and VRT strongly cooperated on the state aid investigation, which triggered doubts as to who was really in charge of the negotiations. VRT indeed played a key role in the procedure. This should be nuanced to some extent, however, as the recipient of the aid is often involved, as in other countries. In addition, many Commission questions could only be answered by VRT. The Commission's concerns were certainly justified, but in the end the Flemish government took ownership of the case opting for a speedy closure, rather than sticking to its principles like VRT and its Dutch neighbours would have preferred. Pragmatism had triumphed.

Besides the mutual mistrust, the approval of the new management contract in the middle of the state aid procedure was another complicating factor. The Commission did not welcome the approval of a new management contract without any prior consultation. For Flanders, there was no problem at all. A new contract was necessary as the old one was about to expire. The negotiation of the management contract is a competency of the Flemish government. Hence, the latter did not deem it strictly necessary to consult the Commission in this matter. Although this issue led to some irritation on both sides, it was eventually pushed aside.

Leaving aside the suspicion among the negotiation partners, there were also diverging ideas about the substance of the case. On the proportionality issues, a consensus was rather easily reached – albeit that the specificities thereof required some textual adaptations in the final decision. In particular *ex ante* evaluation was a difficult nut to crack. In spite of pressure from the VRT, the Flemish government decided to go along with the idea of an *ex ante* evaluation in a pragmatic way (see later in this chapter). In exchange, the Commission agreed to rather minimalistic provisions in the Media Decree concerning the test, this being in contrast to other cases in which rather detailed steps of the test can be found.

In short, the state aid procedure concerning the Flemish public broadcaster VRT was characterised by three elements. Firstly, the negotiations were rather difficult. There was a lot of suspicion on both sides, which finally resulted in a search for pragmatism and, hence, limited commitments. Secondly, the Flemish government and VRT joined forces in this procedure, sharing the same perspective on most issues. Thirdly, the involvement of the private sector was more limited than in other cases. This was probably due to a smaller number of stakeholders and the fact that there was only one active complainant. The latter was not entirely familiar with the possibilities for lobbying within the framework of European state aid control and was, above all, frustrated with the (perceived) limited outcome of the Commission's investigation. Director General (DG) Competition, as one of the interviewees said, 'trusted too much on the promises of the Flemish government and the VRT; commitments were not tested by the Commission that, from a substantial point of view, devoted very limited attention to the specific issues in the complaint filed' (Private broadcaster representative, 2009). This is not to say that private sector influence was irrelevant in this procedure; however, it was considerably less than in other cases.

A modest list of commitments

The Commission closed its procedure on 22 February 2008. Flanders agreed to a number of commitments (EC, 2008b) to be implemented within a period of 12 months. Some of the Commission's demands had already been implemented during the state aid procedure. Although not mentioned in the list of appropriate measures, these anticipatory commitments are taken into account in the analysis of the Commission's impact on the Flemish regulation of VRT.

Definition of the remit

Commitments with regard to the definition of the remit are, certainly given the Commission's critical remarks in this regard, limited in scope. First, before agreeing on the public service remit in a new management contract, a public consultation is organised by the Flemish Sectoral Council for Media ('Sectoral Council'). The latter is an independent advisory body, advising the Flemish government on all changes in media legislation. It consists of 19 members, 5 of whom are independent; the 14 others represent the public broadcaster, private broadcasters, publishers, consumer interest groups, distributors and so on. The consultation, also invoking academic expertise, precedes the renewal of the management contract every five years. On the basis of the consultation, the Sectoral Council gives advice to the Flemish government and this is made publicly available. Secondly, Flanders has to delineate better the difference between commercial and public services, specifying further its framework on merchandising and side activities.

Vagueness on the *ex ante* test prevails

Most importantly, an *ex ante* evaluation for new media services is foreseen:

> In [the] first instance, the Flemish government will adapt the Mediadecree [sic] by means of a provision that prohibits the VRT to deliver [sic] new services or activities, which are not covered by the Beheersovereenkomst, without prior evaluation and without explicit entrustment by the Flemish government. The authorities will also determine which criteria qualify a service as a new service that is not

covered by the present Beheersovereenkomst and, therefore, requires a prior evaluation. (EC, 2008b: §239)

Three elements can be discerned in the above quotation. Firstly, the requirement of an *ex ante* evaluation for new media services that are not covered by the management contract is to be introduced in the media decree. Secondly, new media services that are not covered by the management contract require an *ex ante* evaluation. Without an evaluation and, subsequently, consent and formal entrustment of the Flemish government, VRT is not allowed to launch new services. Thirdly, the criteria on the basis of which a service is 'new' and, hence, requires an *ex ante* evaluation are to be determined by the Flemish government. The decision also spells out that the Flemish Sectoral Council will be consulted by the Flemish government in regard to every new service requiring an *ex ante* evaluation. Moreover, the Sectoral Council has to take into account a number of criteria when being consulted, that is changes in the Flemish media market, technological evolutions, changes in the Flemish media landscape and the role of the public broadcaster therein, the economic situation in the Flemish media sector, the offer of particular services on the market, international trends, the promotion of Flemish culture and identity, and the expectations of the media consumer. The Council also has to take into account the comments of third parties.

It is apparent that the commitments of the Flemish government are far less specific than the commitments made in the German or Irish cases (for Germany, see previous chapter; for Ireland, see EC, 2008d: §141–50). There is no (strict) identification of separate steps in the required *ex ante* evaluation. Also, less attention is devoted to third party involvement. Moreover, the list of criteria that is included as part of the appropriate measures is not new, as in the management contract 2007–11 (in which the Flemish government and public broadcaster anticipated several of the Commission's desires) similar criteria are listed for the three-yearly evaluation of the management contract (Vlaamse Regering en VRT, 2006: Article 3, §2). Excepting third party involvement, the list of criteria that have to be taken into account in every *ex ante* test for new media is nearly identical to that quoted from the 2007–11 management contract. The difference is that the listed criteria should not only apply for a three-yearly evaluation of the management contract, but also for possible *ex ante* tests.

A commitment with regard to control that is not mentioned in the list of appropriate measures concerns the establishment of an independent body that measures and evaluates the performance of VRT. This body is the Flemish Regulator for the Media (VRM), created in April 2005 and commenced activities in 2006 – thus during the Commission's procedure. Although VRM finds its origins in plans of the Flemish government to rationalise the different regulatory bodies in place, it is generally regarded as a fulfilled commitment on the side of the Flemish government. DG Competition concluded that the body indeed acts as an independent regulator, sanctioning or alerting VRT to breaches of the Media Decree (VRM, 2007a, 2007b, 2007c).

Proportionality and transparency

Finally, with regard to the issue of proportionality, three specific commitments have been made. Firstly, the Flemish government will introduce mechanisms that avoid possible overcompensation. A financial auditing body is to monitor these mechanisms and approve the annual accounts of the public broadcaster. Secondly, reserves will be limited. The accumulation of reserves cannot, under normal circumstances, exceed 10 per cent of annual government compensation. If reserves exceed this limit, the excess is transferred to a special account of the Flemish government. This account can be used only to cover for possible future deficits of the public broadcaster. Thirdly, and already mentioned, a framework on merchandising and side activities will be made publicly available. This framework clarifies under which conditions VRT can be involved in commercial activities.

A *de iure* implementation

The appropriate measures listed above resulted in three concrete alterations to the Flemish Media Decree. The Decree was amended on 18 July 2008 and introduced three new Articles, 16bis, 17bis and 20quater. After making the transposition of the AVMS directive, these Articles became 18, 20 and 26 respectively (Vlaamse Regering, 2009a) (used throughout the chapter). In addition, the framework on merchandising and side activities was published in February 2009 (VRT, 2009). In June 2009, the Flemish government also published a clarifying addendum to the management contract on the definition of new services not covered by the management contract (Vlaamse Regering and VRT, 2009).

Alterations to the Media Decree

Article 18 introduces the principle of an *ex ante* evaluation for new media services. It states, 'The VRT can launch new services or activities that are not covered by the management contract only after an explicit approval of the Flemish government' [translated from Dutch]. In that sense, it literally transposes the Commission's demand in most state aid cases for a more explicit entrustment of the remit to public broadcasters. The entrustment of the Flemish government must be based on an advice (not binding) of the Sectoral Council. In its recommendation, the Council must take into account the opinion of third parties. Advice must also be published on the Council's website. The operationalisation of the test is addressed in both §2 and §3 of Article 18, and repeats almost literally the appropriate measures in the state aid decision. Article 18 does not depict a two-legged test embodying a public value assessment and a market impact evaluation; it meets the appropriate measures to the letter. In current discussions on the design of an *ex ante* test, the Sectoral Council accepts the need for a market impact assessment. However, it is far from clear what the requirements are for such an assessment and what budget is available for a market impact assessment.

Article 20 legally enshrines a five-yearly public consultation on the role of VRT – to be conducted before the renewal of the management contract. A public consultation already preceded the management contract for the period 2007–11. This procedure is now legally anchored in the Media Decree, however. The framework of this consultation is also defined in a more specific manner. Again, it is the Sectoral Council that is responsible for the organisation of the consultation. In this consultation, similar parameters are used as in the *ex ante* test. The consultation should also depend on scientific expertise and result in an advice of the Sectoral Council. This advice is the basis for negotiations of a new management contract between the Flemish government and the VRT.

A final alteration is introduced in Article 26; this provides for a 10 per cent cap on reserves accumulation by the public broadcaster. Although there was no fundamental disagreement about this provision, it took quite some time before the Flemish government and DG Competition agreed on the specific formulation of all the concepts used in this article. It was, in particular, important for the Commission to ensure that reserves would amount to 10 per cent of the annual government compensation (not, for example, all public revenue streams). One should not overlook, that although the introduction of this article results in more legal certainty, the current financial situation of the Flemish public broadcaster is not one in which reserves will be accumulated. Rather it is likely that existing reserves will, given the financial difficulties of VRT, continuously decrease.

The framework on merchandising and side activities: What framework?

Bearing in mind the substantial savings that have to be made by VRT, its commercial revenues are becoming increasingly relevant. The management contract 2007–11 already stipulates that 38 per cent of the VRT's overall budget should come from commercial revenues, asking for an active commercial policy from VRT while adhering to its public service obligations. This puts pressure on the relations between the public broadcaster and private media companies.

In order to formulate clear rules for VRT's commercial activities, a framework on merchandising and side activities has been developed by the public broadcaster itself (VRT, 2009); this framework needs the approval of the Board of Governors. The public version of the framework was published in February 2009, one year after the state aid procedure. The reason for the delayed publication was threefold. Firstly, the Board of Governors did not perceive the publication as a priority, which is rather bizarre given the growing importance of commercial revenues for VRT. Secondly, VRT awaited the approval of the new Media Decree, incorporating the concepts used in the AVMS directive. Thirdly, and more substantially, VRT had hoped to include some provisions on previews in the framework. The Board of Governors resists a pay-model for previews, however.

The framework on merchandising and side activities, *in casu* commercial activities, consists of two big parts. The first part briefly explains what the framework is about and explains that the framework is an elaboration of the relevant provisions in the Media Decree and the management contract. The second part contains the actual framework on merchandising and side activities.

From part one, it is clear that the framework's goal is not so much to limit what the public broadcaster can do with regard to commercial activities, but to clarify what VRT is doing in commercial markets (note that the Commission also never asked for a limitation of VRT's commercial activities).

Part two lists the conditions on the basis of which commercial services can be provided. A distinction is made between the exploitation of VRT's programmes via different distribution modes, messages of general interest and commercial communication, Line Extensions and a rest category of commercial activities. The framework also clarifies how VRT can engage in commercial communication markets. A distinction is made between VRT's linear and non-linear offers. For linear offers, conditions with regard to commercial communication are somewhat stricter. This is in line with the AVMS directive that also makes a distinction between a light-touch regulation for non-linear offers and more rules for linear services (see Chapter 5 in this book). For both television sponsoring and radio advertising, there are caps. Product placement is, with the exception of children's programmes, accepted. The framework stresses that commercial communication is not allowed on thematic Internet sites for news and children. On all other websites, commercial communication is allowed.

In spite of the caps on television sponsoring and radio advertising, most private broadcasters consider the regulatory framework too loosely defined (i.e. it is not limiting, it is enabling). In their opinion, VRT is involved in television advertising (defined as 'sponsoring') albeit prohibited, caps on radio advertising are circumvented with special offers, various forms of commercial communication are not capped at all, and on the Internet VRT experiments freely with commercial communication. Most interviewees, excepting the representatives of the public broadcaster, admit that VRT certainly explores the margins of Flemish regulation concerning commercial communication. This seems to be unavoidable due to a combination of factors. Firstly, the VRT was obliged to raise its commercial revenues from 32 per cent in 2007 to 38 per cent of its total revenues in 2011. Over those four year, revenues were required to increase by 6 per cent while the market was not doing well at all. Secondly, due to the financial problems of the public broadcaster, reliance on commercial revenues is expected to increase even further and the Flemish government does not seem likely to renegotiate public compensation of VRT. Thirdly, VRT is a competitor (unlike any other, but a competitor nevertheless) in a commercial market environment. It would be odd if it were not to attempt to explore possible additional revenue streams. Therefore, it is the Flemish government's job to better regulate the commercial communication activities of VRT and monitor compliance with the regulatory framework. The role of VRM needs strengthening in this regard, but the Flemish government itself has the right to define further the rules for commercial communication activities carried out by VRT.

The framework for merchandising and side activities does not define too many rules; it basically illustrates that nearly everything is possible. The Flemish government needs to regulate VRT's commercial communication activities more carefully. However, there is no single financial incentive for the Flemish government to introduce stricter rules and improve the framework on merchandising and side activities. If VRT manages to increase its commercial revenues to 38 per cent of its total revenues, the Flemish government is satisfied. But what about the public service remit? Is it desirable that a public broadcaster risks prioritising its search for new commercial communication strategies over the renewal of its public service project in a digital age? Moreover, what about private media companies' difficulties in finding sustainable business models online? Commercial communication activities of VRT on the Internet deserve additional attention, as one can hardly defend a public broadcaster that receives public funding distorting markets that are far from developed. Any prohibition to engage in Internet advertising, sponsoring and so on. should be accompanied by a renegotiation of VRT's public budgets.

In short, the framework consolidates the de facto situation with regard to the commercial activities of VRT. It is an interpretation of the management contract and Media Decree provisions by VRT management itself. Therefore, it should not be elevated to the level of 'rules' applying to commercial activities of VRT as no parliamentary control applies nor was the Sectoral Council of Media consulted to illustrate the framework.

The consultation before the management contract renewal

When looking more closely at the Media Decree, the introduction of an *ex ante* evaluation for new services in Flanders should not be considered the most important alteration of Flemish public broadcasting regulation after Commission interference. It might well be that the *ex ante* evaluation will never take place in practice and that, in fact, the consultation before the renewal of the management contract every five years appears to be more important.

The consultation for the management contract 2012–16 began in mid-2009. The Flemish administration and the Sectoral Council ordered three research reports, dealing with citizens' and stakeholders' views on the public broadcaster and its market impact, respectively. The administration was involved in the capacity of the Sectoral Council, of which some members are part of a research group, and could not choose between the different proposals. The Sectoral Council was granted rather extensive competencies after the state aid procedure. However, given the representation within of sector interests, it might not be the most suitable body for the consultation and the *ex ante* evaluation.

Leaving that aside, the results of independent research showed an enormous public support for a holistic public broadcaster, with over 80 per cent of the Flemish citizens supporting VRT (Dhoest et al., 2010). The consultation of stakeholders concluded that most actors in the Flemish media and cultural sector agreed with the relevance of a public broadcaster that delivers high-quality, Flemish content. Some were less enthusiastic in advocating for a more rigid regulatory framework, certainly for new media services (Donders et al., 2010). For its advice, the Sectoral Council did not take into account the market study (criticizing its quality). On the basis of the audience and stakeholder studies, the Council published an advice advocating unanimously for a strong public broadcaster active in all genres with an emphasis on high-quality, Flemish content. It supports a multimedia role, albeit that the public service remit was deemed to focus mainly on audiovisual content (Sectorraad Media, 2010). Parliamentary discussions will proceed from this advice.

A feeble *ex ante* test

Whereas the consultation is 'up and running', the *ex ante* evaluation has not yet been implemented. There is not even a procedure that outlines the different steps to be followed should a new service necessitate evaluation. The impression exists that the *ex ante* test is not too important within the Flemish legal order for PSB. There are two elements explaining why an *ex ante* evaluation will probably not become a standard procedure for the evaluation of certain public broadcasting activities.

The first element relates to the provision that only new services or activities not covered by the public service contact require an *ex ante* evaluation. Every five years the management contract is updated. This update requires a public consultation and an advice from the Sectoral Council. The latter should take into account similar aspects as for a possible *ex ante* test. So, as long as VRT's activities are covered by each new management contract, no *ex ante* test is required at all. In that sense, the *ex ante* test is an instrument that is only to be used in the exceptional case that VRT launches a service not covered by the management contract. Whereas in the UK and Germany the test is a dynamic extension of the legal framework for PSB – a standard procedure should the public broadcasters in these countries wish to extend their offers – the Flemish test is a tool to be used in exceptional circumstances only. If the management contract covers all the services of VRT, this is not problematic from a European state aid point of view. An explicit entrustment is foreseen. Since the contract is updated every five years and consultations begin one year before that (these precede the actual negotiations between the Flemish government and VRT), all possible new services might be included in VRT's remit via this procedure. Note that the consultation does not discuss distinct services. The remit and performance of VRT are discussed as a whole. In that sense, some sort of 'Amsterdam test' – even in the form of a broader consultation – has not been implemented in Flanders. This means that competitors, and also other stakeholders, will have to rely on informal lobbying to alter aspects of the management contract. A formalised procedure for particular contested services, in which competitors and other relevant stakeholders (such as content producers, museums and libraries) have the opportunity to question possible market impacts and the public value of VRT's services, is more desirable in comparison with the system put in place.

A second element relates to the Flemish government's definition of 'new services'; in other words: Which services are covered by the management contract and which are not? The Flemish government had to develop criteria to determine the definition of new services. In June 2009, the Flemish government and VRT (Vlaamse Regering and VRT, 2009) agreed on a so-called clarifying addendum to the management contract of 2007–11. This addendum listed the services covered by the management contract. All other services require an *ex ante* test. From a legal point of view, this seems to be in line with the appropriate measures made in this regard. There are two problems with this addendum, however; these relate to the way in which the addendum was developed and its contents.

Bypassing the Sectoral Council

Firstly, the addendum is in fact developed by VRT. On the basis of earlier, non-public, documents circulating within VRT, one can conclude that VRT itself developed a list of services that were covered by the management contract. This list was entirely taken over by the Flemish government. Although one can accept that VRT takes an initiative in this regard, it is questionable that the affected public broadcaster draws up a list of services covered by the management contract that is subsequently entirely taken over by the Flemish government. As such, the public broadcaster has the power to prevent an *ex ante* evaluation from happening.

The Sectoral Council was not consulted about the addendum. The Flemish government and VRT maintained that such a consultation was not necessary, as the addendum merely clarifies the management contract between the two parties also agreeing on the addendum. In the opinion of several members of the Council, the addendum is a fundamental reinterpretation of the management contract, however. Various members of the Council (not only private sector representatives!) did not accept that the Council was being bypassed. This position is understandable because the Council is responsible for conducting an *ex ante* evaluation and, moreover, received the addendum only after it had been signed.

The fact that there is such a limited control on a soft law instrument is not acceptable from a broader democratic point of view. It is at least desirable that a parliamentary debate is possible about this issue. It is not suggested that the Flemish government and VRT deliberately avoided discussion about the addendum. Both parties wanted to close the procedure of implementing the appropriate measures, following which the Flemish government was obliged to develop those services covered by the management contract and those not. In order to prevent the implementation process from being prolonged, the addendum was drafted and an agreement reached between the Flemish government and VRT. The intention of the addendum was, as such, to clarify the current management contract and leave discussions about possible new services for the consultation before the next management contract. The intentions underlying the addendum were most likely not malign. However, both private sector representatives and independent members of the Sectoral Council felt pushed aside for the purpose of having a flexible framework for VRT's new media services. Indeed, the Flemish government VRT deviated from the emerging consultation model to develop and adapt media policy in Flanders.

What new services?

The second problematic aspect of the addendum (Vlaamse Regering and VRT, 2009) is its lack of clarity. Even though the interpretative addendum is in fact a list of services covered by the management contract, many questions remain. How future-proof is the interpretative addendum? It is not entirely clear why the Flemish government did not opt to draft a list of criteria qualifying a service as a significant new service not covered by the management contract. This would be more in line with practices in the UK, Germany and the Netherlands.

Which services are exactly covered? At first sight, it seems that the list of services that are covered by the management contract is rather straightforward. This is not necessarily the case, however. For example, services like VRT's sports and news websites are covered by the management contract. On the news website, a number of different services are offered, however. The website is, as such, a platform (and brand) offering a variety of public services. The audience can consult VRT's Videozone (comparable to the BBC's iPlayer) and watch the public broadcasters' news and current affairs online. The website also offers text services providing the most up-to-date news. In addition, files are compiled on specific news topics such as, for example, the Flemish elections. These files contain a lot of background information on the Flemish political system, while the services obviously contribute to fulfilling the public service remit. Blogs and forums are also accessible via the news website. It is sometimes less clear what the added value of these services is. It is not suggested that these services do not have any public value but, nevertheless, they might require an *ex ante* test. The current addendum ensures that the entire variety of services that is offered via VRT's news website is covered by the management contract. The same logic can be applied to other websites. Whereas it is not entirely sure that all services that are currently offered, taking again the example of the news website, should effectively fall within the ambit of the interpretative addendum, it is even less clear whether new services (currently not offered on the news website) are covered by this addendum. It seems undesirable that new services, which one cannot even imagine today, are covered by an interpretative addendum simply because they are offered on a platform that is covered by the addendum. This criticism is in part countered by the fact that the addendum is explicitly linked to the management contract, which means that the services listed in the addendum must be interpreted in the light of their description in the management contract. One should thus read the addendum and the management contract together. Reading the addendum in isolation, one could get the impression that VRT enjoys an overly broad flexibility; this is certainly not the case. Yet, the remark that it is not entirely clear which services are covered by, for example, the news website remains valid. This does not mean that one should define all services in an overly precise manner. VRT should be flexible in order to adapt its websites and launch new innovative public services. An *ex ante* test does not necessarily undermine the flexibility of the public broadcaster. It could, on the contrary, provide a solid basis to expand services on different platforms.

What is a channel? The addendum obliges a test for new linear radio and/or television channels. New linear channels are channels not covered by the list of services incorporated in the 2007–11 management contract following the interpretative addendum. For the moment, there are no new channels that would require an *ex ante* evaluation. In the interpretative addendum, the digital channels Canvas+ and Één+ are defined as linear enrichments of the television channels Één and Canvas. Therefore, they are covered by the management contract and do not require an *ex ante* evaluation. At the moment, Één+ can be regarded as enrichment and an ad hoc offer of services. It is not certain, however, whether future developments of Één+ can still fit the label of enrichment only. It seems that such developments are not taken into account, however. The addendum covers Één+ regardless of serious adaptations. This seriously impairs the future-proof character of the addendum, or at least shows that the addendum is in fact nothing more than an ad hoc solution to an issue that demands a structural regulatory answer.

Canvas+ should already be classified as a channel if one follows VRT's own definition of the channel. The interpretative addendum classifies Canvas+ as being covered by the management contract 2007–11. The definition of Canvas+ in the addendum does not match VRT's definition and practical organisation of Canvas+, however. The addendum states that the '+' channels are 'a temporary decoupling' (Vlaamse Regering and VRT, 2009) of Één and Canvas. The '+' channels offer enriched content that fits within the third track of VRT's triple-track policy, or broadcast a programme that cannot be broadcast on Één or Canvas due to an alternative programmation. VRT defines Canvas+ as a 'permanent digital additional folder of Canvas' (for this, see http://multiblog.vrt.be/ canvasprogrammas/het-najaar-van-canvas/, accessed 12 October 2010). Canvas+ has a fixed, though limited, programme schedule. It is thus not entirely clear how strictly the definitions in the interpretative addendum are to be interpreted. If Canvas+ does not fit within the definition of linear enrichments of the addendum, is an *ex ante* evaluation required after all?

Is there any audience limit for pilot projects? The new Broadcasting Communication specifies that pilot projects do not require an *ex ante* evaluation if they are tested for a limited amount of time and targeted at a restricted part of the audience (EC, 2009a: §90). Leaving aside whether a two-year period for pilot projects is too generous, the interpretative addendum does not specify that services can only be offered to a restricted part of the audience. So, in theory, it is possible to offer a new service (within a pilot project) to the entire audience. If such a service turns out to be very successful, it is not sure whether the Sectoral Council or the Flemish government would deprive the audience from such a service after two years. This is not to say that VRT would actually decide to follow such an expansive strategy, nor can one assume that the Flemish government would not control this. However, the addendum should be more specific on this point.

Implementing to the letter, not to the spirit

One has to wait to ascertain whether the Commission, whose representatives claim that in Ireland, Flanders and Germany *ex ante* tests are being implemented or at least in the pipeline (e.g. Repa, 2009), will accept the system above. Does this design meet the demands of the Commission? DG Competition assumes that the Flemish government will decide on criteria for 'new' services and operationalise a test. Yet, this is not the case. VRT developed a list of services covered by the management contract and the Flemish government agreed to this. The list is so broad that it is not clear whether a test will be performed in the next two years. Many questions also exist about the test itself. How will the test be conducted? Who will be responsible for all the steps? What will the different steps be? What will be the involvement of third parties? How much time will it take? Is there a budget foreseen for the test? Overall, a fixed test will not be implemented immediately.

It should be stressed that the Flemish government has – from a legal perspective – correctly implemented its commitment to define which services are not covered by the management contract (and can, hence, be considered as new services). In addition, the competencies of the Commission to intervene in the process of implementation of the appropriate measures are limited. Of course, DG Competition can ask the Flemish government for clarification of certain rules or instruments, but it cannot ask the Flemish government to follow a specific strategy for implementing the appropriate measures. The limited powers of the Commission to put pressure on the Flemish government in this regard do not *a priori* exclude that an *ex ante* test will become operational in Flanders. Other actors, like the Sectoral Council, can try to push for a test and are actually doing so. The question remains whether an *ex ante* test, even if in theory completely developed and operational, will be applied if the current interpretative addendum is upheld by VRT and the Flemish government and is taken up in the management contract 2012–16.

Evaluation: Much ado about nothing?

Pauwels and De Vinck (2007, p. 52) argue that VRT and the Flemish authorities are no longer solely competent to formulate public broadcasting policy. Public broadcasting policy, so they contend, is increasingly subject to investigations and the scrutiny of the Commission.

The investigations of the Commission indeed show that there is at least the potential for a supranational institution to question specific financing arrangements between the Flemish government and VRT. This is in itself a relevant observation, since public broadcasting policy fell traditionally within the sovereign competences of national or regional authorities (see Chapter 2 of this book). The new Flemish government explicitly recognises the importance of the European state aid rules in its agreement to form a new government. Defining policy challenges for the media sector, the agreement specifically says that the VRT must exploit technological evolutions but cannot, in doing so, go beyond the boundaries of its public service remit. Explicit reference is hereby made to European state aid rules (Vlaamse Regering, 2009b). This was not the case before the state aid procedure (Vlaamse Regering, 2004).

Does this mean that the state aid procedure under which the Commission investigated the funding of VRT has indeed affected the policy framework for public broadcasting in Flanders. The various stakeholders differ in opinion. In Germany, all stakeholders agreed that the European state aid procedure 'moved' things and resulted in a number of significant changes in the policy framework. The introduction of the three-step test was identified as the most important alteration in the Interstate Treaty on Broadcasting and Telemedia (see previous chapter). In Flanders, both the Flemish government and public broadcaster VRT maintain that, although significant adaptations were made, there were not too many far-reaching commitments. In addition, they also contend that, given the specific arrangements in the management contract, there was no need for extensive commitments. Private sector representatives even claim that no fundamental changes, which they deem necessary, have been made. In their opinion, the European state aid procedure is a lost opportunity. This appreciation of Commission intervention is erroneous, as relevant changes have been made. Reference can be made to the legal enshrinement of a consultation process before the revision of the management contract, the publication of the framework on merchandising and side activities, the possibility of conducting an *ex ante* evaluation before VRT launches a service that is not covered by the management contract and the requirement to limit reserves to 10 per cent of annual public funding.

Did these changes result in a marginalisation of VRT's activities or contribute to a transfer from a PSB to public service media policy framework? There is no evidence suggesting that the European state aid procedure marginalised VRT's scope of activities. The Commission indeed questioned aspects of VRT's expansion into new media markets. It doubted in particular that this expansion was supported by an official entrustment of the Flemish government. A new provision in the Media Decree (i.e. an *ex ante* test is required when VRT offers a service that is not covered by the management contract) alleviated the Commission's concerns. This questioning of the legal basis of VRT's expansion cannot be equated with an intention to limit VRT's scope of activities, however. Possible limitations of VRT's remit will only come from the Flemish government or result from the public broadcaster's own strategic choices. The danger of the public broadcaster gradually limiting instead of genuinely expanding its own remit is a possible over-focusing on increasing commercial revenues in new media markets.

It is equally difficult to conclude that the Commission's intervention fostered a complete transfer from a PSB to a public service media policy framework. Public broadcasting regulation was already technology neutral and the remit quite elaborately described in the management contract for 2007–11. Some alterations of the Media Decree and the management contract were indeed introduced, but it remains difficult to pinpoint whether the concretisation in these documents was entirely caused by the Commission. Several stakeholders admitted that the 2007–11 management contract was, *minimum minimorum*, revised with the demands of the Commission in mind. An interviewee involved in the negotiations with the Commission stressed that the latter had no intention of pushing the public broadcaster into the margin of service delivery. Rather, setting out from a dominantly economic approach, it wanted to avoid the possibility of market distortion.

The immediate effects of the Commission procedure are indeed minimal. Yet, at the level of control, several initiatives have been taken after the state aid procedure that might induce a more balanced relation between the evaluation of VRT and its programmation independence. The advice of the Sectoral Council, for example, stressed that control of VRT is too dispersed and, hence, not effective. A rationalisation and centralisation of control within a limited amount of bodies was put forward, and this on the basis of the ordered studies (Sectorraad Media, 2010). The entire consultation exercise also warranted scientific research, validating and invalidating common claims made in public debate about VRT, and asked stakeholders to sustain their claims with valid arguments. This, and also the *ex ante* evaluation for new media services, which is indeed still in its infancy, could potentially further a consultation- rather than a conflict-based regime for developing public broadcasting policy in Flanders.

Overall, the Commission's investigation did not provoke serious discussion about how to improve the regulation for public service media in Flanders. Debates dealt only with minimising the Commission's impact and maintaining the *status quo*. The European state aid procedure was not an incentive for the Flemish government to improve the regulation of public broadcasting in Flanders. Was it much ado about nothing, then? Admittedly, regulation was adapted more to the letter than to the spirit of the Commission's demands. Nevertheless, these adaptations – even if minor – could have an impact in the future and should, hence, be closely monitored.

11
The Netherlands

On 26 January 2010, the Commission issued its decision on the funding of the various Dutch public broadcasters. The decision was preceded by a lengthy procedure initiated in May 2002 following complaints from private broadcasters, later joined in their grievances by the Dutch publishing sector. As had been the case with other state aid cases, agreement between the Commission and the Dutch authorities appeared extremely difficult. The Dutch refused to accept the competencies of the Commission in the area of public service broadcasting (PSB), and negotiations were temporarily suspended on numerous occasions. The Netherlands attempted to convince other governments to fight Commission intervention. They were somewhat disappointed when the Flemish government eventually opted for a pragmatic compromise with the Commission (see previous chapter). When the Commission was updating the 2001 Broadcasting Communication, the Dutch even initiated and coordinated Member State (MS) resistance. The former Dutch Minister for Media Plasterk insisted that MS retained control over their own public broadcasting regimes, expressing a fear for marginalisation as a consequence of EU intervention. He stressed MS' right to distort the market if they deemed this fit for safeguarding democratic values (in NN, 2008). The Commission was not appreciative of the initiative.

Negotiations between the Commission and the Netherlands were also difficult, as these were permeated by another case (EC, 2006a) dealing with specific, compartmentalised subsidies to the Dutch public broadcasters. In 2006, the Commission concluded that these subsidies were new aid and illegal, which warranted the reimbursement of nearly €80 million from the public broadcasters to the Dutch government. While negotiating on the annual funding of the public broadcasters, the Netherlands was confronted with this unwelcome decision. In addition, both the Netherlands and the Commission were faced with a legal procedure before the General Court after it became clear that the Dutch government had decided to file an action against the Commission's decision. The Court issued a judgment on 16 December 2010, dismissing all grounds for the action. The ruling itself had no influence on the Commission's decision, as it followed the latter by almost a year after it had been issued.

The aim of this chapter is to identify the reasons for the difficult negotiations, focusing on the different steps in the case and the final result. In a manner similar to which the Flemish government opposed Commission intervention and settled eventually for a rather concise list of commitments, a similar outcome could have been expected for the Dutch case. However, the chapter will point out that the commitments of the Netherlands were more far-reaching.

The chapter consists of five parts and mimics the structure of the chapters on Germany and Flanders. In part one, the basic features of PSB in the Netherlands are discussed. Part two provides a chronology of the state aid procedure, devoting attention to the diverging interests of all involved stakeholders. In part three, the commitments of the Dutch government are listed, after which an evaluation of the implementation of these commitments follows in part four. Finally, some provisional conclusions are outlined.

A pluralistic, but highly complex, system

The public broadcasting system in the Netherlands is rather complex. It developed along the lines of the political, ethical and religious polarisation of Dutch society. PSB is not owned by the state, and is also not entrusted to the market. Rather, it is organised by several social organisations. These jointly operate a number of radio and television channels, and were initially funded on the basis of a licence fee (Bardoel, 2008, p. 200). For the sake of uniformity, the chapter will refer to these social organisations as public broadcasters.

Development, reform and preservation of the pluralistic broadcasting system

The distinguishing feature of the Dutch PSB system since its inception in the 1920s is its pluralistic organisation. In 1919, private initiatives for radio emerged in the Netherlands. Social organisations, aspiring to have a stake in the new medium, laid the foundations of the pluralistic organisation of PSB in the Netherlands. Initially, these organisations hired airtime from the private companies that first explored radio. Prior to 1930 there were already five social organisations concerned with radio: NCRV (Calvinist), KRO (Catholic), VARA (socialist), VPRO (liberal–Protestant) and AVRO (liberal–bourgeois). The latter attempted to unite all the organisations under one umbrella public broadcaster. This attempt failed, after which the government intervened, dividing airtime between the different groups and formally establishing the polarised system in radio (Brants, 2004, p. 146). The so-called radio decree remained in place until the 1960s, when the Broadcasting Act (*cf. infra*) was approved (Bardoel, 2008, p. 201; Katsirea, 2008, p. 101).

The pluralistic organisation of the Dutch broadcasting system was preserved in the 1960 broadcasting Act. It allowed for new licences, granting more social groups (representing among others youngsters and migrant communities) the right to broadcast. The expansion of groups was due to the secularisation of society. Three broadcasting channels were made available for all social organisations. The time and money allocated to each organisation depended on the number of members they were able to recruit, and this remains the rule to date. Besides social organisations, existing by virtue of their members, the Dutch government created an additional broadcasting organisation in 1995. This organisation, NPS, is entrusted with programmes related to the arts, culture, youth and minorities (Katsirea, 2008, p. 102).

Private television started in 1989, with the Luxembourg group RTL broadcasting via satellite (Bardoel, 2008, p. 204). The introduction of competition put considerable pressure on the pluralistic organisation of PSB in the Netherlands. The three public broadcast channels lost 35% of their market in the first five years of RTL's activities (Barker, 1997, p. 39; Brants, 2004, p. 149; Bardoel, 2008, p. 204). It should be stressed that RTL's broadcasting activities were in fact not deemed legal by the Dutch government which, in 1988, had approved an amended Broadcasting Act, keeping the public broadcast monopoly intact. The Netherlands was of the opinion that the pillarised system best protected the diversity in society and the needs of its citizens. The introduction of private broadcasters outside the carefully constructed pluralistic system was seen as a threat. This perception of danger was strengthened by the inability of the Dutch government to regulate advertising on incoming broadcast signals (which was the case with RTL, broadcasting from Luxembourg) (Price, 1995, p. 35). The country of origin principle in the Television without Frontiers (TWF) directive prohibits MS to do so (see Chapter 5). Competition in the Dutch market became a reality (Heuvelman, 1994, pp. 133–4) and broadcasting was conceptualised more and more as a commodity for consumers, rather than as a public service to citizens (Bardoel, 2003, p. 83).

Dutch politicians acknowledged the public broadcasters' problems in coping with competition and, hence, policy reforms became inescapable. The Dutch government introduced rules for private television in the 1990s and, subsequently, reformed the public broadcasting system. Management practices were introduced, potential for advertising increased and the licence fee became indexed in order to match increasing production costs (Bardoel, 2008, pp. 204–7). These changes were introduced after the public broadcasters, herein supported by government, consulted McKinsey on how to professionalise in order to cope with competition. The report most ardently argued against the imitation of private broadcasters' programming. In genres catered for by both the private and public sectors, quality should be the distinguishing feature of the latter's offer. McKinsey also advised better branding of the three television channels, which lacked an identity. Consequently, the first television channel was rebranded as the generalist channel offering news and entertainment for a wider audience. The second television channel was to focus on in-depth informative programmes and culture. The third television channel was supposed to be innovative, attracting mainly younger audiences. Not only McKinsey's advice, but also the report of the Commission *Ververs* of 1996 – an evaluation committee resembling the UK *Peacock* and German *De Witte* Committees (Potschka, 2010) – provided input for the reforms. Its advice most importantly stressed that the public broadcasters had to 'go back to the public', offering 'comprehensive, reliable, attractive and innovative programmes which function as a point of reference in an ever more complex and rapidly changing information society' (Bardoel, 2003, p. 84).

Pressure on the public broadcasting system

At present, the licensed public broadcasters are KRO, NCRV, EO, VARA, AVRO, TROS, VPRO, BNN and Max. They need a minimum of 50,000 members in order to apply for funding and broadcasting time on one of the three main television channels. Complementary to these organisations, there are several non-member organisations. NPO is the umbrella public broadcaster responsible for coordinating all other organisations, being in charge of the execution of the provisions on PSB in the Media Act and catering for news and information programmes in the main. Previously, NPO was part of NOS, one of the various broadcasting organisations, but now NOS has been split up: NPO takes care of organisation and coordination, while NOS, RTV takes care of programming and television activities. As already mentioned, NPS is concerned with the programming of the arts, culture and minority groups. After NOS, RTV and NPS, other organisations cater for educational programming (Bardoel, 2008, pp. 207–8).

NPO, which is charged with the execution of the Media Act's provisions, has a concession for ten years. The system of concessions was introduced in 2000, and was somewhat revolutionary. It implies that only one organisation is accountable for the fulfilment of the Media Act's provisions and the provisions in the concession. Concession-holders are thus no longer the individually licensed public broadcasters (Bardoel, 2003, p. 84). Admittedly, this is a step away from a fully fledged pluralistic organisation model. Nonetheless, it has considerably enhanced transparency, accountability and efficiency. In exchange for its delivery of public services (on three television and five radio channels), NPO receives government subsidies. These replaced the license fee in 2000. Together with advertising revenues, the Dutch public broadcasters have an overall budget of slightly over €840 million (as of 2009, NPO, 2010, p. 33). Advertising revenues account for approximately 25%. On a more technical note, it should be mentioned that the sales, management and exploitation of commercial communication are the responsibility of the STER, which is a specific organisation that sells airtime on public radio and television to advertisers. The Minister of Media appoints its board. The revenues of the STER are transferred to the Ministry of Media, after which part of the revenues are transferred to public broadcasters (Van Eijk, 2007, p. 152). In other words, not all advertising revenues generated by selling airtime on public radio and television are effectively going to the public broadcasters; some of the money can also be used to subsidise other initiatives in the media or cultural sector.

In recent years there has been an increasing pressure on the otherwise somewhat stable PSB system in the Netherlands. Indeed, there have been several commissions evaluating public broadcasters and some ground-breaking reports (e.g. the WRR report) have been published. Several consecutive budget cuts may be observed, which seem to have resulted from an instable political landscape since 2002 (Brants, 2004, p. 146). In 2010, the newly elected right-wing cabinet decided on a comprehensive review of Dutch cultural and media policies, announcing significant budget cuts for both domains to take effect immediately. These budget cuts would follow the previous cuts in 2002 under the government of former Prime Minister Balkenende (Bardoel, 2010). Some government parties have even expressed their desire to limit the number of television channels from three to two, arguing that entertainment does not have a place on public broadcast channels. These pleas were inspired by an aversion against what these parties perceive to be leftist and elitist programming strategies (a claim that is, in turn, difficult to align with the desire to eliminate entertainment from public broadcasters' programme schedules). Political pressures are also reinforced by public criticism. Citizens feel the present polarised system is no longer representative of society, which is reflected in lower membership numbers (Bardoel, 2008, p. 209). Diminishing memberships are problematic indeed as the entire system, clinging to the idea of a genuine public sphere creation, depends on representative and popular support.

Overall, one particular group of policy makers and citizens were of the opinion that the public broadcasters did not sufficiently serve the needs of society. This appreciation is supported by the conclusions of the first evaluation committee of the PSB system in 2004. The concession plan, renewed every ten years, oversees an evaluation of the public broadcaster every five years. In 2004, the first evaluation was conducted. As Bardoel points out, the evaluation was a substantial exercise, involving self-assessments for public broadcasters regarding different aspects of their operation. On the basis of these self-assessments and on over 100 interviews with stakeholders, the evaluation committee concluded that all separate organisations performed reasonably to well. However, cooperation between the organisations was deficient, resulting in a disappointing audience reach (less than 40% market share), a lack of complementarity between the different offers and an inefficient deployment of resources (Bardoel, 2008, p. 210). As a consequence of these criticisms, several measures were taken to enhance cooperation.

Political criticism is fuelled by private broadcasters and, increasingly so, by publishers. Competition in the Dutch broadcasting market is stable, as the public broadcasters RTL and SBS divide most of the market among themselves, holding a combined market share of 85% (van Cuilenburg and van der Wurff, 2007, p. 82). This relatively comfortable situation has not prevented private broadcasters like RTL filing complaints with the Commission against the funding of Dutch public broadcasters, nor lobbying against this at the national level. The commercial broadcasters oppose the holistic public service remit of the Dutch public broadcasters. Essentially, the remit of the Dutch public broadcasters can be summarised by referring to three values, that is variety, quality and diversity. The public broadcasters are supposed to be active in all different genres (with a percentage defined for each genre) (Bakker and Vasterman, 2007, p. 151), to reach as many people as possible with high-quality content, and to provide their offerings over all relevant platforms (van Cuilenburg en van der Wurff, 2007, p. 82). In particular, this last provision has provoked contention from publishers. Whereas private broadcasters, who have not been very active on the Internet to date, are still relatively silent on the issue (Bardoel, 2008), Dutch publishers oppose any public presence online. They have lobbied fiercely against it – successfully as it would appear, as several right-wing parties have expressed doubts about the necessity of an online presence of public broadcasters.

Independent control

The Dutch public broadcasting system is at present regulated on the basis of the Media Act, which contains the main provisions for the various public broadcasters. The public service remit is defined in a holistic manner, requiring the Dutch public broadcaster to deliver media services over different platforms in the fields of information, education, culture and entertainment (Het Koninkrijk der Nederlanden, 2008: Article 2.1, §1). Rephrasing the Amsterdam Protocol, the Media Act requires all public services to meet the democratic, social and cultural needs in society. A number of objectives, referring to pluralism, independence, universality, accessibility, diversity, quality and reach are also made explicit (Nederlandse Regering, 2008: Article 2.1, §2). The legitimacy of public broadcasters' new media offers, which is already made explicit in Article 2.1, §1, is emphasised again in §4 of the same article.

Public broadcasters transpose the obligations of the Media Act into concrete programming strategies. Government has no right to intervene in the contents of public broadcasters' services (as stressed in Nederlandse Regering, 2008: Article 2.22). Indeed, freedom of programming and the total prohibition of censorship is a core element of the Dutch PSB system (Bakker and Vasterman, 2007, p. 151). The provisions of the Media Act are enforced by the Dutch Media Authority, which is an independent body 'policing' both public and private broadcasters (Brants, 2004, p. 153). The existence of this independent regulatory authority reinforces the independence of public broadcasters.

The last Dutchman standing

The Netherlands did not welcome the state aid control of their PSB system. There were three reasons for the excessive length of the procedure:

fierce Dutch opposition, the obstinate stance of the Commission and the added pressures from public broadcasters and private media players.

Dutch opposition

The first reason for the length of the procedure was the Dutch opposition to Commission intervention. The Netherlands adhered to the same argument as the Flemish and German governments (see previous chapters); they refused Commission competencies in the area, emphasising the sovereign powers of MS in the area of PSB. Moreover, they initially rejected all proposals that could result in a harmonisation of broadcasting policies. There were manifold frustrations permeating the Dutch position.

Firstly, the Dutch government was taken by surprise when RTL filed an initial complaint about the funding of the public broadcasting regime. There was certainly some annoyance concerning RTL, a Luxembourg-based company not bound by Dutch regulations, going against Dutch public broadcasting. Nevertheless, they were well aware of certain frustrations in the private sector. The subjects of this complaint and other subsequent complaints were thus far from being a revelation.

Secondly, the Commission decided to split the procedure into two separate investigations. One investigation, closed by 2006, dealt with so-called new aid mechanisms and resulted in the Commission's request of a reimbursement of €76,327 million (EC, 2006a: §179). The Dutch government complied with the demand for the reimbursement. It disputed the classification of new aid, however, arguing that all support mechanisms were existing aid and should, therefore, have been part of one procedure. This mode of classification would have prevented the demand for a reimbursement, as existing aid does not need to be reimbursed.

Thirdly (and similar frustrations were heard from the Flemish government), the Netherlands questioned the continuous stream of questions coming from the Commission. Answering these questions required a lot of human resources but, more importantly, the perception existed that the continuous stream of private sector complaints about the Commission fuelled the stream of Commission questions.

Fourthly, and related to this, the entire transparency of the procedure was considered doubtful. Concept versions of the 2006 decision were sent to the Dutch government before publication. However, allegedly, these concept versions differed from the final published version in several respects, resulting in a lack of trust between the two negotiating parties.

Fifthly, there were also some substantive opinions of difference between the Commission and the Dutch government. With regard to the new aid, the time period included for the calculation was disputed. The Dutch government also disputed that unused reserves could distort the market in any way. These complaints were all refuted in the General Court's judgment on the case on 16 December 2010 (General Court, 2010) – a considerable blow to the Dutch government. With regard to the investigation into the existing aid scheme, the demand for an *ex ante* evaluation was particularly difficult to swallow. The Dutch considered it an instrument of harmonisation across MS – a standpoint they also fiercely defended while opposing the approval of the 2009 Broadcasting Communication. Former Minister of Media Plasterk (2008) wrote a letter to the Commission questioning the need for clarification of the 2001 Broadcasting Communication. Most MS supported the initiative (see Chapter 7). At a gathering in September 2008, Plasterk stressed that the choice for PSB implied the acceptance of some degree of market distortion. At the same time, he warned against the atrocity of American public broadcasters and their niche programming (NN, 2008).

Hence, the opposition to the Commission was severe. The Dutch did not perceive this to be a problem in itself, but rather intrinsic to the nature of state aid control. However, they did perceive the stance of the Commission as problematic. It should be stressed that the Netherlands did not opt for a fully fledged political conflict. Although there was a meeting with former Commissioner for Competition Neelie Kroes, most discussions were held between the responsible cabinet and Commission unit. Admittedly, different case handlers from the Commission dealt with the procedure. This complicated matters as new case handlers have to become acquainted with the specificities of the broadcasting systems with which they are dealing. In fact, several interviewees – as in other countries – considered the circulation of Commission staff as problematic. At national ministries, people stay in their respective positions for much longer. Given the duration of these cases, this seems indeed more convenient from a negotiation point of view.

The symbolic value of the Dutch case for the Commission

The Commission was perhaps equally as 'difficult' as the Dutch government. The Dutch case was indeed considered as an exemplary one, which had to follow the line of argumentation in the German, Flemish and Irish cases. Also, from the point of view of the Commission, some frustrations with regard to the Dutch position existed.

First of all, the Dutch position was felt to be overly rigid. The Flemish decided to be much more pragmatic in the end and got away with fairly limited commitments. The Dutch played their cards more publicly and, in the end, had to swallow a list of much further-reaching commitments. The more extensive list of commitments should also be seen in the light of the commissionership of Dutchwoman Neelie Kroes. Obviously, no commissioner would be tempted to give the impression of being more lenient towards her home country. According to some, this resulted in a more unbending attitude of the Commission towards the Netherlands. Moreover, the Commission was far from happy with the public stance taken on the case by certain Dutch political figures. For example, former State Secretary for Media Medy Van Der Laan heavily criticised the Commission's decision to demand a reimbursement of nearly €80 million of government funding. Van Der Laan (in NN, 2006) said that the Dutch government would find a way around the decision, compensating the public broadcasters for the reimbursement. The Commission did not appreciate this statement. The public statement complicated the negotiations on the existing aid as the same negotiators dealt with the new and existing aid procedures. Another point of concern for the Commission was the Dutch opposition to the 2009 Broadcasting Communication. Put simply, the Dutch could only oppose the Communication. The latter put forward the same principles and instruments that the Netherlands were opposing in the case with which they were involved. This did not necessarily mean that the Dutch government had to trigger and coordinate MS resistance to the 2009 Communication, however. Some Commission officials considered such a public outcry inappropriate because of the direct interest the Dutch had in the matter.

The case did not only revolve around 'nitty-gritty' mutual frustrations, as the Commission also had some substantive points of view from which it did not wish to deviate. Because it was asking all MS to implement an *ex ante* evaluation of new media services, it was difficult to abandon this principle in order to reach a consensus with the Dutch government.

Additional pressure from public broadcasters and private sector

The positions of the public broadcasters and the private sector can be seen as a third reason for the lengthy procedure. Essentially, the public broadcasters opposed most of the Commission's requests, insisting on their programming freedom and withstanding all possibilities of harmonising Dutch practices with instruments in other MS. In so doing, they referred to MS' sovereign right to organise their public broadcasting system (as acknowledged by the Amsterdam Protocol), the right to freedom of expression and the respect for media pluralism (Article 11 of the Charter of Fundamental Rights of the EU), and countries' sovereign right to install cultural policies (the UNESCO Convention on Cultural Diversity) (Vecht, 2010).

The private sector was equally militant, repeatedly filing complaints with the Commission. By late 2008, when a decision was nearly in sight, a stream of additional complaints from the publishing sector was added to the list of complaints that had previously been filed by both publishers and private broadcasters. They were of the same opinion, questioning the vagueness of the remit, the proportionality of the public funding in place, the commercial communication activities of the public broadcasters and its new media activities. Specifically in relation to the latter, the publishers complained that the revision of the Media Act in 2008 made the public service remit more vague, instead of clarifying it (EC, 2010: §72–3). The new stream of complaints added to the workload of the Commission and delayed the entire procedure. Furthermore, it added to the pressure on the negotiators. This is not to say that both the public broadcasters and the private sector did not have valid arguments. It can be doubted, however, whether their arguments aided the attempts to close the procedure.

On 26 January 2010 a decision was finally issued. The Dutch government made considerable concessions. The compromise was reached as both the Commission authorities and the Dutch government sought to end the lengthy procedure before the installment of the new Commission. It was felt that a new commissioner might complicate the case, emphasising new action points in the field of state aid control. In that sense, a closure of the procedure during the mandate of Neelie Kroes was preferable for all parties involved.

Commitments

The commitments made by the Dutch government relate to the definition of the remit, the control of the various public broadcasters and the proportionality of their funding. Most importantly, an extensive procedure for the approval of new services was introduced, accompanied by a more detailed description of the public service remit.

In fact, the public service remit had already been clarified in the Media Act of 2008, in which the core concept of the remit is media service, rather than the previous difference between main and side tasks. The remit is confined to electronic services (i.e. no printed matter), which are required to be a mix of information, education, culture and entertainment. Merchandising, e-commerce, travel agency services, web shops, the exploitation of television guides and so on are all considered commercial services. A register of commercial activities is also to be published by the Media Authority (EC, 2010: §216–18). The Dutch government agreed, and had already included this in the 2008 Media Act to evaluate the public broadcasters strategy plans. The latter must be submitted every five years, describing public broadcasters' intentions for the coming five years.

In a specific part of the strategy plans, the public broadcasters will – and this is a new measure – explain which new offers they want to launch within their overall strategy. Subsequently, the public value and market impact of these offers is assessed. The first step in the relevant procedure is the description of the new offers, as well as similar market offers, by the public broadcasters. On this basis, the Media Authority and the Council for Culture will formulate advices to the Ministry for Media. The Minister of Media takes a provisional decision on the basis of these advices and the public broadcasters' proposals. This draft decision is published, after which third parties are invited to provide comments heard at public or bilateral meetings. Comments have to be submitted within six weeks of the publication of the draft decision. The Minister can, but is not obliged to, consult experts. The Minister will then publish a final decision, carefully balancing the added value of the service against its possible adverse market impact. A final decision, in which the Minister can approve, reject or amend the proposed service, is published and should adequately explain its conclusions. The entire procedure is not part of the Media act, but of the General Administrative Law Act (*Algemene Wet Bestuursrecht*) (EC, 2010: §219–22, §234–9). The choice for this option is precise as the *ex ante* procedure, which seems to be specific to PSB, is not subject to sector-specific legislation. The strategy is understandable, however, as it avoids difficult amendments to the Media Act (Figure 11.1).

Other commitments made by the Dutch government relate to pilot projects and proportionality mechanisms. With regard to the former, the Commission expects the Dutch government to limit the scope and duration of pilot projects as much as possible (EC, 2010: §240). This is a more rigid approach towards pilot projects when compared with the Flemish decision, in which there were no restrictions on pilot projects included (see previous chapter). With regard to the latter, the Dutch government most importantly committed to limit reserves accumulation to 10 per cent of annual public funding. When an exception to

Figure 11.1   Procedure for the *ex ante* assessment in the Netherlands (see also Bardoel and Vochteloo, 2010: slide 8)

this rule is made, the Dutch government will notify the Commission thereof (EC, 2010: § 232–3).

More political intervention?

Turning to the implementation of the commitments made, the analysis can be rather brief. Most commitments made by the Dutch government had already been implemented in the Media Act or awaited some amendments of the General Administrative Law Act. In that sense, the Dutch played 'safe', agreeing mainly to commitments that already implemented in legislation and the Commission assured itself of an effective implementation. Consequently, the implementation of the appropriate measures corresponds very well with the measures listed in the decision issued. In this, the Dutch case differs from the Flemish case (see previous chapter).

The *ex ante* evaluation of new media services

When looking at the *ex ante* evaluation of new media services, the Dutch government approved new services from the Dutch public broadcasters in 2009 and 2010. The approval of 2010 concerns the concession asked (and eventually granted) by the Dutch public broadcasters for the period 1 September 2010 to 31 December 2015. The concession plan was presented on 1 March 2010; the State Secretary approved the concession plan and the new services contained within it on 31 August 2010. The approval of these new services has been granted for one year only. Public broadcasters are compelled to evaluate their new offers within this 12-month period and require an additional approval should they wish to continue the delivery of these new services on a permanent basis. The services approved on 31 August 2010 concern on-demand services, the exploration of mobile platforms for service delivery and the development of 12 digital radio channels. In 2009, the Minister of Media approved two digital television channels (one focusing on children and parents, the other on politics and sports), 12 digital radio channels, narrowcasting services and various other services (see http://www.rijksoverheid.nl/onderwerpen/omroepen/publieke-omroep/nieuwe-diensten-publieke-omroep).

Private media companies opposed several of the public broadcasters' proposals for new media services. However, few of their claims were sustained by solid evidence. This shows the limits of *ex ante* evaluation to some extent. Its market impact assessment depends heavily on information provided by third parties. If the latter are not willing to share this information, fearing it might be disclosed, a fully fledged market impact assessment is difficult to perform. Nevertheless, most private television, radio and publishing companies filed an action against the decisions of the Dutch government to approve the new services. On 24 December 2010, the Court of Amsterdam decided that the decisions to accept the new services were unfounded. It agreed with the Dutch government and the public broadcasters that the new services were adequately defined and could rightfully be considered a part of the public service remit (Rechtbank van Amsterdam, 2010: §3.4, §3.9). This conclusion went against the private sector's allegations. The Court mainly criticised the market impact assessment that was part of the overall analysis. For the market impact assessment, the Dutch government limited itself to an interpretation of the analyses conducted by market parties. The Court said that such an approach was inadequate. The government itself should have data (possibly from an external expert) and not rely only on an interpretation of private sector data (Rechtbank van

Amsterdam, 2010: §3.15). The Dutch government did not agree with this appraisal and will file an action against the Court's decision.

Consultation on the public broadcasting system

Following *ex ante* evaluation of new media services, the Media act 2008 also foresaw a consultation on the future of the public broadcasting system every five years. Basically, The Dutch government compiled a list of questions on the future of the PSB system (ranging from priority tasks to impact on the market). In June 2010, the State Secretary for Media, Marja van Bijsterveldt-Vliegenthart (2010) presented the results of this consultation. These results will be used to update the regulation in place for PSB only in 2016, when the current Concession Act expires. As expected, the results of the consultation are very divergent.

Private broadcasters and publishers questioned an allegedly vague public service remit, asking for a clearer definition of priorities and more adequate control, while respecting the independence of the public broadcasters. The private media companies advocated against the commercial communication activities of the public broadcasters (e.g. NDP, 2010; NRC Handelsblad, 2010; Telegraaf Media Nederland, 2010). Moreover, several private broadcasters and publishers expressed doubts about the starting point of the consultation. Indeed, the questions from the former Dutch government seem to suggest that they wanted to retain the established polarised organisation of the system (e.g. Elsevier, 2010). Most private media companies rejected such an attachment, however, arguing for a more comprehensive re-evaluation of the system. Several suggestions were formulated in this respect. For example, MTVN advocated for a more restricted area of activities for the public broadcasters. The private broadcasters referred to a report from the Scientific Council for Government Policy (WRR, 2005), assigning a restricted set of functions (i.e. information, culture, arts and education) to the public broadcasters (MTVN, 2010; see also CLT-UFA, 2010). NDP (2010), the interest group of the publishing sector, suggested exploring the possibility of a more distributed model in which the current social organisations responsible for production compete with each other and private players, in reaction to tendering for public programmes.

The public broadcasters were far more positive, appreciating the government's basic attachment to the current PSB model in the Netherlands. They presented their views on their future in a joint reaction to the consultation, starting with a summary of their vision on the public broadcasting system. Essentially, a holistic and qualitative vision that would easily fit within most social democratic public service media literature (see Chapter 3) was presented. Following that, the public broadcasters answered the government's questions, most interestingly accepting some of the private sector's criticism, but also – and at the same time – declining it, arguing that the eventual aim of the private sector is to undermine the entire PSB (NPO, 2010).

Since the consultation has been launched and will now be concluded by a different government, it remains to be seen what the outcome of the entire exercise will be. For now, the impact on public broadcasting remains unclear – all the more so because the results of the consultation will be implemented in 2016 when the new Concession Act is agreed upon. This means that five years after stakeholders were asked to comment on PSB policy, some of their comments might actually be used in adapting regulation. Only in the case of 'urgency' can some earlier amendments of the Media Act or Concession Act be made.

So far, the most important observation to be made on the outcome of the Commission's state aid procedure is the extensive role the Ministry of Media plays in both the *ex ante* evaluation of new media services and the consultation on the future role of the public broadcaster. In other countries, the role of the Minister of Media is very much limited to eventually approval or rejection of the service (see previous chapters on Germany and Flanders), responding to the advice of an independent authority that controls the entire procedure. In the Netherlands, the procedure is organised by the Ministry and gives the wherewithal to the Minister to influence the programming of the public broadcaster. This is interesting in the light of the Dutch emphasis on programming freedom, and could give the impression of a politicisation of public broadcasters' editorial strategies (Bardoel and Vochteloo, 2010). It is too early to make far-reaching conclusions in this regard. However, it is certainly a trend to watch closely.

Provisional conclusions

The outcome on the Dutch state aid procedure was long awaited. In 2006, the Commission still aspired to close the German, Flemish, Irish, Dutch and Austrian procedures simultaneously. All procedures dealt with the definition of the remit (and new media services in particular), the ways in which public broadcasters were controlled and the proportionality of their funding. For all procedures, the Commission strived after the realisation of the same action points: the introduction of an *ex ante* evaluation, a clear demarcation between public and commercial services and transparency of funding mechanisms. In spite of all the parallels between the different state aid procedures, the German state aid procedure was closed in April 2007. The Flemish and Irish cases were closed in February 2008; Austria followed at the end of October 2009 and the Netherlands only in January 2010. Why did the procedure take so long, and does the outcome reflect the length of the procedure in any way?

Firstly, the procedure took so long because all stakeholders involved disagreed on very fundamental aspects of the state aid procedure. The Dutch government refused most substantive aspects of the Commission's questions. Contrary to the Flemish case, the latter was not inclined to settle for a limited number of commitments. The stakeholders involved added considerably to the pressures. Certainly at the end of the procedures, Dutch publishers kept insisting on more stringent regulation of the public broadcaster by the Commission.

When evaluating the eventual commitments made by the Dutch government, it is fair to say that these were substantial although, admittedly, the commitments were less numerous than the commitments made by the German Länder (see Chapter 9). Nevertheless, the numerous changes in the public service remit in the Media Act, the introduction of an *ex ante* evaluation for new media services and the five-yearly consultation on the future of the public broadcasting system are far from 'easy' promises for the Dutch government. It is less clear whether all commitments made have fostered a policy environment that is more supportive of a public service media project.

On the positive side, the abolition of the distinction between core tasks (i.e. traditional radio and television) and side activities (i.e. new media activities) can be considered a step in the right direction. In the new Media Act, services have to fit the public service remit, referring to core public values rather than platforms. Such an approach is technology neutral and is better suited to ensuring that all services delivered by public broadcasters actually meet some pre-set standards. These are, in the eyes of the private sector, still too vaguely defined. However, the Media Act specifies a number of public objectives such as universality, pluralism, quality, diversity and so on. One might indeed argue for more elaboration. This could be the consequence of the consultation on the future of the public broadcaster. Moreover, more elaboration can be found in the Concession Acts, which are more specific public management contracts between the Dutch government and the public broadcasters (represented in this by NPO, *cf. supra*). Furthermore, at the level of transparency, the involvement of more stakeholders in the debates on PSB is also a positive evolution. The complex maze of public broadcasters is more closely watched and rationalised. Even if private broadcasters and publishers are the most vigilant of watchdogs, a review of structures that stem from a period in which polarisation was the dominant way of organising society indeed seems necessary.

On the negative side, it is regrettable that the Ministry of Media holds a major responsibility for both the *ex ante* evaluation of new media services and the five-yearly consultation on the future of the public broadcasting system. Politics are subject to electoral processes; they tend to shift very easily and could, hence, jeopardise the stability on which public broadcasting systems thrive. Also, the possibility of more dependence on politics is somewhat frightening. In that regard, the implementation of these instruments needs to be closely watched. Related to this, it is noteworthy that the Commission's state aid procedure might have created the impression of 'Europe' changing certain aspects of PSB policy – herein responding to private sector interests. However, the subsequent government changes in the Netherlands have affected public broadcasting policies more substantially. Political elites have appeared to be rather opportunist when discussing the future of the PSB system. In that sense, it might be advisable in the Dutch context to consider more seriously Europe's plea for more independent regulation and more objective parameters to measure public broadcasters' performance.

12
Conclusion

Contrary to dominant beliefs, the Commission's policies do not provide evidence of a master plan against public service broadcasting (PSB). State aid control has to some extent contributed to the furthering of good governance principles and could contribute further to the ongoing transfer from PSB to public service media policies. This is a good thing as it is certain that PSB will not survive in the twenty-first century unless 'it fundamentally transforms itself' (Jakubowicz, 2007a, p. 44).

Evaluation of the Commission's policies

Tectonic plates moving in opposite directions

Buendia Sierra (2006, p. 543) argues that the application of the state aid rules in public service sectors is difficult. When public objectives and internal market objectives meet, he speaks of 'tectonic plates' moving in opposite directions. Other scholars (e.g. Bardoel and Vochteloo, 2008; Moe, 2008a) echo his observation, maintaining that competition goals and public broadcasting objectives are opposites.

One cannot deny that public broadcasting is an exception within the framework of competition policy. Its funding has to be legitimised as an acceptable market distortion. Public interest objectives are taken into account in the application of the competition rules. They are not the driver of competition policy, however. There is thus an asymmetric treatment of public interest and competition objectives. The Commission also has no strong legal basis to pursue public interest objectives. In fact, Member States (MS) do not want the Commission to meddle with cultural and public policies. Subsidiarity is one of the most important concepts used in state aid control of public broadcasters, which at times gives the impression that not so much the contents of state aid control, but rather its executor is found problematic by countries and scholars alike. Without doing an injustice to the importance of the division of competencies, the Commission's policies should be evaluated more on their substance.

In spite of the substantial difficulties when applying state aid rules to the funding of public broadcasters, the tectonic plates of Buendia Sierra (2006) do not always move in opposite directions. Indeed, there is regular seismic movement, but these do not result in constant eruptions. The European treaty embraces the balancing act that has to be made when applying mainstream competition rules to public sectors (supposedly) near and dear to the heart of MS. The fact that there is a special regime for public services makes clear that their importance is recognised.

The Amsterdam Protocol is the most obvious example of how the balance between different objectives is established. Pushed by MS, the Amsterdam Protocol stresses the link between public broadcasting and European democratic societies. It thus recognises the importance of PSB from a social–democratic, and not from a market failure, perspective. No other institution has such a special status in the Treaty. Some public broadcast representatives see the Amsterdam Protocol only as the sole attempt of national governments to curb Commission intervention. However, the Protocol is about more than competencies. It is a truly exceptional part of the Treaty in which a political choice for public values, having to be balanced against economic objectives, is made. In so doing, the Protocol is exemplary for the complex processes and multiple institutions that, together, are the EU.

Finally, seismic movement is manageable too because stakeholders have succeeded in adapting their approaches. In the 1990s, some Commission officials took a rather aggressive stance towards entertainment and sports. In both the 2001 and 2009 Broadcasting Communications, all genres were accepted as a part of public broadcasters' remit. Its approach on new media was also adapted and became more nuanced, focusing on MS' responsibilities to define the public service remit. In a similar vein, MS have also come to accept the application of the state aid rules. When updating their public broadcasting policy frameworks, they take these rules into account, knowing they have to comply with them.

The distinction between public and commercial services

In the application of the state aid provisions, the Commission has focused on a number of issues. The strict delineation between public and commercial services has been its absolute priority. In order to ensure fair competition and, related to this, prevent unnecessary market distortions, MS have to ensure that they fund public and not commercial services.

It is for that reason that the Commission has consistently emphasised the necessity of a clearly defined remit and an explicit entrustment of activities to the public broadcaster. Its concern about new media services should also be seen in the light of the Commission's concerns in regard to mission creep, that is commercial services becoming publicly funded. The Commission's demands for independent control and transparency of public broadcasters' organisation and funding are all tied to its quest for targeted state aid.

Trends in the Commission's state aid policy

Whereas the emphasis on a clear demarcation between public and commercial services is a constant factor in the Commission's policies, some changes and trends can also be discerned.

Firstly, the Commission's involvement with public broadcasting has evolved from a political to a more legalistic approach. After stalling decision taking in the 1990s, the General Court forced the Commission to take action on the issue of PSB. As a consequence, a more legalistic approach gradually emerged. This strengthened the position of the Commission and also enhanced legal certainty. The legal parameters of the procedure do not prevent state aid cases in the area of PSB from staying primarily politically determined. Most interviewees, except for the representatives of the Commission, admitted that the state aid and public broadcasting 'story' remains highly political.

Secondly, to some extent Commission intervention has also resulted in a harmonisation of MS' public broadcasting policies. Gromnicka's (2005) more general observation that MS are pressured to transpose European principles into national legislation concerning services of general economic interest (SGEI) is validated. The Commission has formulated a number of common principles (e.g. transparency, a clear definition, the *ex ante* test for new services) that are taken over by most MS. Does this superficial harmonisation automatically mean that the Commission tries to impose a 'one size fits all' approach on MS, as is feared by the latter and most representatives of public broadcasters? Not at all. The claim of harmonisation should not be taken too far. Several examples illustrate how the historical, social, cultural, economic and political embeddedness of public broadcasting policy is persistent even when the Commission intervenes. The case studies of the German, Flemish and Dutch implementation of appropriate measures show that, for example, the *ex ante* evaluations in Germany, Flanders and the Netherlands differ significantly at the levels of means, procedures, services covered and stakeholder involvement.

Thirdly, there is an evolution towards a more proactive intervention with MS' public broadcasting regimes. In the 1990s, the Commission attempted to refrain from decision taking. After the adoption of the 2001 Broadcasting Communication, the hesitant approach of the Commission gradually disappeared. The post-2001 decisions provide evidence of a vision on PSB.

A fourth trend concerns the evolution towards a more economic approach. More specifically, the demands for a market impact assessment and involvement of third parties in *ex ante* evaluations is a very concrete example of the way in which PSB is approached from an economic angle by the Commission. Although a market impact assessment in itself not a bad idea and one can only argue for third party (when not exclusively private sector) involvement, it should also be recognised that the Commission's own market assessments are at best fragmentary and face considerable empirical problems.

Fifthly, the Commission has come to accept PSB as a holistic project. In that regard, the more active stance of the Commission on state aid to public broadcasting should not be equated with a more negative stance on the issue. On the contrary, the Commission has never recognised the holistic character of PSB more explicitly than it does today. In the 1990s it took few decisions, yet its stance was more extreme as certain genres and forms of funding were not found permissible. In addition, some decisions at the beginning of the twenty-first century held that information society services were not part of the public service remit. The Commission does not uphold such an approach any more. It's more recent decision practice – and also the 2009 Broadcasting Communication, in line with the Amsterdam Protocol – accept a holistic public broadcasting system.

Finally, the Commission is increasingly succesful in striking a balance between the need for coherence and a case-specific approach. It is vital that, precisely because of the diverging broadcasting regimes in the specific MS and the latter's extensive competences to organise a PSB system, the increasingly coherent approach of state aid cases is not taken too far. During the first ten years of state aid intervention in this area, MS, public broadcasters and private media companies did not know what to expect from state aid policy. Gradually, an approach materialised. A clearly defined remit, an official entrustment and proportionality were put forward as the criteria on the basis of which state aid cases were to be assessed. Yet, these criteria leave considerable room for a case-by-case implementation (as is shown in the chapters on Germany, Flanders and the Netherlands) and, as such, ensure that one does not strive for coherence for the sake of it. A case-by-case approach is absolutely necessary taking into account that, for example, larger and smaller MS vary considerably when it comes to PSB policy. Hence, one should continue to strive for a balance between legal certainty on the one hand and a case-by-case approach on the other hand.

Marginalisation of public service broadcasting

When looking at the intentions of the Commission in applying the state aid rules and the eventual outcome of state aid procedures, is there indeed any evidence of a marginalisation of public broadcasters? Is the Commission pushing public broadcasters from the mainstream into the margin, as suggested by Bardoel and Vochteloo (2008)?

European scepticism about public service media

The discourse of the Commission indeed exemplifies scepticism about a public service media project. State aid is not considered a 'normal' situation. Perhaps paradoxically, PSB policies are considered the cornerstones of MS' media policies. In that sense, they are 'normal'. The idea that the funding of public broadcasters is not normal is reinforced by the European liberalisation policies in the audiovisual sector. The Television without Frontiers (TWF) directive (1989) and its successor the Audiovisual Media Services (AVMS) Directive (2007) strove for the creation of an internal market in broadcasting. Most forms of government intervention go against this internal market project. Certainly for new media services, this claim can be made as the AVMS directive foresees a lighter regulatory regime for new media services, assuming the market is functioning optimally here. This shows there is a much more cautious approach towards government intervention when it concerns new media services. Consequently, it would make little sense for Director General (DG) Competition to defend government intervention in the area of new media services when a European, sector-specific, directive finds intrusive regulation less necessary in this area.

Not so much scepticism after all?

Several factors, often neglected in other contributions on state aid and public broadcasting, explain for the Commission's scepticism with regard to new media services. Firstly, the Commission faced considerable difficulties in developing an approach towards new media services. Often, it took over fragments of MS' own policies. As the latter have largely failed to develop sustainable public service media policies, the sometimes flawed approach of the Commission is understandable.

Moreover, the Commission's approach to public broadcasting has never been static. The Commission has gradually adapted its approach – certainly when dealing with the definition of public broadcasters' remit – in order to find the equilibrium between enforcing competition rules and respecting MS' competencies in the area of public broadcasting.

Furthermore, the majority of state aid decisions do not deal with new media services. In other procedures, the Commission has dealt with tax exemptions, loan restructuring measures, the launch of regional channels and so on. Hence, it is erroneous to claim that there has been a full-frontal, European attack on public service media.

Finally, the Commission has rarely questioned a holistic, public service media project. In 1998, the Commission indeed wrote a draft paper on the application of the state aid rules in the area of PSB, arguing that sports and entertainment could be catered for by the private sector. However, this initiative by some individuals was immediately retracted by former Commissioner Karel Van Miert. Since then, the Commission accepts all genres as part of the public service remit, assigning definition competencies to the MS. With regard to new media, a somewhat sceptical attitude indeed prevailed, but also on that topic, the Commission increasingly focuses on MS' competencies to ensure there is an adequate definition of the public service remit. The General Court has backed the Commission's acceptance of a holistic PSB system, arguing that it is part of European traditions, acknowledged by the Amsterdam Protocol and should not be limited to those offers for which the private sector does not cater. In that sense, a market failure approach is rejected on a legal basis (CFI, 2008a, 2008b). Consequently, Michalis' (2010, p. 40) assessment that the Commission sees market failure as a determining criterion is inaccurate, as the Commission's own policies do not provide evidence thereof. In fact, looking at the offer made to Western European public broadcasters today, we observe that it is still varied, covering multiple genres and platforms. Moreover, a marginalisation approach would be incompatible with the General Court's vision in this matter.

Enhancement of a public service media project

The hypothesis followed in this book is that state aid control could in fact foster the development of a sustainable public service media project. This project was defined, referring to six criteria:

1. Cross-media: public broadcasters' offers are determined in a technology-neutral way.
2. Core: public broadcasters' services are part of the remit in so far they meet clearly spelled-out public service objectives, not because they are linked to traditional radio or television programmes.
3. Cost: public broadcasters are funded in a sustainable way; there is no over-reliance on commercial revenues.
4. Clarity: public broadcasters' financial and structural organisation is transparent; accountability mechanisms are in place.
5. Control and command: a balance is struck between the adequate and coherent control of public broadcasters on the one hand and the need for independence of programming strategies on the other.
6. Checks and balances: public broadcasters do their job, while not preventing others from doing theirs; policies aim to ensure fair competition.

Was it possible to validate the hypothesis and observe a strengthening of all these criteria? Decision practice (see Chapter 8) indeed shows that good governance principles at the level of clarity, control and command, and checks and balances were stimulated. The requirement of having a separation of accounts was a major improvement in many public broadcasters' organisation. Nevertheless, there is no straightforward answer to the question raised above. The case studies on Germany, Flanders and the Netherlands resulted in diverging results, with one case study (Germany) providing ample evidence of the strengthening of a holistic public service media project, whereas the case studies on Flanders and the Netherlands gave somewhat different results. In Flanders, government resisted too many changes as a consequence of Commission intervention. Admittedly, the multi-stakeholder negotiation of public broadcasting policies was strengthened. The *ex ante* evaluation for new media services exists only in theory, however. In the Netherlands, many changes were introduced; the remit was indeed clarified, but of several other changes, the eventual impact remains to be seen. In particular, the more extensive control possibilities for government are worrying and not in line with the Commission's demand for more independent control.

Essentially, the Commission at least forced MS and other actors to reflect on the evolution from PSB to public service media. This is of intrinsic value for the project. Public service media is thus a work in progress, determined by the Commission. There is no denial of the significant impact of Commission policies on PSB possible. Nevertheless, one should bear in mind that the diverging results of the case studies convincingly illustrate that the eventual outcome of state aid procedures depends on a number of external factors that are even more important than the Commission's intervention. MS' own domestic preferences, political power balances, the lobbying strength of private media companies, the relation between a national government and its public broadcasters and so on are all factors that have an affect on the outcome of a European state aid procedure.

For that reason, scholars should continue closely to watch national developments as MS, in spite of their grudge against the Commission, are in the driver's seat when defining the contours of public broadcasters' activities. After all, one should not forget that MS are those putting pressure on many public broadcasters' finances. The Commission has rarely questioned the level of funding of public broadcasters. The Commission's state aid procedures have introduced certain elements in MS' public broadcasting policies, and it remains to be seen whether these seeds will materialise in the future.

Some recommendations for public service media and policy in Europe

On the basis of the findings in this book, five sets of recommendations can be presented. Firstly, MS and other stakeholders have to live with the idea of European intervention in the area of PSB. Although resistance can be necessary during negotiations, one should realise that public broadcasting and competition goals are not always in opposition. A number of competition principles have furthered good governance practices in public broadcasting. MS should embrace the opportunities of state aid control in order to review and adapt their public broadcasting policies if necessary. Now, they principally overlook all relevant aspects of the Commission's suggestions, opposing the latter's intervention *per se*. It is counterproductive that state aid procedures are so overly focused on subsidiarity questions. As Arino (2004, p. 125) points out, 'The distribution of competences in the media arena should not be a power struggle between MS to avoid interference by the Community. It is not an "either or" question. On the contrary, action by the EU should support and supplement MS and vice versa'. Related to this, private companies can be criticised for instrumentalising state aid policy for their own benefit. Obviously, some circumstances justified private broadcasters' decision to take matters to 'Brussels'. The first forum for discussion should remain the MS, however. The Commission has, itself, emphasised this claming that it does want to be involved in the micro-management of public broadcasting regimes (Repa, 2009).

Secondly, MS should invest more in multi-stakeholder-based policies. MS have a responsibility towards shaping transparent consultation and not conflict-based policy-making environments. Public service media policy is no longer the consequence of a largely bilateral negotiation between politicians and public broadcasters. Increasingly, other stakeholders have to be and are becoming involved. The trend towards multi-stakeholder-based policies has certainly been reinforced by the Commission, emphasising the right of third parties to be consulted on important policy changes. However, the category of third parties should not be limited solely to private media companies. Far too often citizen representation groups, the cultural sector, unions and so on are not sufficiently included in debates on PSB.

Thirdly, there is a need for more evidence-based policies. These require more targeted research, ordered with independent academic institutions. These should investigate the scope of public service media, the services required to realise public interest objectives and indicate which activities of public broadcasters are indispensable in contributing to a democratic society. Such research efforts will strengthen the basis of public service media and illustrate why public service media are an important project in a media ecology where abundance has become a buzzword. Not only public broadcasters' performance, but also policy-makers' performance, should be measured. There is a need to evaluate whether policies are delivering. If certain instruments, such as *ex ante* tests, are deficient in some respects, deficiencies have to be restored.

Fourthly, and related to the former recommendation, policies need to become more rational. Public service media policies lack coherence. Policy makers need to decide whether they want a public service media project or whether they want to adhere to a PSB project. If they opt for a public service media project, they have to decide on the goals such a project serves and the services that fit within the project. There needs to be a link between the two. Finally, there is a future for public service media. This needs to be debated and the Commission, sometimes staying within and sometimes going beyond its competencies, has contributed to the necessary debates. Public broadcasting regimes are far from perfect; yet, setting out from the idea that European welfare states are still prepared to invest in the realisation of public values irrespective of profit motives, PSB – and, by extension public service media – is a policy project worth continuing in so far as such a project is holistic in nature, based on evidence, supported by rational accountability mechanisms and made possible through adequate funding mechanisms that do not unnecessarily harm markets. A pluralistic media ecology requires both public and private players.

References

ACT, EPC and AER. (2004). Safeguarding the future of the European audiovisual market: a white paper on the financing and regulation of publicly funded broadcasters.

Agence Europe. (1998). Karel Van Miert drops plans for guidelines on aid to public televisions but will directly attack aid that seems irregular.

Anestis, P. and Drakakis, S. (2006). State aid policy and services of general economic interest: shedding some light on a controversial area. *The European Antitrust Review*, 60–6.

Antoniadis, A. (2006). The financing of public service broadcasting. In M. S. Rydelski (ed.), *The EC State aid regime: distortive effects of State aid on competition and trade* (pp. 591–630). London: Cameron May.

Antoniadis, A. (2008). The financing of public service broadcasting. In M. Mederer, N. Pesaresi and M. Van Hoof (eds), *State aid* (pp. 1285–349). Brussels: Claeys & Casteels.

Appelman, M., van Dijk, M., Nahuis, R., Vollaard, B. and Waagmeester, D. (2005). Een economisch vooronderzoek ten behoeve van het rapport van de WRR over de media. In W. B. H. J. van de Donk, D. W. J. Broeders and F. J. P. M. Hoefnagel (eds), *Trends in het medialandschap: vier verkenningen* (pp. 11–66). Amsterdam: Amsterdam University Press.

Arhold, C. (2007). The case law of the European Court of Justice and the Court of First Instance on State aids in 2006/2007. *European State aid Law Quarterly*, 2, 151–214.

Arino, M. (2004). Media regulation and the knowledge economy – competition law and pluralism in European digital broadcasting: addressing the gaps. *Communications and Strategies*, 54, 97–130.

Armstrong, M. and Weeds, H. (2007). Public service broadcasting in the digital world. In P. Seabright and J. von Hagen (eds), *The economic regulation of broadcasting markets: evolving technology and challenges for policy* (pp. 81–149). Cambridge: Cambridge University Press.

Aslama, M. (2010). Re-thinking PSM audiences. Diversity of participation for strategic considerations. In G. Ferrell Lowe (ed.), *The public in public service media* (pp. 87–100). Gothenburg: Nordicom.

Aslama, M. and Syvertsen, T. (2006). Policies of reduction or renewal? European public service broadcasting in the new media era. In U. Carlsson (ed.), *Radio, TV and Internet in the Nordic countries. Meeting the challenges of new media technology* (pp. 29–41). Gothenburg: Nordicom.

Bakker, P. and Vasterman, P. (2007). The Dutch Media Landscape. In G. Terzis (ed.), *European media governance: national and regional dimensions* (pp. 145–56). Bristol: Intellect Books.

Ballon, P., Donders, K., Evens, T., Bannier, S. and Rucic, H. (2010). *Naar een Ecosysteem-Model voor Onderzoek en Innovatie rond Audiovisuele Consumptie in Vlaanderen. Deliverable I: Scopebepaling, omgevingsanalyse en archetypische modellen voor innovatie in Vlaanderen.* Brussels/Ghent: IBBT-SMIT, VUB/MICT, UGent.

Barber, B. R. and Thorburn, D. (2004). Which technology and which democracy? In H. Jenkins (ed.), *Democracy and new media* (pp. 33–48). Cambridge: MIT Press.

Bardoel, J. (2003). Back to the public? Assessing public broadcasting in the Netherlands. *Javnost The Public*, 10 (3), 81–96.

Bardoel, J. (2008). Dutch television: between community and commodity. In D. Ward (ed.), *Television and public policy: change and continuity in an era of global liberalization* (pp. 199–222). New York: Lawrence Erlbaum.

Bardoel, J. (2010). Are we being served? Reflections on public service broadcasting in transition. Presentation at the IBBT-SMIT Lecture Series, Brussels.

Bardoel, J. and D'Haenens, L. D. (2004). Media responsibilty and accountability: new conceptualizations and practices. *Communications: the European Journal of Communication Research*, 29 (1), 5–25.

Bardoel, J. and D'Haenens, L. D. (2008). Reinventing public service broadcasting in Europe: prospects, promises and problems. *Media, Culture and Society*, 30 (3), 337–55.

Bardoel, J. and Ferrell Lowe, G. (2007). From public service broadcasting to public service media. The core challenge. In G. Ferrell Lowe and J. Bardoel (eds), *From public service broadcasting to public service media* (pp. 9–28). Gothenburg: Nordicom.

Bardoel, J. and Vochteloo, M. (2008). *Squeezing European public service broadcasting from the mainstream to the margin? EU State aid policy vis à vis public service broadcasting.* Paper presented at the 2nd ECREA Conference, Barcelona.

Bardoel, J. and Vochteloo, M. (2009). *Media policy between Europe and the nation-state: the case of the EU Broadcast Communication 2009.* Paper presented at the ECREA-CLP Workshop on 'new direction for communication policy research', Zürich.

Bardoel, J. and Vochteloo, M. (2010). *Conditional access for PSB to new media platforms: EU State aid policy vs. PSB: the Dutch case.* Paper presented at the Conference 'Exporting the Public Value Test', Brussels.

Barker, C. (1997). *Global television: an introduction.* Oxford: Blackwell Publishers.

Barnett, S. (2002). Which end of the telescope? From market failure to cultural value. In J. Cowling and D. Tambini (eds), *From public service broadcasting to public service communications* (pp. 34–45). London: IPPR.

Barnett, S. (2006). *Public service broadcasting: a manifesto for survival in the multimedia age (a case study of the BBC's new charter).* Paper presented at the RIPE Conference, Amsterdam.

Barnett, S. (2007). Can the public service broadcaster survive? Renewal and compromise in the new BBC Charter. In G. Ferrell Lowe and J. Bardoel (eds), *From public service broadcasting to public service media* (pp. 87–104). Gothenburg: Nordicom.

Barnett, S. and Docherty, D. (1991). Purity or pragmatism: principles and practice of public service broadcasting. In J. G. Blumler and T. J. Nossiter (eds), *Broadcasting finance in transition: a comparative handbook* (pp. 23–37). New York: Oxford University Press.

Bartosch, A. (2002). State aid. In C. Koenig, A. Bartosch and J. D. Braun (eds), *EC competition and telecommunications law* (pp. 161–224). The Hague: Kluwer Law International.

Barwise, P. (2002). What are the real threats to public service broadcasting. In J. Cowling and D. Tambini (eds), *From public service broadcasting to public service communications* (pp. 16–33). London: IPPR.

Bavasso, A. (2002). Public service broadcasting and State aid rules: between a rock and a hard place. *European Law Review*, 27, 340–350.

Bavasso, A. (2003). *Communications in EU Antitrust law: market power and public interest*. The Hague: Kluwer Law International.

Bavasso, A. (2006). Chapter 17: Broadcasting. In L. Hancher, T. Ottervanger and P. J. Slot (eds), *EC State aids* (pp. 420–38). London: Thomson Sweet and Maxwell.

BBC Trust (2009). Local video: Public Value Test final conclusions.

Biggam, R. (2009). Public broadcasting and State aid in the new media environment. In C. Pauwels, H. Kalimo, K. Donders and B. Van Rompuy (eds), *Rethinking European media and communications Policy* (pp. 165–87). Brussels: VUB Press.

Blauberger, M. (2008). From negative to positive integration? European State aid control through soft and hard law. Cologne: Max-Planck-Institut für Gesellschaftsforschung.

Blumler, J. G. (1991). *Broadcasting finance in transition: a comparative handbook*. Oxford: Oxford University Press.

Blumler, J. G. (1993). The British approach to public service broadcasting: from confidence to uncertainty. In R. K. Avery (ed.), *Public service broadcasting in a multichannel environment* (pp. 1–28). New York: Longman.

Bonte, L. (22 November 2005). Schaf de openbare omroep af, *De Standaard*. Retrieved from http://www.standaard.be/Artikel/Detail.aspx?artikelId=GQMK JPJT&word=Schaf+de+openbare+omroep+af.

Brants, K. (2004). The Netherlands. In M. Kelly, G. Mazzoleni and D. McQuail (eds), *The media in Europe: the Euromedia handbook* (pp. 145–56). London: Sage Publications.

Brevini, B. (2010). Towards PSB 2.0? Applying the PSB ethos to online media in Europe: a comparative study of PSBs' internet policies in Spain, Italy and Britain. *European Journal of Communication*, 25 (4), 348–65.

Broeders, D., Huysmans, F. and Verhoeven, I. (2006). Setting the scene: ontwikkelingen in het medialandschap. *Tijdschrift voor Communicatiewetenschap*, 34 (2), 116–32.

Brown, A. (1996). Economics, public service broadcasting, and social values. *The Journal of Media Economic*, 9 (1), 3–15.

Buckley, S., Duer, K., Mendel, T., Monroe, P. and Raboy, M. (2008). *Broadcasting, voice and accountability: a public interest approach to policy, law and regulation*. Michigan: University of Michigan Press.

Buendia Sierra, J. L. (2006). An analysis of Article 86(2) EC. In M. S. Rydelski (ed.), *The EC state aid regime: distortive effects of state aid on competition and trade* (pp. 541–74). London: Cameron May.

Burda, H. (2007, 22 November). Was ist Grundversorgung?, *Die Zeit*. Retrieved from http://www.zeit.de/2007/48/Forum-Burda

Burgelman, J.-C. (1990). *Omroep en politiek in België. Het Belgisch audio-visuele bestel als inzet en resultante van de naoorlogse partijpolitieke machtsstrategieën (1940–1960).* Brussels: BRT.

Burgelman, J.-C. and Perceval, P. (1995). Belgium: the politics of public broadcasting. In M. Raboy (ed.), *Public broadcasting for the 21st century* (pp. 87–102). London: John Libbey Publishing.

Cabrera Blazquez, F. J. (2000). Commission: approval of the EBU-Eurovision system. *IRIS Legal Observations*, 6 (4/5).

Castells, M. (1996). *The rise of the network society.* Oxford: Blackwell Publishers.

CFI (Court of First Instance) (1998). Telecinco v Commission.

CFI (1999). TF1 v Commission.

CFI (2000). SIC v Commission.

CFI (2008a). SIC v Commission.

CFI (2008b). TV2/Danmark and others v Commission.

Chakravarty, P. and Sarikakis, K. (2006). *Media policy and globalisation.* Edinburgh: Edinburgh University Press.

CLT-UFA. (2010). Reactie op de toekomstigverkenning landelijke publieke omroep.

Coase, R. H. (1947). The origin of the monopoly of broadcasting in Great Britain. *Economica*, 14(55), 189–210.

CoE (Council of Europe). (1994). Resolution no.1 on the future of public service broadcasting. CoE, Strassbourg.

CoE (2009). Recommendation 1878(2009) on the funding of public service broadcasting. CoE, Strassbourg.

Coe, R., Priest, J. and Hutton, D. (2002). Evaluation of BBC Digital Curriculum: summary of findings. Durham: University of Durham, Educational Evaluation Group.

Cole, M. D. (2009). Rechtsgrundlagen der elektronischer Medien. In D. Dörr, J. Kreile and M. D. Cole (eds), *Handbuch Medienrecht: Recht der elektronischen Massenmedien* (pp. 83–104). Frankfurt am Main: Verlag Recht und Wirtschaft.

Coleman, S. (2002). From service to commons: re-inventing a space for public communication. In J. Cowling and D. Tambini (eds), *From public service broadcasting to public service communications* (pp. 88–98). London: IPPR.

Collins, R. (1994). Unity in diversity? The European single market in broadcasting and the audiovisual, 1982–92. *Journal of Common Market Studies*, 32(1), 89–102.

Collins, R. (1998). From satellite to single market. London: Routledge.

Collins, R. (2002). Public service broadcasting: too much of a good thing? In J. Cowling and D. Tambini (eds), *From public service broadcasting to public service communications* (pp. 131–51). London: IPPR.

Collins, R. (2007). The BBC and 'public value'. *Medien und Kommunikationswissenschaft*, 65 (2), 164–84.

Collins, R. (2010). *Exporting the Public Value Test: assessing EU MS' evaluation of public broadcasters' new media services.* Paper presented at the Conference 'Exporting the Public Value Test', Brussels.

Collins, R., Finn, A., McFayden, S. and Hoskin, C. (2001). Public service broadcasting beyond 2000: is there a future for public service broadcasting? *Canadian Journal of Communication*, 26(1).

Coppens, T. (2003). Digital public broadcasting in Flanders: walking the tightrope. *Telematics and Informatics*, 20, 143–59.

Coppens, T. and Saeys, F. (2006). Enforcing performance: new approaches to govern public service broadcasting. *Media, Culture and Society*, 28 (2), 261–84.

Coppieters, S. (2003). The financing of public service broadcasting. In A. Biondi, P. Eeckhout and J. Flyn (eds), *The law of state aid in the EU* (pp. 265–79). Oxford: Oxford University Press.

Coppieters, S. (2010). *Ex ante test in the Flemish Community*. Paper presented at the Conference 'Exporting the Public Value Test', Brussels.

Craufurd-Smith, R. (2001). State support for public service broadcasting: the position under European Community Law. *Legal Issues of Economic Integration*, 38 (1), 3–22.

Crocioni, P. (2006). Can State aid policy become more economic friendly? *World Competition*, 29 (1), 89–108.

Croteau, D. R. and Hoynes, W. (2002). *Media/Society: industries, images and audiences*. London: Pine Forge Press.

Curran, J. (2008). Media diversity and democracy. In T. Gardam and D. Levy (eds), *The price of plurality* (pp. 103–9). Oxford: Reuters Institute for the Study of Journalism.

Curwen, P. (1999). Television without Frontiers: can culture be harmonized? *European Business Review*, 99 (6), 368–75.

Da Silva, F. (1995). Public service broadcasting in the European market place. In B. Groombridge and J. Hay (eds), *The price of choice: public service broadcasting in a European competitive market place* (pp. 38–43). London: John Libbey Publishing.

Dahlgren, P. (2001). Public service media, old and new: vitalizing a civic culture? *Canadian Journal of Communication*, 24 (4), 1–19.

De Bens, E. and Paulussen, S. (2005). Hoe anders is de VRT? De performantie van de Vlaamse publieke omroep. *Tijdschrift Communicatiewetenschap*, 33 (4), 365–386.

De Vinck, S. and Pauwels, C. (2008). Cultural diversity as the final outcome of EU policymaking in the audiovisual sector: a critical analysis. In H. Schneider and P. Van den Bossche (eds), *Protection of cultural diversity from a European and international perspective* (pp. 263–316). Antwerp/Oxford/Portland: Intersentia.

Debrett, M. (2007). *Reinventing public service television: from broadcasters to media content companies*. Paper presented at the ANZCA Conference, Melbourne.

Depypere, S. and Tigchelaar, N. (2004). The Commission's state aid policy on activities of public service broadcasters in neighbouring markets. *Competition Policy Newsletter*, (2), 19–22.

Dhoest, A. and Van den Bulck, H. (2003). Vijftig jaar openbare televisie in Vlaanderen: weldaad of verschrikking? *Tijdschrift voor Communicatiewetenschap*, 31(4), 279–97.

Dhoest, A. and Van den Bulck, H. (2007). Inleiding. In A. Dhoest and H. Van den Bulck (eds), *Publieke televisie in Vlaanderen: een geschiedenis* (pp. 3–22). Ghent: Academia Press.

Dhoest, A., Van den Bulck, H., Vandebosch, H. and Dierckx, M. (2010). *De publieke opdracht gewikt en gewogen*. Antwerp: Universiteit Antwerpen.

Donders, K. (2009). Staatssteun, Europese Commissie, TV/Danmark, publieke omroep, arrest Gerecht van Eerste Aanleg: krachtlijnen. *Auteurs en Media* (pp. 1–2), 135–8.

Donders, K. and Lamensch, M. (2010). The introduction of a 'tax-and-fund' system to subsidise public television in France: cultural revolution or legal swamp? *Journal of Media Law*, 2 (2), 227–44.

Donders, K., Loisen, J. and Pauwels, C. (2008). Het Europese staatssteunbeleid en de openbare omroep: welke antwoorden voor de VRT? Antwerp: Vlaams Steunpunt voor Buitenlands Beleid.

Donders, K. and Pauwels, C. (2008). Does EU policy challenge the digital future of public service broadcasting? An analysis of the Commission's State aid approach to digitization and the public service remit of public broadcasting organizations. *Convergence, The International Journal of Research into New Media Technologies*, 14 (3), 295–311.

Donders, K. and Pauwels, C. (2009). European State aid rules and the public service broadcasting remit in the digital age: analyzing a contentious part of European policy and integration. In I. Garcia-Blanco, S. Van Bauwel and B. Cammaerts (eds), *Media agoras: democracy, diversity and communication* (pp. 178–97). Cambridge: Cambridge Scholars Publishing.

Donders, K. and Pauwels, C. (2010a). The introduction of an ex ante evaluation for new media services: 'Europe' asks it or public broadcasters need it? *International Journal of Media and Cultural Politics*, 4 (2).

Donders, K. and Pauwels, C. (2010b). What if competition policy assists the transfer from public service broadcasting to public service media? An analysis of EU State aid control and its relevance for public broadcasting. In J. Gripsrud and H. Moe (eds), *The digital public sphere: challenges for media policy* (pp. 117–32). Gothenburg: Nordicom.

Donders, K. and Raats, T. (2011). *Analyzing national practices after European State aid control: are multistakeholder negotiations beneficial for public service broadcasting?* Paper presented at the IAMCR conference, Istanbul.

Donders, K., Raats, T., Walravens, N. and Moons, A. (2010). *De rol van de openbare omroep in Vlaanderen: stakeholderbevraging*. Brussels: IBBT-SMIT.

Donders, K., Van Rompuy, B. and Pauwels, C. (2007). *Concurrentie in het concurrentiebeleid? Op zoek naar coherentie in het Europese mededingingsbeleid voor de publieke omroep: een perspectief op de posities van de Europese Commissie en het Europees Hof van Justitie.* Paper presented at the Etmaal van de Communicatiewetenschappen, Antwerp.

Dony, M. (2005). Les compensations d'obligations de service public. In M. Dony and C. Smits (eds), *Aides d'état* (pp. 109–52). Brussels: Institut d'Etudes Européennes.

Dörr, D. (2009a). *Das Verfahren des Drei-Stufen Tests: Stellungnahme angefertigt im Auftrag des Verbandes Privater Rundfunk und Telemedien.* Mainz: Mainzer Medieninstituts.

Dörr, D. (2009b). Eine Chance: ARD und ZDF sollten den Drei-Stufen-Test ernst nehmen. In V. Lilienthal (ed.), *Professionalisierung der Medienaufsicht: Neue Aufgaben für Rundfunkräte – Die Gremiendebatte in epd medien* (pp. 161–7). Wiesbaden: VS Verlag.

Dörr, D. (2009c). Grundsätze der Medienregulierung. In D. Dörr, J. Kreile and M. D. Cole (eds), *Handbuch Medienrecht: Recht der elektronischen Massenmedien* (pp. 133–84). Frankfurt am Main: Verlag Recht und Wirtschaft.

Doyle, G. (2002a). *Media ownership: the economics and politics of convergence and concentration in the UK and European media.* London: Sage Publications.

Doyle, G. (2002b). *Understanding: media economics.* London: Sage Publications.

Doyle, G. (2007). Undermining media diversity: inaction on media concentrations and pluralism in the EU. *European Studies*, (24), 135–56.

Drijber, B. J. (1999). The revised television without frontiers directive: is it fit for the next century? *Common Market Law Review*, 36, 87–122.

Duff, A. (1997). *The Treaty of Amsterdam.* London: The Federal Trust.

Dyson, K. (1985). The politics of cable and satellite broadcasting: some West European comparisons. In R. Kuhn (ed.), *Broadcasting and politics in Western Europe* (pp. 152–71). London: Routledge.

Dyson, K. and Humphreys, P. (1988a). Regulatory change in Western Europe: from national cultural regulation to international economic statecraft. In K. Dyson and P. Humphreys (eds), *Broadcasting and new media policies in Western Europe* (pp. 92–160). London: Routledge.

Dyson, K. and Humphreys, P. (1988b). The context of new media politics in Western Europe. In K. Dyson and P. Humphreys (eds), *Broadcasting and new media policies in Western Europe* (pp. 1–61). London: Routledge.

EBU (2008). Response to the Commission's questionnaire on the revision of the Broadcasting Communication.

EC (European Commission) (1984). Green paper on television without frontiers: the establishment of a European single market for broadcasting, especially by satellite and cable.

EC (1997). Green paper on the convergence of the telecommunications, media and information technology sectors, and the implications for regulation: towards an information society approach.

EC (1998). Draft proposal guidelines on public service broadcasting (unpublished).

EC (1999a). Financing of 24-hour advertising-free news channels out of the licence fee by the BBC.

EC (1999b). Phoenix/Kinderkanal.

EC (2001). Communication on the application of State aid rules to public service broadcasting.

EC (2002a). BBC Licence fee.

EC (2002b). ZDF Medienpark.

EC (2003a). Ad hoc measures implemented by Portugal for RTP.

EC (2003b). BBC Digital Curriculum.

EC (2003c). Measures implemented by Italy for RAI.

EC (2003d). State aid implemented by France for France 2 and France 3.

EC (2004a). Measures implemented by Denmark for TV2/Danmark.

EC (2004b). Recapitalisation of TV2/Danmark.

EC (2005a). Article 17 letter: Staatliche Beihilfe: Die Finanzierung der öffentlich-rechtlichen Rundfunkanstalten.

EC (2005b). Ayuda estatal en favor del RTVE.

EC (2005c). Canone di abbonamento RAI.

EC (2005d). Chaîne française d'information internationale.

EC (2005e). Redevance radiodiffusion.

EC (2006a). Ad hoc financing of Dutch public service broadcasters.

EC (2006b). Artikel 17 brief: financiering van openbare omroep VRT.

EC (2006c). Compensation payments to public service broadcaster RTP.

EC (2006d). Financial support to restructure the accumulated debt of RTP.

EC (2007a). Financing of workforce reduction measures of RTVE.

EC (2007b). Licence fee funding of German public broadcasters ARD and ZDF.
EC (2008a). Aid to channel 4 linked to digital switchover.
EC (2008b). Annual funding of Flemish public broadcaster VRT.
EC (2008c). Review of the Commission from the Communication on the application of State aid rules to public service broadcasting: questionnaire.
EC (2008d). State financing of RTE and TG4.
EC (2009a). Communication on the application of the State aid rules to public service broadcasting.
EC (2009b). Financing of the Austrian public service broadcaster ORF.
EC (2009c). Subvention budgétaire pour France Télévisions.
EC (2010). Annnual funding of the Dutch public service broadcasters.
European Council (1989). Television without Frontiers Directive, 89/552/EEC.
European Council (2007). Audiovisual Media Services Directive, 2007/65.
ECJ (2001). PreussenElektra.
ECJ (2002). Stardust.
ECJ (2003). Altmark Trans GmbH and Regierungspräsidium Magdeburg vs. Nahverkehrsgesellschaft Altmark GmbH.
Elsevier. (2010). Reactie op de toekomstverkenning landelijke publieke omroep.
Elstein, D. (2008). How to fund public service content in the digital age. In T. Gardam and D. A. Levy (eds), *The price of plurality: choice, diversity and broadcasting institutions in the digital age* (pp. 86–90). Oxford: Reuters Institute for the Study of Journalism.
Elstein, D., Cox, D., Donoghue, B., Graham, D. and Metzger, G. (2004). *Beyond the charter: the BBC after 2006.* London: the Broadcasting Policy Group.
EP (European Parliament) (1996). The future of Public Service Television in a multi-channel digital age.
Erk, J. (2003). Federalism and mass media policy in Germany. *Regional and Federal Studies*, 13(2), 106–26.
Fairbairn, C. (2004). Commentary: why broadcasting is still special. In A. Peacock (ed.), *Public service broadcasting without the BBC?* (pp. 58–70). London: Institute for European Affairs.
Fechner, F. (2009). *Medienrecht* (10th edn). Tübingen: Mohr Siebeck.
Fell, J. (2005). *Broadcasting regulation in Germany.* Paper presented at the Communications Regulatory Authority, Sarajevo.
Ferrell Lowe, G. (2010). Beyond altruism. Why public participation in public service media matters. In G. Ferrell Lowe (ed.), *The public in public service media* (pp. 9–36). Gothenburg: Nordicom.
Flyvbjerg, B. (2006). Five misunderstandings about case-study research. *Qualitative Inquiry*, 12(2), 219–45.
Friederiszick, H. W., Röller, L.-H. and Verouden, V. (2005). European State Aid Control: an economic framework. Working paper, downloaded from https://www.esmt.org/fm/312/European_State_Aid_Control.pdf.
Galperin, H. (2004). *New television, old politics: the transition to digital TV in the United States and Britain.* Cambridge: Cambridge University Press.
Garnham, N. (1990). *Capitalism and communication: global culture and the economics of information.* London: Sage Publications.
Garnham, N. (1994). The broadcasting market and the future of the BBC. *The Political Quarterly*, 65 (1), 11–19.

Garnham, N. and Locksley, G. (1991). The economics of broadcasting. In J. G. Blumler and T. J. Nossiter (eds), *Broadcasting financing in transition: a comparative handbook* (pp. 8–22). New York: Oxford University Press.

General Court (2010). Netherlands and Nederlandse Omroep Stichting v Commission.

George, A. L. and Bennett, A. (2004). *Case studies and theory development in the social sciences.* Cambridge: MIT Press.

German Länder (2009). Begründung zum Zwölften Staatsvertrag zur Änderung rundfunkrechtlicher Staatsverträge (Zwölfter Rundfunkänderungsstaatsvertrag).

Gerring, J. (2007). *Case study research: principles and practices.* Cambridge: Cambridge University Press.

Gibson, O. (2003, 27 January). BBC Digital Curriculum judicial review dropped, *The Guardian.* Retrieved from http://www.guardian.co.uk/media/2003/jan/digitalmedia.bbc/print.

Goossens, C. (1998). *Radio en televisie in Vlaanderen: een geschiedenis.* Leuven: Davidsfonds.

Goossens, C. (2009). *De macht van de media: de markt is de baas.* Leuven: Uitgeverij van Halewijck.

Grade, M. (2005). The future of the BBC. In B. Franklin (ed.), *Television policy: the MacTaggart lectures* (pp. 157–64). Edinburgh: Edinburgh University Press.

Graham, D. (2005). It's the ecology, stupid!, In J. Heath and D. Levy (eds), *Can the market deliver? Funding public service television in the digital age?* (pp. 78–100). Eastleight: John Libbey Publishing.

Grespan, D. (2008a). Services of general economic interest. In W. Mederer, N. Pesaresi and M. Van Hoof (eds), *EU Competition Law: Volume IV – State aid* (pp. 1123–208). Brussels: Claeys & Casteels.

Grespan, D. (2008b). State aid procedures. In W. Mederer, N. Pesaresi and M. Van Hoof (eds), *EU Competition Law: Volume IV – State aid* (pp. 551–708). Brussels: Claeys & Casteels.

Grespan, D. and Bellodi, L. (2006). State aid. In G. L. Tosato and L. Bellodi (eds), *EU Competition Law – Volume I: Procedure anti-trust, merger, State aid* (pp. 327–430). Brussels: Claeys & Casteels.

Grespan, D., and Santamato, S. (2008). Favouring certain undertakings or the production of certain goods: advantage. In W. Mederer, N. Pesaresi and M. Van Hoof (eds), *EU Competition Law: Volume IV – State aid* (pp. 273–368). Brussels: Claeys & Casteels.

Gromnicka, E. (2005). Services of general economic interest in the State aids regime: proceduralisation of political choices. *European Public Law*, 11 (3), 429–61.

Hakenberg, W. and Erlbacher, F. (2003). State aid law in the European courts in 2001 and 2002. *ECLR* 24 (9), 431–48.

Hansen, M., Ysendyck, A. and Zühlke, S. (2004). The coming of age of EC State aid law: a review of the principal developments in 2002 and 2003. *ECLR* 25 (4), 202–33.

Harcourt, A. (2005). *The EU and the regulation of media markets.* Manchester: Manchester University Press.

Harrison, J. and Woods, L. M. (2007). *European broadcasting law and policy.* Cambridge: Cambridge University Press.

Harvey, S. (2010). *No jam tomorrow? State aid rules and the legitimacy of public service media: the closure of the BBC's digital curriculum project ('Jam')*. Paper presented at the RIPE Conference, London.

Herman, E. S. (1993). The externalities effects of commercial and public broadcasting. In K. Nordenstreng and H. I. Schiller (eds), *Beyond national sovereignty: International communication in the 1990s* (pp. 85–115). New York: Ablex Publishing Corporation.

Herold, A. (2009). The new Audiovisual Media Services Directive. In C. Pauwels, H. Kalimo, K. Donders and B. Van Rompuy (eds), *Rethinking European media and communications policy* (pp. 99–126). Brussels: VUBPress.

Herrgesell, O. and Kotsch, R. (1999, 19 January). Die ARD is nicht das Eichma: Gespräch mit ZDF-Intendant Stolte über Kollegen, Konkurrenten und die Konvergenz der Programme, *Berliner Zeitung*. Retrieved from http://www.berlinonline.de/berliner-zeitung/archiv/.bin/dump.fcgi/1999/0119/none/0002/index.html

Hesse, A. (2003). *Rundfunk Recht* (3th edn). Munich: Verlag Vahlen.

Hettich, P. (2008). Youtube to be regulated? The FCC sits tight, while European broadcast regulators make the grab for the Internet. *St. John's Law Review*, (82), 1447–508.

Het Koninkrijk der Nederlanden, 29 december 2008, «Mediawet 2008», Staatsblad 583.

Heuvelman, A. (1994). Communication science and broadcasting in the Netherlands. In D. French and M. Richards (eds), *Media education across Europe* (pp. 129–38). London: Routledge.

Hieronymi, R. (2004). *Key note speech*. Paper presented at the 'The key role of public service broadcasting in European society in the 21st century', Amsterdam.

Hilmens, M. (2002). Who we are, who we are not: battle of the global paradigms. In L. Parks and S. Kumar (eds), *Planet TV: a global television reader* (pp. 53–73). New York: New York University Press.

Hitchens, L. (2006). *Broadcasting pluralism and diversity: a comparative study of policy and regulation*. Oxford: Hart Publishing.

Hoffmann-Riem, W. (1991). Rundfunk als public service – ein überaltertes Konzept. In R. Weiss (ed.), *Aufgaben und Perspektiven des öffentlich-rechtlichen Fersnsehens* (pp. 21–47). Hamburg: Nomos Verlagsgesellschaft.

Hoffmann-Riem, W. (1995). Germany: the regulation of broadcasting. In M. Raboy (ed.), *Public broadcasting for the 21st century* (pp. 64–86). London: John Libbey Publishing.

Hoffmann-Riem, W. (2000). Thesen zur Regulierung der dualen Rundfunkordnung. *Medien & Kommunikationswissenschaft*, 48 (1), 7–19.

Hoffmann-Riem, W. (2006). Rundfunk als Public Service: anmerkungen zur Vergangenheit, Gegenwart und Zukunft öffentlich-rechtlichen Rundfunks. *Medien & Kommunikationswissenschaft*, 53 (1), 94–104.

Hollick, C. (1995). Keynote address: broadcasting regulation: choice and the public interest. In B. Groombridge and J. Hay (eds), *The price of choice: public service broadcasting in a competitive European market place* (pp. 5–20). London: John Libbey Publishing.

Holtz-Bacha, C. (2005). The EU, the MS and the future of public broadcasting. *Doxa*, (3), 231–7.

Holznagel, B. (2009). *The public service remit in Germany: clarification by the three-step-test?* Paper presented at the European Competition law and public service broadcasting, Budapest.

Holznagel, B., Dörr, D. and Hildebrand, D. (2008). *Elektronische Medien: Entwicklung und Regulierungsbedarf.* Munich: Verlag Franz Vahlen.

Hoskins, C., McFayden, S. and Finn, A. (2004). *Media economics: applying economics to new and traditional media.* London: Sage Publications.

Hughes, R. (1988). Satellite broadcasting: the regulatory issues in Europe. In R. Negrine (ed.), *Satellite broadcasting: the politics and implications of the new media* (pp. 49–74). London: Routledge.

Hulten, O. and Brants, K. (1992). Public service broadcasting: reactions to competition. In K. Siune and W. Truetzschler (eds), *Dynamics of media politics: broadcast and electronic media in Western Europe* (pp. 116–28). London: Sage Publications.

Humphreys, P. (1994). *Media and media policy in Germany: the press and broadcasting since 1945.* Oxford: Berg.

Humphreys, P. (1996). *Mass media and media policy in Western Europe.* Manchester: Manchester University Press.

Humphreys, P. (1999). Germany's dual broadcasting system: recipe for pluralism in the age of multi-channel broadcasting? *New German Critique*, (78), 23–52.

Humphreys, P. (2003). *EU policy on State aid to public service broadcasting.* Paper presented at the SMIT-CEAS-TELENOR Conference of the ICT and Media Sectors within the EU Policy Framework, Brussels.

Humphreys, P. (2007). The EU, communications liberalisation and the future of public service broadcasting. *European Studies*, 24(1), 91–112.

Humphreys, P. (2008a). *Digital convergence, European competition policy and the future of public service broadcasting: the UK and German cases.* Paper presented at the 58th Annual Conference of the ICA, Montreal.

Humphreys, P. (2008b). *Globalization, Digital Convergence, De-regulatory competition, Public service broadcasting and the 'Cultural Policy Toolkit'; the Cases of France and Germany.* Paper presented at the ECREA, Barcelona.

Ingves, M. (2010). *The ex ante test in the Nordic countries.* Paper presented at the Conference 'Exporting the Public Value Test', Brussels.

Iosifidis, P. (2008). Public television policies in Europe: the cases of France and Greece. *International Journal of Media and Cultural Politics*, 4 (3), 349–67.

Iosifidis, P. (2010). Pluralism and funding of public service broadcasting across Europe. In P. Iosifidis (ed.), *Reinventing public service communication: European broadcasters and beyond* (pp. 23–35). New York: Palgrave Macmillan.

Jakubowicz, K. (2003). Bringing public service broadcasting to account. In G. Ferrell Lowe and T. Hujanen (eds), *Broadcasting and convergence: new articulations of the public service remit* (pp. 147–66). Gothenburg: Nordicom.

Jakubowicz, K. (2004). A square peg in a round hole: the EU's policy on public service broadcasting. In I. Bondebjerg and P. Golding (eds), *European culture and the media* (pp. 277–301). Bristol: Intellect Books.

Jakubowicz, K. (2007a). Public service broadcasting in the 21st century. What chance for a new beginning? In G. Ferrell Lowe and J. Bardoel (eds), *From public service broadcasting to public service media* (pp. 29–50). Gothenburg: Nordicom.

Jakubowicz, K. (2007b). Public service broadcasting: a new beginning, or the beginning of the end. Retrieved from http://www.knowledgepolitics.org.uk knowledge politics.

Jakubowicz, K. (2010). PSB 3.0: Reinventing European PSB. In P. Iosifidis (ed.), *Reinventing public service communication: European broadcasters and beyond* (pp. 9–22). New York: Palgrave Macmillan.

Katsirea, I. (2008). *Public broadcasting and European law: a comparative examination of public service obligations in six MS.* New York: Wolters Kluwer International.

KEF. (2008). Zusatzinformation 3: Gesamtaufwand Online überschreitet Selbstbindungen der Anstalten.

Kleist, T. (2003). *Die Entwicklung des Gemeinschaftsrechts und ihre Auswirkung auf die Gebührenfinanzierung des öffentlich-rechtlichen Rundfunks.* Paper presented at the Muünchener Medientage, Munich.

Kleist, T. and Scheuer, A. (2006). Public Service Broadcasting and the EU. From Amsterdam to Altmark: the discussion on EU State Aid Regulation. In S. Nissen (ed.), *Making a difference: Public service broadcasting in the European media landscape* (pp. 163–82). Eastleigh: John Libbey Publishing.

Knox, F. (2005). The doctrine of consumers' sovereignty. *Review of Social Economy,* 63 (3), 383–94.

Koehler, L. (2008). *Current challenges for PSBs in Germany and ZDF's digital strategies.* Paper presented at the RIPE Conference 'Public Service Media in the 21st Century', Mainz.

Koenig, C. and Haratsch, A. (2003). The licence-fee-based financing of public service broadcasting in Germany after the Altmark Trans judgment. *European State Aid Law Quarterly,* 2 (4), 569–78.

Koenig, C. and Kühling, J. (2001). How to cut a long story short: das PreussenElektra-Urteil des EuGH und die EG Beihilfenkontrolle über das deutsche Rundfunkgebührensystem. *Zeitschrift für Urheber- und Medienrecht,* 45 (7), 537–46.

Kops, M., Sokoll, K. and Bensinger, V. (2009). *Rahmenbedingungen für die Durchführung des Drei-Stufen-Tests: Gutachten erstellt für den Rundfunkrat des Westdeutschen Rundfunks.* Cologne: Institut für Rundfunkökonomie.

Kroes, N. (2008). The way ahead for the Broadcasting Communication. Speech at the Conference on *Public service media in the digital age,* 17 July, Strasbourg.

Kuhn, R. (1988). Satellite broadcasting in France. In R. Negrine (ed.), *Satellite broadcasting: the politics and implications of the new media* (pp. 176–95). London: Routledge.

Latzer, M., Braendle, A., Just, N. and Saurwein, F. (2009). *SRG Online Beobachtung: Konzessionskonformität von Webseiten und elektronischen Verbindungen.* Zurich: University of Zurich.

Leurdijk, A. (2007). Public service media dillemas and regulation in a converging landscape. In G. Ferrell Lowe and J. Bardoel (eds), *From public service broadcasting to public service media* (pp. 71–86). Gothenburg: Nordicom.

Levy, D. (1999). *Europe's digital revolution: broadcasting revolution, the EU and the nation state.* London: Routledge.

Leys, C. (2001). *Market-driven politics: neoliberal democracy and the public interest.* London: Verso.

Lilienthal, V. (2009). *Professionalisierung der Medienaufsicht: neue Aufgaben für Rundfunkräte – Die Gremiendebatte in epd medien.* Wiesbaden: VS Verlag für Sozialwissenschaften.

Lilley, A. (2008). The fertile fallacy: new opportunities for public service content. In T. Gardam and D. A. Levy (eds), *The price of plurality: choice, diversity and broadcasting institutions in the digital age* (pp. 95–100). Oxford: Reuters Institute for the Study of Journalism.

Loisen, J. (2009). *Het audiovisuele dossier op de agenda van de Wereldhandelsorganisatie. Een institutioneel en politiek-economisch onderzoek naar de teneur, vorm en marges van de WTO interventie in audiovisueel beleid.* PhD, Vrije Universiteit Brussel, Brussels.

Lowe, L. (2008). *Participation in the debate, organized by the Vertretung des Landes Rheinland Pfalz in Brüssel and the Mainzer Medieninstitut.* Paper presented at the Brüsseler Mediengespräch: die Rundfunkmitteilung der Kommission auf dem Prufstand, Brussels.

Lyons, M. (2008). *Putting audiences at the heart of the BBC review.* Paper presented at the IPPR Media Convention Conferenc, Oxford.

Marsden, C. and Arino, M. (2004). From analogue to digital. In A. Brown and R. G. Picard (eds), *Digital terrestrial television in Europe* (pp. 3–36). London: Routledge.

Mazzocco, D. (1998). *Networks of power: corporate TV's threat to democracy.* Cambridge: South End Press.

McChesney, R. W. (2002). Public broadcasting: past, present and future. In M. P. McCauley, B. L. Artz, D. Halleck and E. E. Peterson (eds), *Public broadcasting and the public interest* (pp. 10–24). New York: M.E. Sharpe.

McChesney, R. W. (2008). *The political economy of media: enduring issues, emerging dilemmas.* New York: Monthly Review Press.

McDonnell, J. (1991). *Public service broadcasting: a reader.* London: Routledge.

McGonagle, T. (2009). Council of Europe: Committee of Ministers: recommendation on promotion of democratic and social contribution of digital broadcasting. *IRIS Plus,* 2009 (06), 25–6.

McQuail, D. (1991). Broadcasting structure and finance: the Netherlands. In J. G. Blumler and T. J. Nossiter (eds), *Broadcasting finance in transition: a comparative handbook* (pp. 144–57). New York: Oxford University Press.

McQuail, D. (1998). Media and sociocultural change. In D. McQuail and K. Siune (eds), *Media policy: convergence, concentration and commerce* (pp. 107–79). London: Sage Publications.

McQuail, D. (2003). Public service broadcasting: both free and accountable. *Javnost The Public,* 1 (3), 13–23.

McQuail, D., de Mateo, R. and Tapper, H. (1992). A framework for analysis of media change in Europe in the 1990s. In K. Siune and W. Truetzschler (eds), *Dynamics of media politics: broadcast and electronic media in Western Europe* (pp. 8–24). London: Sage Publications.

Meier, H.-E. (2006). Die Regulierungskrise des öffentlich-rechtlichen Rundfunks. *Medien & Kommunikationswissenschaft,* 54 (2), 258–87.

Meza, E. (9 July 1999). German casters blast ARD, ZDF Retrieved October, 2009, from http://www.variety.com/article/VR1117503853.html?categoryid=14&cs=1.

Michalis, M. (2007). *Governing European Communications: from unification to coordination.* Lanham: Lexington Books.

Michalis, M. (2010). EU broadcasting governance and PSB: between a rock and a hard place. In P. Iosifidis (ed.), *Reinventing public service communication: European broadcasters and beyond* (pp. 36–48). New York: Palgrave Macmillan.

Moe, H. (2008a). Between supranational competition and national culture? Emerging EU policy and public broadcasters' online services. In I. Bjondeberg and P. Madsen (eds), *Media, democracy and European Culture* (pp. 215–39). Bristol: Intellect Books.

Moe, H. (2008b). Discussion forums, games and second life: exploring the value of public broadcasters' marginal online activities. *Convergence: the International Journal of Research into New Media Technologies*, 14 (3), 261–76.

Moe, H. (2009a). *Public broadcasters, the Internet and democracy: comparing policy and exploring public service media online*. PhD, University of Bergen, Norway.

Moe, H. (2009b). Status und Perspektiven öffentlich-rechtlicher Online-Medien. *Media Perspektiven* (4), 189–200.

Moe, H. (2010). *The Norwegian ex ante test*. Paper presented at the Conference *Exporting the Public Value Test*, Brussels.

Morris, P. F. and Peterson, P. E. (2000). *The new American democracy*. New York: Addison Wesley.

Mortensen, F. (2008). Altmark, Article 86(2) and public service broadcasting. *European State Aid Law Quarterly* 2, 239–49.

Mosco, V. (1996). *The political economy of communication: rethinking and renewal*. London: Sage Publications.

MTVN. (2010). Reactie op de toekomstverkenning landelijke publieke omroep.

Munoz Saldana, M. (2008). The future of public service broadcasting in Community Law. *Media and Cultural Politics*, 4 (2), 203–19.

Murdoch, R. (2005). Freedom in broadcasting. In B. Franklin (ed.), *Television policy: the MacTaggart lectures* (pp. 131–8). Edinburgh: Edinburgh University Press.

Murdock, G. (2000). Digital futures: European television in the age of convergence. In J. Wieten, G. Murdock and P. Dahlgren (eds), *Television across Europe: a comparative introduction* (pp. 35–58). London: Sage Publications.

Murdock, G. (2004). *Building the digital commons: public broadcasting in the age of the Internet*. Paper presented at the 2004 Spry Memorial Lecture, Montreal.

NDP (2010). Reactie op de toekomstverkenning landelijke publieke omroep.

Negrine, R. (1985). Introduction. In R. Negrine (ed.), *Cable television and the future of broadcasting* (pp. 1–14). London: Croom Helm.

Nicolaides, P. (2003). Compensation for public service obligations: the floodgates of state aid? *ECLR* 24 (11), 561–73.

Nicolaides, P., Kekelekis, M. and Buyskes, P. (2005). *State aid policy in the European Community: a guide for practitioners*. The Hague: Kluwer Law International.

Nihoul, P. (1998). Les services d'intérêt général dans le Traité d'Amsterdam. In Y. Lejeune (ed.), *Le Traité d'Amsterdam: espoirs et déceptions* (pp. 341–55). Brussels: Bruylant.

Nikolinakos, N. (2006). *EU Competition law and regulation in the converging telecommunications, media and IT sectors*. The Hague: Kluwer Law International.

Nitsche, I. (2001). *Broadcasting in the EU: the role of public interest in competition analysis*. The Hague: TCM Asser Press.

NN. (2006). Publieke omroep moet 80 miljoen terugbetalen. Retrieved from http://www.nu.nl/algemeen/761179/publieke-omroep-moet-80-miljoen-terugbetalen.html.

NN. (4 September 2008). Plasterk wil geen strengere EU-regels omroep, *NRC Handelsblad*. Retrieved from http://vorige.nrc.nl/media/article1972021.ece/Plasterk_wil_geen_strengere_EU-regels_omroep.

Noam, E. (1991). *Television in Europe*. New York: Oxford University Press.

Nossiter, T. J. (1991). British television: a mixed economy, pp. 95–143. In J. G. Blumler and T. J. Nossiter (eds). *Broadcasting finance in transition: a comparative handbook*. New York: Oxford University Press.

NPO (2010). Meerjarenbegroting 2011–2015.

NRC Handelsblad (2010). Reactie op de toekomstverkenning landelijke publieke omroep.

OFCOM (2004). OFCOM review of public service broadcasting: Phase 1 – Is television special?

OFCOM (2005). OFCOM review of public service television broadcasting – Phase 3 – competition for quality.

OFCOM (2007). A new approach to public service content in the digital media age: the potential role of the public service publisher.

Papathanassopoulos, S. (1990). Broadcasting and the European community: the commission's audiovisual policy. In K. Dyson and P. Humphreys (eds), *The political economy of international communications: international and European dimensions* (pp. 107–24). London: Routledge.

Papathanassopoulos, S. (2007a). Financing public service broadcasters in the new era. In E. De Bens (ed.), *The media between culture and commerce* (pp. 151–66). Bristol: Intellect Books.

Papathanassopoulos, S. (2007b). The mediterranean/polarized pluralist media model countries. In G. Terzis (ed.), *European media governance: national and regional dimensions* (pp. 191–200). Bristol: Intellect Books.

Paulu, B. (1981). *Television and Radio in the United Kingdom*. Minnesota: University of Minnesota Press.

Pauwels, C. (1995). *Cultuur en economie: de spanningsvelden van het communautair audiovisueel beleid. Een onderzoek naar de grenzen en mogelijkheden van een kwalitatief cultuur en communicatiebeleid in een economisch geïntegreerd Europa. Een kritische analyse en prospectieve evaluatie aan de hand van het gevoerde Europees audiovisueel beleid*. PhD, Vrije Universiteit Brussel, Brussels.

Pauwels, C. (2000). De creatie van een competitieve Europese audiovisuele programma-industrie: mission impossible? In D. Biltereyst and H. de Smaele (eds), *Transformatie en continuïteit van de Europese televisie* (pp. 25–52). Ghent: Academia Press.

Pauwels, C. and Cincera, P. (2001). Concentration and competition policies: towards a precarious balance wtihin the global audiovisual order. In L. D'Haenens and F. Saeys (eds), *Western broadcasting at the dawn of the 21st century* (pp. 49–82). New York: Mouton de Gruyter.

Pauwels, C. and De Vinck, S. (2007). De openbare omroep in nauwe schoentjes? Een blik op de impact van het liberaliseringsbeleid van de EU. In A. D'Hoest and H. Van Den Bulck (eds), *Publieke Televisie in Vlaanderen: Een Geschiedenis* (pp. 132–65). Ghent: Academia Press.

Pauwels, C. and Donders, K. (2011). Let's get digital: From Television without Frontiers to the digital Big Bang: the EU's continuous efforts to create a future proof internal media market. In R. Mansell and M. Raboy (eds), *Media and communications policies in a globalised context*. New York: Maxwell Publishing.

Peacock, A. (1986). *Report of the Committee on financing the BBC*. London: Her Majesty's Stationary Office.

Peacock, A. (2000). Editorial: market failure and government failure in broadcasting. *Economic Affairs*, 20(4), 2–6.

Peacock, A. (2004). Public service broadcasting without the BBC? In A. Peacock (ed.), *Public service broadcasting without the BBC?* (pp. 33–53). London: Institute for Economic Affairs.

Peeters, B. (2009). Der 'Drei-Stufen-Test': Die Zukunft der öffentlich-rechtlichen Onlineangebote. *Kommunikation und Recht*, 1(2), 6–34.

Perceval, P. (1995). De omroepsector: waarom oorlog en waarom vrede? In J.-C. Burgelman, D. Biltereyst and C. Pauwels (eds), *Audiovisuele media in Vlaanderen: analyse en beleid* (pp. 13–56). Brussels: VUBPress.

Pesaresi, N. and Van Hoof, M. (2008). Chapter 1: State aid control: and introduction. In W. Mederer, N. Pesaresi and M. Van Hoof (eds), *EC Competition Law: Volume IV, State aid* (pp. 1–17). Brussels: Claeys & Casteels.

Plasterk, R. (2008). Letter: Broadcasting Communication/State aid for public service broadcasting.

Potschka, C. (2010). *The liberal tradition and communications policy-making in the UK and Germany*. Paper presented at the 3rd European Communication Conference, Hamburg.

Price, M. (1995). *Television, the public sphere and national identity*. Oxford: Oxford University Press.

Price, M., and Raboy, M. (2003). *Public service broadcasting in transition: a documentary reader*. The Hague: Kluwer Law International.

Psychiogopoulou, E. (2006). EC State Aid Control and Cultural Justification. *Legal Issues of Economic Integration*, 33(1), 3–28.

Psychogiopoulou, E. (2008). *The integration of cultural considerations in EU law and policies*. Leiden: Koninklijke Brill NV.

Pérez Gomez, A. (2006). Spain: new act on national public radio and television. *Iris Legal Observations*, 2006(6), 11–19.

Quigley, C. and Collins, A. M. (2003). *EC State Aid Law and Policy*. Oxford: Hart Publishing.

Raats, T. and Pauwels, C. (2010). 'The Cultural Remit Renaissance?' Conceptualizing and assessing public service broadcasting as a hub in a networked media ecology. Paper presented at the RIPE @ 2010 Conference 'Public Media After The Recession', London.

Raboy, M. (1995). Public service broadcasting in the context of globalisation. In M. Raboy (ed.), *Public broadcasting for the 21st century* (pp. 1–22). London: John Libbey Publishing.

Rechtbank van Amsterdam. (2010). AWB 10/1169, 10/1181, 10/1195, 10/1291, 10/1293, 10/1294, 10/1295, 10/1296, 10/1297, 10/1298,10/1299, 10/1300, 10/1301, 10/1302, 10/1303, 10/1304, 10/1305, 10/1306, 10/1307, 10/1308, 10/1310, 10/1311, 10/1312, 10/1313,10/1314,10/1316, 10/4954, 10/4955 en 10/4956 BESLU.

Reding, V. (2005). Better regulation for Europe's media industry: the Commission's approach. Audiovisual Conference 'Between Culture and Commerce', 22 September, Liverpool.

Reding, V. (2006). Audiovisual Media Services Directive: the right instrument to provide legal certainty for Europe's media businesses in the next decade. Speech at the seminar 'Regulating the new media landscape', 7 June, Brussels.

Regourd, S. (1999). Two conflicting notions of audiovisual liberalisation. In M. Scriven and M. Lecomte (eds), *Television broadcasting in contemporary France and Britain* (pp. 29–45). New York: Berghahn Books.

Repa, L. (2009). *The broadcasting communication*. Paper presented at the IES and IBBT-SMIT workshop on 'EU State aid policy and its impact on MS' regulation of public service broadcasting', Brussels.

Ritten, L. and Braun, W. D. (2004). Chapter IX: Government-induced distortions of competition. In L. Ritten and W. D. Braun (eds), *European competition law: a practioner's guide* (pp. 951–1023). The Hague: Kluwer Law International.

Rizza, C. (2003). The financial assitance granted by MS to undertakings entrusted with the operation of a service of general economic interest. In A. Biondi, P. Eeckhout and J. Flynn (eds), *The law of state aid in the EU* (pp. 67–84). Oxford: Oxford University Press.

Robinson, B., Raven, J. and Low, L. P. (2005). Paying for public service television in the digital age. In J. Heath and D. Levy (eds), *Can the market deliver? Funding public service television in the digital age* (pp. 101–28). Eastleight: John Libbey Publishing.

Saeys, F. and Antoine, F. (2007). Belgium. In L. D'Haenens and F. Saeys (eds), *Western broadcasting models: structure, conduct and performance.* New York: Mouton De Gruyter.

Saeys, F. and Coppens, T. (2003). Business of corebusiness: de opdracht van de West-Europese publieke omroepen nogmaals ter discussie. *Tijdschrift voor Communicatiewetenschap*, 31 (4), 338–55.

Santa Maria, A. (2007). *Competition and State aid: an analysis of the EC Practice.* The Hague: Kluwer Law International.

Sawers, D. (2000). Public service broadcasting: a paradox of our time. *Economic Affairs*, 20 (4), 33–5.

Scannel, P. (1995). Britain: public service broadcasting, from national culture to multiculturalism. In M. Raboy (ed.), *Public broadcasting for the 21st century* (pp. 23–41). Luton: John Libbey Publishing.

Scheuer, A. (2006). Traditional paradigms for new services? The commission proposal for a 'Audiovisual Media Services Directive'. *Communications and Strategies*, 62 (2), 71–91.

Schultz, W. (2008). Der Programmauftrag als Prozess seiner Begründung. *Media Perspektiven* (4), 158–65.

Schultz, W. (2009). The legal framework for public service broadcasting after the German State aid case: Procrustean Bed or Hammock? *Journal of Media Law*, 1 (2), 219–41.

Schüller-Keber, V. (2009). Die Kommunikationsfreiheiten in der Verfassung. In D. Dörr, J. Kreile and M. D. Cole (eds), *Handbuch Medienrecht: Recht der elektronischen Massenmedien* (pp. 63–82). Frankfurt am Main: Verlag Recht und Wirtschaft.

Sectorraad Media (2010). Beheersovereenkomst tussen de openbare omroep en de Vlaamse Gemeenschap voor de periode 2012–2016. Een duidelijke keuze voor kwaliteitsvolle invulling. Statement of advisory body. Retrieved from *www.cjsm.vlaanderen.be/.../media/.../20101214_MED_advies_beheersovereenkomst_VRT_2012-2016.pdf*.

Sepstrup, P. (1990). *Transnationalization of television in Western Europe.* London: John Libbey Publishing.

Shah, S. (27 January 2003). RM leads fight against BBC digital curriculum, *The Independent*. Retrieved from http://www.independent.co.uk/news/business/news/rm-leads-fight-against-BBC-digital-curriculum-604426.html.

Siune, K. and McQuail, D. (1992). Conclusion: wake up, Europe! In K. Siune and W. Truetzschler (eds), *Dynamics of media politics: broadcast and electronic media in Western Europe* (pp. 190–9). London: Sage Publications.

Smith, M. P. (2001). How adaptable is the Commission? The case of State aid regulation. *Journal of Public Policy*, 21 (3), 219–38.

Sokoll, K. (2009). Der neue Drei-Stufen-Test für Telemedienangebote öffentlich-rechtlicher Rundfunkanstalten. *NJW* (13), 885–92.

Soltèsz, U. and Bielesz, H. (2004). Judicial Review of State Aid Decisions – Recent Developments. *ECLR* (3), 133–52.

Steemers, J. (1999). *Changing channels: the redefinition of public service broadcasting for the digital age*. Paper presented at the ECPR Joint Research Sessions, Mannheim.

Steemers, J. (2001). In search of a third way: balancing public purpose and commerce in German and British public service broadcasting. *Canadian Journal of Communication*, 26 (1), 69–87.

Steemers, J. (2003). Public service broadcasting is not dead yet: strategies in the 21st century. In G. Lowe and T. Hujanen (eds), *Broadcasting and convergence: new articulations of the public service remit* (pp. 123–36). Gothenburg: Nordicom.

Suter, T. (2008). *Setting public goals, defining public value, securing public support – the challenge for Europe's PSBs*. Paper presented at 'Public service media in the digital age', Strasbourg.

Syvertsen, T. (1997). Paradise lost: the privatisation of Scandinavian broadcasting. *Journal of Communication*, 47(1), 120–7.

Szyszczak, E. (2004). Public services in the new economy. In C. Graham and F. Smith (eds), *Competition, regulation and the new economy* (pp. 185–206). Portland: Hart Publishing.

SWR (2009). Telemedienkonzepte des SWR.

Tambini, D. and Cowling, J. (2004). Introduction: redefining public service broadcasting for the 21st century. In D. Tambini and J. Cowling (eds), *From public service broadcasting to public service communications* (pp. 1–4). Oxford: Institute for Public Policy Research.

Telegraaf Media Nederland (2010). Reactie op de toekomstverkenning landelijke publieke omroep.

Tongue, C. and Harvey, S. (2004). Citizenship, culture and public service broadcasting. Response to Ofcom's review of public service relevision broadcasting, Phase 1: 'Is television special'.

Tracey, M. (1995). The role of listeners and viewers in the future of broadcasting. In B. Groombridge and J. Hay (eds), *The price of choice: public service broadcasting in a competitive European market place* (pp. 124–7). London: John Libbey Publishing.

Tracey, M. (1998). *The decline and fall of public service broadcasting*. Oxford: Clarendon Press.

Valcke, P. and Lievens, E. (2009). Rethinking European broadcasting regulation. In C. Pauwels, H. Kalimo, K. Donders and B. Van Rompuy (eds), *Rethinking European media and communications policy* (pp. 127–64). Brussels: VUBPress.

Valcke, P. and Stevens, D. (2007). Graduated regulation of regulatable content and the European Audiovisual Media Services Directive: one small step for the industry and one giant leap for the legislator? *Telematics and Informatics*, 24 (4), 285–302.

Van Audenhove, L., Morganti, L. and Vanhoucke, J. (2007). *The cultural industries and upcoming forms of regulation and self-regulation*. Paper presented at the GigaNet Symposium (Global Internet Governance Academic Forum), Rio De Janeiro.

Van Bijsterveldt-Vliegenthart, M. (2010). Consultatie toekomst landelijke publieke omroep. Avaialable on www.rijksoverheid.nl.

van Cuilenburg, J. and van der Wurff, R. (2007). Netherlands. In E. De Bens (ed.), *Media between culture and commerce* (pp. 81–9). Bristol: Intellect Books.

Van Den Bulck, H. (2007). Het beleid van de publieke televisie: van hoogmis van de moderniteit naar postmodern sterk merk? In A. Dhoest and H. Van Den Bulck (eds), *Publieke televisie in Vlaanderen: een geschiedenis* (pp. 59–84). Ghent: Academia Press.

Van den Bulck, H. (2008). Can PSB stake its claim in a media world of digital convergence? *Convergence The International Journal of Research into New Media Technologies*, 14 (3), 335–49.

Van Den Bulck, H. (2010). *Making ends meet: developing ex ante assessments in Flanders*. Paper presented at the Conference 'Exporting the Public Value Test', Brussels.

Van Eijk, N. (2007). The Netherlands. In S. Nikoltchev (ed.), *The public service broadcasting culture* (pp. 149–58). Strasbourg: European Audiovisual Observatory.

Vandermeersch, P. (2009). Participation in session 'The estabilished media react', *Digital News Affairs*, Brussels.

Vecht, R. (2010). Presentation of the Head of NPO's Legal Department. Conference 'Exporting the Public Value Test', Brussels.

Vedel, T. and Bourdon, J. (1993). French public service broadcasting: from monopoly to marginalization. In R. K. Avery (ed.), *Public service broadcasting in a multichannel environment: the history and survival of an ideal* (pp. 29–51). New York: Longman.

Venturelli, S. (1998). *Liberalising the European media: politics, regulation, and the public sphere*. Oxford: Clarendon Press.

Verhofstadt, D. (1982). *Het einde van het VRT-monopolie*. Antwerp: Kluwer.

Vlaamse Regering (2004). Vertrouwen geven, verantwoordelijkheid nemen.

Vlaamse Regering (2008). Aanpassing mediadecreten beslecht Europees onderzoek rond financiering VRT.

Vlaamse Regering (2009a). Decreten betreffende de radio-omroep en de televisie.

Vlaamse Regering (2009b). Een daadkrachtig Vlaanderen in belissende tijden.

Vlaamse Regering and VRT (2006). Beheersovereenkomst 2007–2011. De opdracht van de openbare omroep in het digitale tijdperk.

Vlaamse Regering and VRT. (2009). Verklarend addendum bij de beheersovereenkomst 2007–2011 inzake de activiteiten en diensten die binnen het toepassingsgebied van de beheersovereenkomst vallen.

Voorhoof, D. (1995). Mediabeleid en mediarecht in Vlaanderen. In J.-C. Burgelman, D. Biltereyst and C. Pauwels (eds), *Audiovisuele media in Vlaanderen: analyse en beleid* (pp. 187–212). Brussels: VUBPress.

VPRT (2003). Beschwerde bei der Europäischen Kommission wegen Online- und E-commerce-Aktivitäten von ARD und ZDF eingereicht Transparenz bei Gebührenverwendung eingefordert – Steuerbegünstigung steht auf dem Prüfstand [Press release].

VRM (Vlaamse Regulator voor de Media) (2007a). Tomas Coppens en Nele Bogaerts v NV VRT. 21 September, nr. 2007/037.

VRM (Vlaamse Regulator voor de Media) (2007b). Tomas Coppens en Timothy Heyninck v NV VRT. 21 September, nr. 2007/039.

VRM (Vlaamse Regulator voor de Media) (2007c). VRM v NV VRT. 22 June, nr. 2007/028.

VRT (2006). Voorlopig oordeel Europese Commissie stelt de VRT gerust. Klachten POF en VMMa niet aangetoond [Press release].

VRT (2009). Kader voor merchandising en nevenactiviteiten.

Ward, D. (2003). State aid or band aid? An evaluation of the Commission's approach to public service broadcasting. *Media, Culture and Society*, 25 (2), 233–50.

Ward, D. (2004a). EU media policy: finding a path between commercial and public broadcasting in a dual system. In F. Columbus (ed.), *European economic and political issues* (pp. 135–54). New York: Nova Biomedical.

Ward, D. (2004b). State aid and public service broadcasting. In D. Ward (ed.), *The EU democratic deficit and the public sphere: an evaluation of EU media policy* (pp. 93–106). Amsterdam: IOS Press.

Ward, D. (2008). The Commission's State aid regime and public service broadcasting. In D. Ward (ed.), *The EU and the Culture Industries* (pp. 59–80). London: Ashgate.

WDR (2009). Telemedienkonzept für das Internetangebot des WDR.

West, T. G. (2004). Free speech in the American founding and in modern liberalism. In E. Frankel Paul, F. D. Miller and J. Paul (eds), *Freedom of speech* (pp. 310–84). Cambridge: Cambridge University Press.

Wheeler, M. (2004). Supranational regulation: television and the EU. *European Journal of Communication*, 19 (3), 349–70.

Wheeler, M. (2010). The EU's competition directorate: State aids and public service broadcasting. In P. Iosifidis (ed.), *Reinventing public service communication: European broadcasters and beyond* (pp. 49–62). New York: Palgrave Macmillan.

Whiters, G. (2003). Broadcasting. In R. Towse (ed.), *A handbook of cultural economics* (pp. 102–13). Cheltenham: Edward Elgar Publishing.

Wiedemann, V. (2004). Public service broadcasting, State aid and the Internet: emerging EU law. Brussels: EBU.

Wolton, D. (1990). La télévision européenne en question. *Médiaspouvoirs*, (20), 87–95.

Woods, L. (2008). The consumer and advertising regulation in the television without Frontiers and Audiovisual Media Services Directive. *Journal of Consumer Policy*, 31 (1), 63–78.

WRR (2005). Focus op functies: uitdagingen voor een toekomstbestendig mediabeleid.

ZDF (2009). Konzept der Telemedienangebote des ZDF.

Index

222 *Index*